2023
9급 전 직렬
공무원
시험 대비

심슨북스

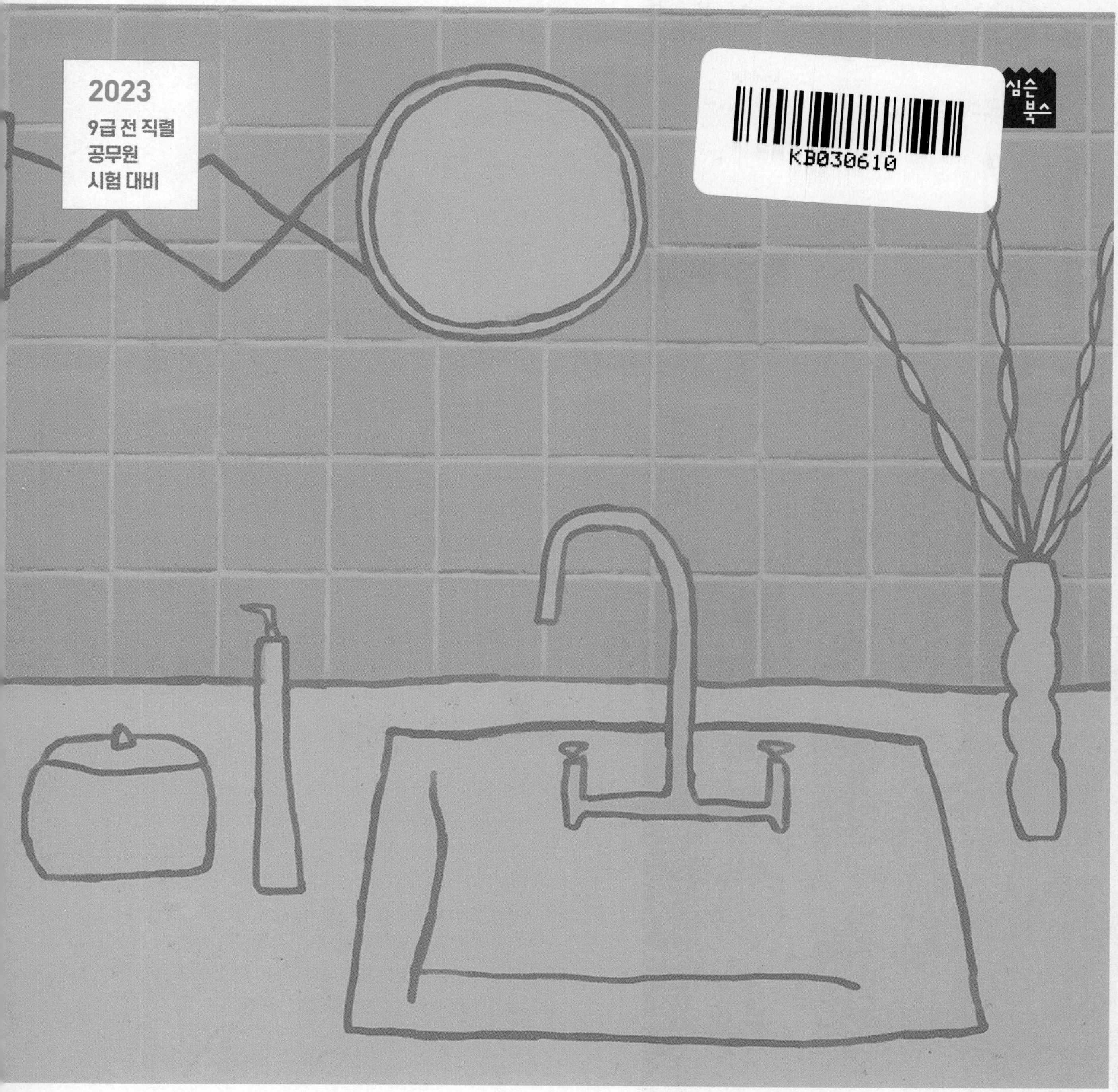

심우철 합격영어 3. 독해

공무원 영어 기본서

유형별 맞춤형 독해 전략을 통한 문제 풀이 시간 단축
수험생의 눈높이에 맞춘 올바른 정답 추론 과정 제시

심우철 지음

커넥츠 공단기
인터넷 강의
gong.conects.com

Preface

머리말

최소시간 X 최대효과

초고효율 심우철 합격영어

책을 내면서...

나는 오랫동안 학원 강사로 학생들을 만났습니다. 시험이라는 전쟁을 치르고 있는 학생들의 책사로서 영어 과목에 대한 전략을 조언하는 일이 내가 하는 일이었습니다. 20년간 매년 치러오는 전쟁이지만 항상 잔혹하게 느껴집니다. 누군가는 승리의 환희를 맛보겠지만 또 다른 누군가는 반드시 패배하게 되어있는 것이 바로 수험이라는 전쟁의 현실입니다.

2012년에 공단기 입성을 준비하면서 스스로에게 약속했습니다. '수험생들의 인생을 좌우하는 공무원 시험이라는 전쟁터에서 학생들의 학습에, 더 나아가 학생들의 미래를 향한 도전에 진정한 길잡이가 되겠노라'고요.

이 책을 완성하기까지 꼬박 4년의 시간이 걸렸습니다. 그리고 몇 차례 개정을 통해 완성도를 높여 왔습니다. 보통 수험서를 집필하는 데 1년이 채 안 걸리는 데 비하면 굉장히 많은 시간을 투자한 셈이지요. '심우철 합격영어'는 20년간 수험영어 최전선에서 살아온 내 노력의 압축입니다. 그리고 당시 스스로에게 한 약속에 대한 응답이기도 합니다. 부디 이 교재가 미래의 공무원을 꿈꾸는 수험생들로 하여금 영어 학습에 대한 답답함에서 벗어나는 데 도움이 되었으면 합니다.

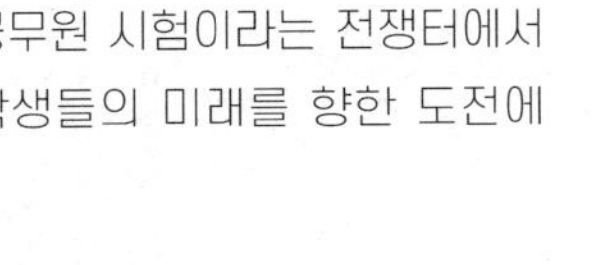

모든 것을 담을 수는 없을까?

공무원 영어 수험서는 이미 시중에 넘쳐납니다.
하지만 기존에 존재하는 딱딱한 영어 이론에 대한 나열만 있을 뿐 학생들이 이것을 더 쉽게 이해할 수 있도록 새로운 형태의 학습법을 제시하는 교재는 찾을 수 없었습니다.
이 책에는 영어 학습에 있어서 핵심이 되는 '구문', '문법', '독해'의 필수 개념을 철저하게 공무원 시험 출제 경향에 맞춰 수록하였습니다.
단순히 열거만 한 것이 아니라 '구문'은 '법칙'으로, '문법'은 '어휘'로, '독해'는 유형별 'Reading Skill'로 풀어내어 학생들의 이해를 한층 도왔습니다.

2022 최신 시험 출제 경향 100% 반영 완료

공무원 시험 출제 경향은 매년 바뀌고 있습니다.
하지만 몇 년째 바뀌지 않는 철밥통 강의와 발행일만 교묘하게 바꾼, 말뿐인 개정 교재로 학생들을 혼동케 하는 현실에 화가 났습니다.
"심우철 합격영어는 2022년까지 시행한 최신 공무원 시험 출제 경향을 철저하게 분석하여 강의와 교재에 녹여냈습니다."

'심우철 합격영어' 하나면 됩니다.

더 이상 어떤 교재로 공무원 영어를 공부해야 하는지 고민하며 시간을 버리지 마십시오.
'심우철 합격영어'에 공무원 영어의 모든 것이 담겨있습니다.
"공무원 영어는 이 책 하나면 완벽하게 끝납니다!"

Preview

교재 특징 / 구성

최소시간 X 최대효과

초고효율 심우철 합격영어

교재 특징

1. 공무원 독해에 100% 적용되는 독해 기술

<심우철 합격영어 독해>는 각 유형에 맞는 명료하고 정확한 독해 전략을 제시합니다. 독해 문항을 푸는 요령뿐만 아니라 시간을 절약할 수 있는 구체적인 전략도 함께 익힐 수 있습니다. <심우철 합격영어 독해>는 오로지 시험장에서 적용 가능한 전략만을 고려한 독해 실전 매뉴얼 교재입니다.

2. 최신 기출 문제와 예상 문제를 통한 실전 연습

학습한 독해 전략을 최신 공무원 문제 및 예상 문제 등의 다양한 난이도의 실전 문제에 적용해 봄으로써 유형별 독해에 대한 적응력을 기를 수 있습니다.

3. 학원 교재 이상의 자세한 해설 제공

기본적으로 <심우철 합격영어 독해>는 온라인 강의 교재이지만, 시중 출판 교재 이상의 콘텐츠를 원하는 공무원 준비 수험생들의 요구에 맞춰 되도록 자세한 내용 설명과 정답에 대한 해설을 제공하기 위해 노력했습니다.

교재 구성

1. 유형별 독해 전략

각 유형에 대한 출제 경향 분석과 자세한 설명을 통해 각각의 유형에 효과적으로 접근하는 방법을 학습합니다.

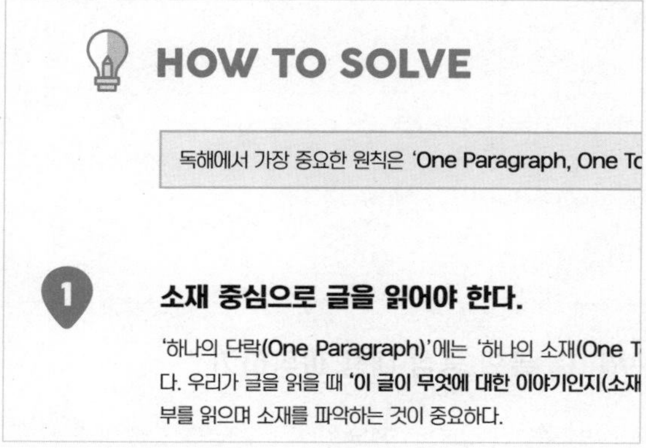
HOW TO SOLVE

독해에서 가장 중요한 원칙은 'One Paragraph, One To

1 소재 중심으로 글을 읽어야 한다.

'하나의 단락(One Paragraph)'에는 '하나의 소재(One T
다. 우리가 글을 읽을 때 **'이 글이 무엇에 대한 이야기인지(소재**
부를 읽으며 소재를 파악하는 것이 중요하다.

2. Skill Example

앞서 학습한 독해 전략을 적용하여 유형 예제를 직접 풀어 보면서 각 유형에 대한 문제 풀이 감각을 기릅니다.

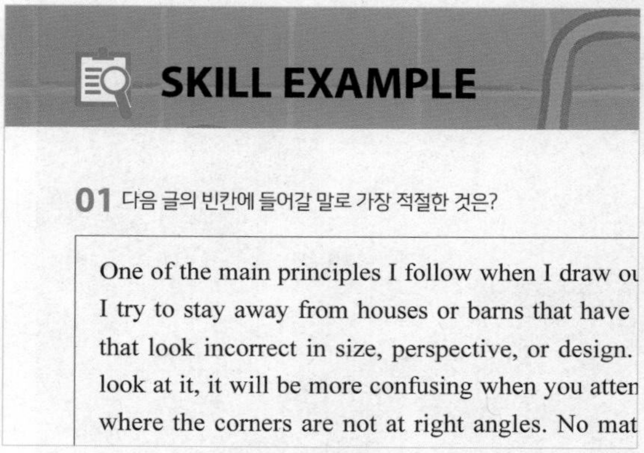
SKILL EXAMPLE

01 다음 글의 빈칸에 들어갈 말로 가장 적절한 것은?

One of the main principles I follow when I draw ou
I try to stay away from houses or barns that have
that look incorrect in size, perspective, or design.
look at it, it will be more confusing when you atten
where the corners are not at right angles. No mat

3. Actual Test

실제 공무원 및 그 밖의 기출 문제를 반복하여 풀어 보면서 실전 적용력을 높입니다.

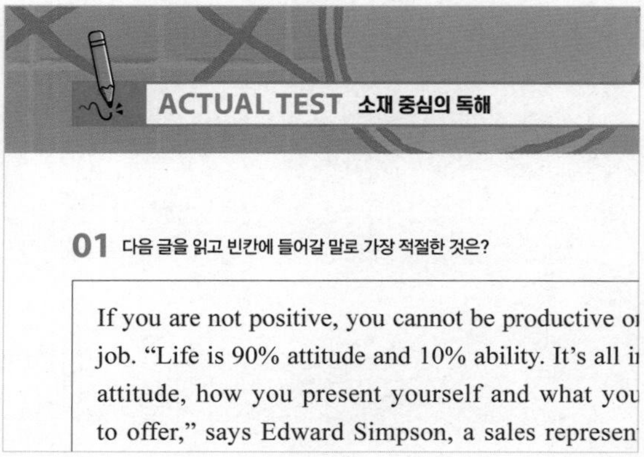
ACTUAL TEST 소재 중심의 독해

01 다음 글을 읽고 빈칸에 들어갈 말로 가장 적절한 것은?

If you are not positive, you cannot be productive o
job. "Life is 90% attitude and 10% ability. It's all i
attitude, how you present yourself and what you
to offer," says Edward Simpson, a sales represen

4. 정답 및 해설

실전 문제에 대한 자세한 해설과 해석을 제공하여 학습한 내용을 완벽하게 소화할 수 있도록 배려하였습니다.

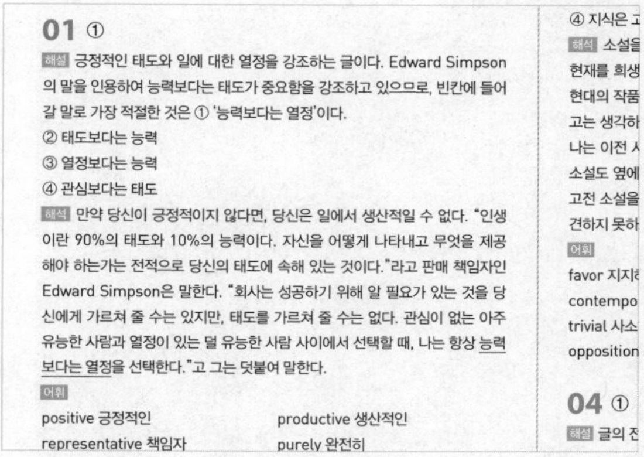
01 ①

해설 긍정적인 태도와 일에 대한 열정을 강조하는 글이다. Edward Simpson의 말을 인용하여 능력보다는 태도가 중요함을 강조하고 있으므로, 빈칸에 들어갈 말로 가장 적절한 것은 ① '능력보다는 열정'이다.
② 태도보다는 능력
③ 열정보다는 능력
④ 관심보다는 태도

해석 만약 당신이 긍정적이지 않다면, 당신은 일에서 생산적일 수 없다. "인생이란 90%의 태도와 10%의 능력이다. 자신을 어떻게 나타내고 무엇을 제공해야 하는가는 전적으로 당신의 태도에 속해 있는 것이다."라고 판매 책임자인 Edward Simpson은 말한다. "회사는 성공하기 위해 알 필요가 있는 것을 당신에게 가르쳐 줄 수는 있지만, 태도를 가르쳐 줄 수는 없다. 관심이 없는 아주 유능한 사람과 열정이 있는 덜 유능한 사람 사이에서 선택할 때, 나는 항상 능력보다는 열정을 선택한다."고 그는 덧붙여 말한다.

어휘
positive 긍정적인 productive 생산적인
representative 책임자 purely 완전히

④ 지식은 고
해설 소설을
현재를 희생
현대의 작품
고는 생각하
나는 이전 시
소설도 옆에
고전 소설을
견하지 못하
어휘
favor 지지하
contempo
trivial 사소
opposition

04 ①
해설 글의 진

Contents

목차

PART 01. 구조 독해

PART 02. 글의 중심 내용 파악하기

최소시간 X 최대효과

초고효율 심우철 합격영어

PART 03. 글의 논리 전개 파악하기

PART 04. 글의 세부 내용 파악하기

Part 01

구조 독해

Reading Skill

01

소재 중심의 독해

HOW TO SOLVE

독해에서 가장 중요한 원칙은 **'One Paragraph, One Topic, One Idea'**이다.

1 소재 중심으로 글을 읽어야 한다.

'하나의 단락**(One Paragraph)**'에는 '하나의 소재**(One Topic)**'와 '하나의 필자의 견해**(One Idea)**'가 있다. 우리가 글을 읽을 때 **'이 글이 무엇에 대한 이야기인지(소재, Topic)'**를 놓치지 말아야 한다. 따라서 글의 도입부를 읽으며 소재를 파악하는 것이 중요하다.

2 연결사 중심의 독해가 되어야 한다.

연결사를 잘 보면 그 지문이 어떻게 전개될지 미리 알 수 있다. 따라서 글을 읽을 때 미리 연결사를 찾아두면 좋다. 특히 앞부분에 위치한 연결사를 미리 찾아두면 그 글의 단락 구조를 알 수가 있기 때문에, 예측 독해가 가능하다. 지문에 연결사가 없으면 두괄식 구조인 경우가 많다.

3 아래의 표현을 알아두면 소재 파악에 도움이 된다.

S + V + that <u>소재 · 주제</u>
It is + 형 + that <u>소재 · 주제</u>
Although A, B(<u>소재 · 주제</u>)

SKILL EXAMPLE

01 다음 글의 빈칸에 들어갈 말로 가장 적절한 것은?

One of the main principles I follow when I draw outside is ______________. I try to stay away from houses or barns that have unusual angles of the roof, or objects that look incorrect in size, perspective, or design. If the subject is confusing when you look at it, it will be more confusing when you attempt to draw it. I know a beautiful barn where the corners are not at right angles. No matter how many times I have drawn it, the perspective does not look right. If I were to make an accurate drawing of this barn and put it in a show, I'm sure I would get all kinds of criticism for my poor perspective. I would not be there to tell my critics that the barn is actually constructed this way. So, I stay away from subjects that do not look right to me.

① not to select a subject that is too difficult or odd
② to draw an object with imagination
③ to get information from abstract subjects
④ to convert inaccurate drawings into accurate ones

지문 분석

One of the main principles I follow when I draw outside is ______________.
내가 야외에서 그림을 그릴 때 준수하는 중요한 원칙들 중 하나는 ______________이다.

첫 문장을 읽으며 글의 소재가 무엇인지 잡아내야 한다. 우선 특별히 눈에 띄는 연결사가 없으므로 이 글은 두괄식 구조임을 알 수 있다. 빈칸에 들어갈 내용은 '밖에서 그림을 그릴 때 내가 따르는 원칙이 무엇인지'에 관한 것이다. 소재는 '그림을 그릴 때의 원칙'이다.

I try to stay away from houses or barns that have unusual angles of the roof, or objects that look incorrect in size, perspective, or design.
나는 특이한 각도의 지붕이 있는 집이나 헛간들, 혹은 크기나 원근, 구성이 맞지 않는 물건들은 그리지 않으려고 노력한다.

'try to stay away from'을 '떨어지려고 노력한다'라고 해석하면 이 글은 이해가 되지 않는다. 소재가 '그림을 그릴 때의 원칙'이므로 '그리지 않으려고 한다'라고 해석을 할 수 있어야 한다. 또한 'unusual(특이한)'과 'incorrect(부정확한)'는 같은 맥락의 단어이다. 결국 이 문장은 '나는 그림 그릴 때 특이한 대상은 그리지 않는다'는 것을 말하고 있다.

If the subject is confusing when you look at it, it will be more confusing when you attempt to draw it.

당신이 그것(대상)을 바라볼 때 대상이 혼란스럽다면, 당신이 그것을 그리려고 시도할 때 그것은 더 혼란스러울 것이다.

이 문장에서 'confusing(혼란을 주는)'은 앞 문장에 나온 'unusual(특이한)'과 'incorrect(부정확한)'와 같은 맥락의 단어이다. 결국 이 문장도 앞 문장과 마찬가지로 '특이한 대상은 그리지 않는다'를 말하고 있다. 같은 소재, 다른 표현일 뿐이다.

I know a beautiful barn where the corners are not at right angles. No matter how many times I have drawn it, the perspective does not look right.

나는 모서리가 직각이 아닌 아름다운 헛간을 알고 있다. 내가 아무리 여러 번 그것을 그려도, 그 원근감은 올바르지 않아 보인다.

'not at right angles(직각이 아닌)', 'does not look right(올바르지 않아 보인다)'도 결국 앞 문장의 'unusual(특이한)'과 'incorrect(부정확한)'와 같은 말이다. 이 문장에서도 결국 말하고자 하는 바는 '특이한 대상은 그리지 않는다'이다.

So, I stay away from subjects that do not look right to me.

그래서, 나는 나에게 올바르게 보이지 않는 대상들을 멀리한다.

마지막 문장에서도 동일한 것을 말하고 있다. 결국 이 지문의 주제는 '나는 그림을 그릴 때 특이한 대상은 가급적 그리려 하지 않는다'이다. 'unusual(특이한)', 'incorrect(부정확한)', 'confusing(혼란을 주는)', 'not at right angles(직각이 아닌)', 'does not look right(올바르지 않아 보인다)'는 결국 같은 말이다.

정답 및 해석

정답 ①

해석 밖에서 그림을 그릴 때 내가 따르는 중요한 원칙들 중의 하나는 너무 어렵거나 이상한 대상을 선택하지 않는 것이다. 난 특이한 각도의 지붕이 있는 집이나 헛간, 혹은 크기와 원근감 또는 디자인이 정확하지 않아 보이는 물체들은 그리지 않으려고 한다. 당신이 대상을 바라볼 때 그것이 혼란스럽다면, 그것을 그리려고 시도할 때는 더 혼란스러울 것이다. 난 모서리가 직각이 아닌 아름다운 헛간을 알고 있다. 내가 아무리 여러 번 그것을 그려도, 그 원근감은 적절해 보이지 않는다. 이 헛간을 정확하게 그려서 사람들에게 보여준다면, 형편없는 원근감 때문에 난 온갖 종류의 비난을 받을 거라고 확신한다. 난 그 헛간이 실제로 이런 식으로 지어졌다고 비평가들에게 말하기 위해 그 자리에 있지는 않을 것이다. 그러므로 난 내게 올바르게 보이지 않는 대상들을 멀리한다.

① 너무 어렵거나 이상한 대상을 선택하지 않는 것
② 상상으로 사물을 그리는 것
③ 추상적인 대상들로부터 정보를 얻는 것
④ 부정확한 그림들을 정확한 그림들로 바꾸는 것

어휘 principle 원칙 barn 헛간 perspective 원근감 subject 대상 confusing 혼란스러운 right angle 직각 accurate 정확한 criticism 비난 construct 건설하다 abstract 추상적인 convert 바꾸다

01 다음 글을 읽고 빈칸에 들어갈 말로 가장 적절한 것은?

> If you are not positive, you cannot be productive on your job. "Life is 90% attitude and 10% ability. It's all in your attitude, how you present yourself and what you have to offer," says Edward Simpson, a sales representative. "A company may be able to teach you what you need to know to succeed, but it cannot teach attitude. When choosing between a purely competent person without interest and a less competent person with zeal, I always choose ____________," he adds.

① zeal over ability
② ability over attitude
③ competence over zeal
④ attitude over interest

02 다음 빈칸에 들어갈 말로 가장 적절한 것은?

Mathematics definitely influenced Renaissance art. Renaissance art was different from the art in the Middle Ages in many ways. Prior to the Renaissance, objects in paintings were flat and symbolic rather than real in appearance. Artists during the Renaissance reformed painting. They wanted objects in paintings to be represented ________________. Mathematics was used to portray the essential form of objects in perspective, as they appeared to the human eye. Renaissance artists achieved perspective using geometry, which resulted in a naturalistic, precise, three-dimensional representation of the real world. The application of mathematics to art, particularly in paintings, was one of the primary characteristics of Renaissance art.

① with accuracy
② in a tradition
③ without reality
④ with symbols

03 다음 빈칸에 들어갈 말로 가장 적절한 것은?

The best way to read fiction is to mix one's reading, neither to favor the present at the expense of the past nor to favor the past at the expense of the present. And do not think contemporary work will appear thin and trivial compared with the great work of the past. It is not necessarily so at all. As a professional reader, I have to try to keep side by side with contemporary fiction while constantly widening and deepening my knowledge of the fiction of earlier times. I'm continually turning from the most vital work of our time to the classic novels, and I find no opposition between them. That is, ______________________.

① classic novels are hard to get
② they are not mutually exclusive
③ we'd better choose one of them
④ knowledge can be found in classic

04 다음 빈칸에 들어갈 말로 가장 적절한 것은?

Soccer is more exciting than any of the top team sports. This is according to the research of a team of scientists. They analyzed the results of over 300,000 games played since 1888. They decided that the likelihood of an "upset" in a game was a good measure of its excitement. An upset is a game in which the weaker team beats the stronger team. They found soccer matches produced more upsets. The survey, however, is not all bad news for enthusiasts of other team sports. It seems that soccer has become ______________________________ over the past fifty years. This suggests that strong teams are becoming stronger and the chance of an upset is lessening.

① less exciting and more predictable
② more thrilling than other team sports
③ a sport which pays athletes too much
④ a sport which produces far more upsets

05 다음 빈칸에 들어갈 말로 가장 적절한 것은?

You suggested that some mestizo people undergo plastic surgery because they believe that their historical faces have no value. That is a preposterous idea because all those involved are merely seeking new and interesting appearances as a vogue. Just think about the white Americans with African hairstyles in order to look special. They definitely do not consider their hairstyles to be shameful. And the Japanese people who undergo surgery to enlarge their eyes obviously do not wish to become a race of people they sometimes describe as pale-complexioned barbarians. Please remember that a Hispanic's or a Mestizo's attempt to look white is just a vogue. You should never describe it as ________________.

*mestizo: 메스티소(스페인인과 북미 원주민의 혼혈)

① lack of self-esteem
② a pattern of vogue
③ a kind of imitation
④ a way of satisfaction

06 다음 빈칸에 들어갈 말로 가장 적절한 것은?

I would like to compare the shift from analog to digital film-making to the shift from fresco and tempera to oil painting in the early Renaissance. A painter making a fresco has limited time before the paint dries, and once it has dried, no further changes to the image are possible. Similarly, a traditional filmmaker has limited means of modifying images once they are recorded on film. Medieval tempera painting can be compared to the practice of special effects during the analog period of cinema. A painter working with tempera could modify and rework the image, but the process was painstaking and slow. The switch to oils greatly liberated painters by allowing them to quickly create much larger compositions as well as to modify them as long as necessary. Similarly, ________________________________, digital technology redefines what can be done with cinema.

① by equating oil painting with analog film-making
② by allowing a filmmaker to treat a film image as an oil painting
③ with the shift from oil painting styles to fresco ones in making films
④ with the introduction of tempera painting methods to cinematic special effects

07 다음 빈칸에 들어갈 말로 가장 적절한 것은?

It is a common misconception among many musicians and non-musicians alike that ________________. This is not surprising as it is natural to associate music with the sounds that create the melody, rather than with the quiet spaces between the notes. Because rests are silent, people often misinterpret these empty spaces as unimportant. But, imagine what would happen if a song was made up of only notes, and no rests. Aside from the fact that the "rests would be history" (pun intended), there would be a wall of sound with no reference point or discernible backbone to the music. This is because the spaces between the sounds provide a baseline and contrast for the piece, and give music structure and texture. In fact, it is a common saying among experienced musicians that a full measure of rest can hold more music than a full measure of blistering notes.

① notes are more important than rests
② rests provide a direct reference point to music
③ silence is no less meaningful than sound in music
④ melody is nothing more than a collection of sounds

Reading Skill **02**

비평·대조 (연결사 중심의 독해)

HOW TO SOLVE

상술(expatiation)과 비평(criticism) 및 대조(contrast)

<상 술>	<비 평>	<대 조>
제3자의 생각 (신(新)정보) ↓ 상술 (예시, 나열) ↓	제3자의 생각 (사회적 통념) ↓ 전환점 ↓ 필자의 생각(주제)	제3자(A)의 생각 ↖ + 주제 ↙ 제3자(B)의 생각

1 상술

글 도입에 제시된 제3자의 생각은 새로운 정보이거나 어려운 내용인 경우가 많다. 그러므로 이하에는 제시된 새로운 정보, 즉 제3자의 생각을 예시나 나열 등을 통하여 보충하거나 다른 말로 풀어서 부연 설명을 한다. 상술의 한 방법으로 예시, 나열 등이 있다. (Reading Skill 03. 예시 · 나열 참고)

제3자의 생각	Tom is a good teacher.
상술 (예시, 나열)	For example, he teaches us English with a zeal. And above all, he often buys us some pizza.

여기서는 2가지 예시를 통해서 Tom이 좋은 선생님이라는 것을 뒷받침한다.

2 비평

비평은 글의 도입 부분에 일반적인 견해나 통념을 제시하고 뒷부분에 반대의 주장을 개진하는 글의 구조이다. 이때 **역접의 연결사**가 많이 나오며, 반드시 **'다수론(제3자의 생각) → 전환점(역접의 연결사) → 필자의 주장'**의 순서로 글이 전개된다. 이때 중반부터 이어지는 필자의 주장이 글의 주제가 된다.

제3자의 생각	Fighting against prejudice is very difficult.
전환점	**But, Yet, However** (그러나) **Nevertheless, Nonetheless, And yet, Still, Even so** (그럼에도 불구하고)
필자의 생각 (주제)	It is important that we try.

3 대조

비평은 제3자의 생각을 비평하면서 뒤에 나오는 필자의 주장을 강조하는 구조이다. 대조 또한 제3자의 생각을 비평하지만, 뒤에는 의미적으로 상반되는 내용이 나온다는 점에서 비평 구조와는 다르다. 특히 앞에 나오는 내용과 뒤에 나오는 내용 모두 똑같이 중요하므로 그 두 개를 포괄한 것이 글의 주제가 된다.

제3자의 생각 1	Some people say that Larry is a good man.
제3자의 생각 2	Other people say that he is an abnormal pervert.
주제	Larry에 대한 다양한 견해가 존재한다.

비평, 대조, 소재 전환의 연결사	A ← But, Yet, However → B But, Yet, However는 가장 널리 쓰이는 연결사로, 비평이나 대조에도 쓰이지만, 소재가 전환될 때도 쓰인다. • Some people say Shimson is rich. However, this is not true. (비평) • Money is important for our happiness. However, health is also essential in leading a happy life. (소재 전환)
대조의 대표적 연결사 및 표현	❶ A ← In[By] contrast, On the contrary, On the other hand → B 위의 연결사가 나오는 경우, 대개 그 연결사 앞뒤의 내용이 대조된다. • Samsung is a Korean company, on the contrary, Apple is a U.S company. ❷ Two(A and B), different(differ, difference) 이 표현들이 문단 앞부분에 나오면, 그 글은 대조 구조가 될 확률이 높다. • Teenage culture and adult culture are **different** from each other. → 이 글은 십 대 문화와 성인 문화의 차이를 다루는 글일 가능성이 크다.

그 외 대조의 연결사 및 표현

❶ A ← while, whereas → B

전체 단락이 두 개로 나누어지는 것이 아니라, 한 문장 안에서 대조가 이루어진다.

• Some people sleep, **while** some people have sleeplessness.

❷ 비교를 통한 대조

A	↔ more ~ than ~er than as ~ as	B

• I am bright**er than** Kevin.

❸ Some vs Others를 통한 대조

• **Some** think Larry is idiotic. **Others** think Larry is smart.

❹ 시간상 대조 (과거와 현재의 차이점을 드러냄)

현재	today, now, nowadays, these days, at present, recently, currently
과거	in the past, those days, ~ ago, once, in + 과거연도
시간상 대조	at first, no longer, used to RV, instead

SKILL EXAMPLE

01 다음 글의 빈칸에 들어갈 말로 가장 적절한 것은?

If you were a butterfly, would you be attracted to a more colorful flower or a less colorful one? Most of you would probably prefer the more colorful option. The same is true for pollinators such as bees and butterflies. For years, biologists have known that flowers use striking colors, scents, elaborately shaped petals, and nectar to attract pollinators. Recent studies, however, reveal another powerful tool of attraction used by flowers: ____________________. Scientists have discovered that mobile flowers are visited more often by pollinating insects than their more static counterparts. It is almost as if the flowers are waving to the insects, saying, "Welcome. Come here and have a drink." Along with this interesting finding, scientists have also concluded that, due to their greater range of motion, flowers with long, thin stalks attract more insects.

① moving in the wind
② fancy color scheme
③ unique tasting nectar
④ having deep roots

지문 분석

For years, biologists have known that flowers use striking colors, scents, elaborately shaped petals, and nectar to attract pollinators.

수년 동안 생물학자들은 꽃들이 꽃가루 매개자들을 유혹하기 위해 눈에 띄는 색, 향기, 정교한 모양의 꽃잎, 그리고 꽃꿀을 사용한다는 것을 알고 있었다.

글의 도입 부분(역접의 연결사가 나오기 전)에는 다수의 견해나 일반적인 사실을 제시한다.

Recent studies, **however**, reveal another powerful tool of attraction used by flowers: ________________. Scientists have discovered that mobile flowers are visited more often by pollinating insects than their more static counterparts.

하지만 최근의 연구들은 꽃들이 사용하는 또 다른 강력한 유혹의 도구인 ________________를 밝힌다. 과학자들은 움직이는 꽃들이 움직이지 않는 꽃들보다 꽃가루를 운반하는 곤충들에 의해 더 자주 방문 받는다는 것을 발견했다.

그리고 전환점(역접의 연결사인 however)이 나오고 앞부분에서 언급되지 않은 새로운 내용이 제시된다. 따라서 빈칸에 들어갈 말에 대한 단서는 however 앞부분이 아닌, 뒷부분에서 찾아볼 수 있다. mobile flowers가 곤충들에 의해 더 많은 방문을 받는다는 설명에서 꽃들의 움직임이 곤충을 유인하는 강력한 수단이라는 것을 알 수 있다.

정답 및 해석

정답 ①

해석 만약 당신이 나비라면, 당신은 색깔이 더 화려한 꽃에 끌리겠는가 아니면 덜 화려한 것에 끌리겠는가? 당신들 중 대부분은 아마도 색이 더 화려한 선택지를 선호할 것이다. 벌이나 나비와 같은 꽃가루 매개자들도 마찬가지이다. 수년 동안, 생물학자들은 꽃이 꽃가루 매개자를 끌어들이기 위해 눈에 띄는 색깔, 향기, 정교한 모양의 꽃잎, 그리고 꿀을 사용한다는 것을 알고 있었다. 그런데, 최근의 연구는 꽃들에 의해 사용되는 다른 강력한 유혹의 도구인 바람에 움직이는 것을 밝혀냈다. 과학자들은 움직이는 꽃들이 움직이지 않는 꽃들보다 꽃가루를 운반하는 곤충들에 의해 더 자주 방문 받는다는 것을 발견했다. 그것은 거의 마치 꽃들이 곤충에게 손을 흔들며 "환영해요. 와서 한잔하세요"라고 말하는 것과 같다. 이 흥미로운 발견에 덧붙여, 과학자들은 또한 더 넓은 움직임의 범위 덕분에, 길고 가는 줄기를 가진 꽃들이 더 많은 곤충을 끌어들인다고 결론지었다.

① 바람에 움직이는 것
② 화려한 색채 배합
③ 독특한 맛이 나는 꿀
④ 깊은 뿌리를 지닌 것

어휘 prefer 선호하다 pollinator 꽃가루 매개자 biologist 생물학자 striking 눈에 띄는 elaborately 정교하게 petal 꽃잎 nectar 꿀 mobile 움직이는 static 움직이지 않는 counterpart 대응물 stalk 줄기 fancy 화려한 scheme 배합, 전략

01 다음 글을 읽고, 빈칸에 들어갈 말로 가장 적절한 것은?

There are good reasons to keep marine fish in the home aquarium. They are diverse, often beautifully colored, and their biology and behavior are endlessly fascinating. Even for the experienced freshwater aquarist, however, marine fish are considered challenging because it's difficult to keep the seawater quality and temperature stable in an aquarium. Unlike freshwater fish, many marine species have little ______________ for variations in water quality and temperature. Therefore, keeping them in a home aquarium demands more monitoring and attention to detail.

① tolerance ② discrimination
③ effect ④ implication

02 글의 흐름으로 보아, 주어진 문장이 들어가기에 가장 적절한 곳은?

However, there are risks associated with teeth whitening.

Most people want sparkling white teeth and beautiful smiles on their faces. This demand for a new beautiful look has led to the popularity of the teeth whitening process. (①) The two most common side effects are temporary increase of tooth sensitivity and irritation of the gums. (②) The sensitivity problem in the teeth usually occurs in the initial stages of the whitening process. (③) The irritation of the gums often occurs during the fitting of a mouthpiece tray. (④) Some other risks associated with teeth whitening are overdose or overuse, addiction, and use of unhygienic or improper instruments.

03 글의 흐름으로 보아, 주어진 문장이 들어가기에 가장 적절한 곳은?

Change in bedtime routines, illnesses, or even the presence of house-guest can cause their sleep patterns to worsen.

Some children are excellent sleepers from birth. In the early weeks they may have to be wakened for feedings. As they grow older, not only do they continue to sleep well, but it becomes difficult to wake them even if one tries. They sleep soundly at night in a variety of situations: bright or dark, quiet or noisy, calm or chaotic. (①) They can tolerate an occasional disruption of their sleep schedules, and they sleep well even during periods of emotional stress. (②) On the other hand, other children seem inherently more restless. These children are much more susceptible to having their sleep patterns disrupted. (③) However, even when these children have always been considered 'non-sleepers,' they also can sleep quite satisfactorily if their routine is respected. (④) In either case, consistent routines should be maintained to provide both types of children with adequate amounts of sleep to ensure both their emotional and physical well-being.

04 글의 흐름으로 보아, 주어진 문장이 들어가기에 가장 적절한 곳은?

> However, recent success in the packaged-cookie market suggests that these may not be the only, or perhaps even the most important, reasons.

Why eat a cookie? Some reasons might be to satisfy your hunger, to increase your sugar level, or just to have something to chew on. (①) It appears that cookie-producing companies are becoming aware of some other influences and, as a result, are delivering to the market products resulting from their awareness. (②) These relatively new product offerings are usually referred to as 'soft' or 'chewy' cookies, to distinguish them from the more typical crunchy varieties. (③) Why all the fuss over their introduction? (④) Apparently much of their appeal has to do with childhood memories of sitting on the back steps devouring those melt-in-your-mouth cookies that were delivered by Mom straight from the oven, while they were still soft.

05 글의 흐름으로 보아, 주어진 문장이 들어가기에 가장 적절한 곳은?

> They appreciated their mothers' constant presence and availability.

My research points to an overwhelming correlation between a mother's working and her daughter's desire to work when she has children of her own. (①) About three quarters of the stay-at-home moms I interviewed had mothers who never worked outside of the home. (②) They also thought that having a job was just an option not a must. (③) On the other hand, all of the women whom I have interviewed whose mothers worked knew that they too would work when they had children. (④) Most of these women felt little hesitation in this decision. They thought that having a job was natural.

Reading Skill

03 예시·나열

HOW TO SOLVE

1 예시(Examples)

상술의 한 방법으로, 앞에 언급된 **추상적 개념을 구체적이고 자세하게 설명**하기 위해서 예시를 드는 단락 구조이다. 이때 **주제는 예시 바로 앞에 있는 문장(추상적이고 큰 개념)**이다. 그러나 그 앞 문장은 보통 어려운 내용이기 때문에 그 앞 문장만 보고서는 답을 찾기가 힘들다. (예시를 드는 이유는 그 개념이 어렵기 때문임을 기억하자.)

따라서 구체적인 예시를 읽어야 하지만, 정확하게 말하면 예시를 들고 있는 부분은 답이 아니다. 하지만 그 예시의 내용을 뒤틀어서 오답 보기로 제시하는 경우가 많기 때문에 예시 구조의 지문을 읽을 때에는 **'예시 앞 문장 → 예시 → 예시 앞 문장'**의 순서로 읽도록 한다.

> ※ 예시의 연결사 생략 (for example, for instance)
>
> 예시의 연결사는 자주 생략된다. 따라서 연결사에만 의존할 것이 아니라 예시 구조의 특징을 잘 알아둘 필요가 있다. 보통 고유명사(지명, 인명), 연도, 구체적인 숫자, if절이 나오면 예시일 확률이 높다.
>
> cf if절이 여러 개일 경우 나열(Listing) 구조일 수 있다.

2 나열(Listing)

❶ **'many, various, several, 구체적인 숫자(one, second, third) + 명사'**가 앞부분에 나오면 나열 구조일 확률이 높다.

이 경우 대개 뒤에는 2개 이상의 내용이 나열되고, 그 나열된 내용의 공통점이나 '명사'가 주제가 된다.

❷ **also, moreover, furthermore, besides, in addition, what is more**이 나오면 두 개 이상의 항목이 나열된다.

이러한 연결사 앞에 나온 내용과 뒤에 나온 내용의 공통된 소재(Topic)가 주제문과 직결된다.

at the same time, similarly, likewise가 나오면 글의 소재가 서로 다른 경우가 많다.

이러한 연결사 앞뒤에는 대개 다른 소재가 나열되며, 또는 글 전체의 맥락이 바뀌어 새로운 화제가 제시된다.

❸ **for example**(예시) 뒤에는 나열 구조가 오는 경우가 많다.

예를 들 때는 하나만 들기보다는 여러 개의 예를 드는 경우가 많으므로 for example(예시) 뒤에 나열이 나오는 경우가 많다.

❹ **another**를 이용하면 앞뒤의 내용이 무엇인지 알 수 있다.

another는 두 번째 나열이고, 첫 번째 나열되고 있는 것과 비슷한 내용이 another 뒤에 이어서 나온다. 가령 another animal이 나왔다고 한다면, 앞에는 어떤 동물(ex. 고양이)이 나왔을 것이고, 뒤에는 또 다른 동물(ex. 개)이 나올 것이다.

SKILL EXAMPLE

01 다음 글의 제목으로 알맞은 것은?

Most people have a vase or two in a cupboard, but lots of things can be turned into stylish containers for a flower arrangement, so before you rush out to buy anything, look around your own home. For instance, goldfish bowls look stunning filled with flower heads or petals, magnifying their contents. Wine, milk, mineral water, or olive oil bottles look particularly good with one or two stems in them. Try a collection of bottles in various shapes and sizes, lined up on a shelf or grouped on a table. An old teapot which has lost its lid becomes an ideal container for a bunch of roses picked from the garden.

① Flower Arrangements and Gardening
② Tips for Planting Flowers in the Garden
③ Decorating a Dining Table with Various Plants
④ Ordinary Things as Flower Containers

지문 분석

Most people have a vase or two in a cupboard, but lots of things can be turned into stylish containers for a flower arrangement, so before you rush out to buy anything, look around your own home. **For instance**, goldfish bowls look stunning filled with flower heads or petals, magnifying their contents.

대부분의 사람들은 찬장 안에 한두 개의 꽃병을 가지고 있지만, 많은 물건들이 꽃꽂이를 위한 세련된 용기가 될 수 있으므로, 무엇인가 사려고 급히 나가기 전에 자신의 집을 살펴보아라. 예를 들어, 금붕어 어항은 내용물을 확대해 보여주기 때문에, 꽃송이나 꽃잎으로 가득 찼을 때 놀라울 정도로 아름답다.

for example, for instance는 예시를 들기 위해 사용되는 대표적인 연결사들이다. 이러한 연결사들은 앞에 나온 말을 보다 더 구체적으로 설명하기 위해 쓰인다. 일반적으로 이러한 예시의 연결사 바로 앞 문장을 보면 글에서 무엇을 말하고자 하는지를 파악할 수 있다. 이 글에서는 꽃을 담기 위해 무엇을 사기 전에 먼저 집안을 살필 것을 말하고 있으며, 꽃병으로 쓸 수 있는 일상적인 사물의 첫 번째 예로 금붕어 어항을 들고 있다.

Wine, milk, mineral water, or olive oil bottles ... 중략 ...
An old teapot which has lost its lid becomes an ideal container for a bunch of roses picked from the garden.
와인, 우유, 미네랄워터, 혹은 올리브오일 병 ... (중략) ...
뚜껑이 없어진 낡은 찻주전자가 정원에서 꺾은 장미 한 다발을 위한 이상적인 용기가 된다.

일반적인 사물들이 꽃병으로 활용될 수 있는 또 다른 사례들을 나열한다. 원래 그 용도가 아닌 물건이더라도 관점을 바꾸면 예쁜 꽃병으로 사용할 수 있다는 것이 이 글의 주제임을 알 수 있다.

정답 및 해석

정답 ④

해석 대부분의 사람들은 찬장에 한두 개의 꽃병을 가지고 있지만 많은 것들이 꽃꽂이를 위한 멋진 용기가 될 수 있으므로 무언가를 사기 위해 달려 나가기 전에, 당신 자신의 집을 둘러봐라. 예를 들어, 금붕어 어항은 내용물을 확대해 보여주기 때문에, 꽃송이나 꽃잎으로 채워지면 굉장히 멋져 보인다. 와인, 우유, 미네랄워터, 혹은 올리브오일 병은 그 속에 한두 줄기를 넣으면 특히 괜찮게 보인다. 선반에 줄지어 늘어놓거나 테이블 위에 모아 놓은 다양한 모양과 크기의 병을 수집해 봐라. 뚜껑이 없어진 낡은 찻주전자가 정원에서 꺾은 장미 한 다발을 위한 이상적인 용기가 된다.
① 꽃꽂이와 정원 가꾸기
② 정원에 꽃 심기를 위한 조언들
③ 다양한 식물들로 식사 테이블 장식하기
④ 꽃병으로서의 일상적인 물건들

어휘 cupboard 찬장 container 용기 flower arrangement 꽃꽂이 goldfish 금붕어 stunning 굉장히 멋진 magnify 확대하다 particularly 특히 lid 뚜껑 ordinary 일상적인

02 다음 빈칸에 들어갈 말로 가장 적절한 것은?

It is not hard to see that a strong economy, where opportunities are plentiful and jobs go begging, ______________________. Biased employers may still dislike hiring members of one group or another, but when nobody else is available, discrimination most often gives way to the basic need to get the work done. The same goes for employees with prejudices about whom they do and do not like working alongside. In the American construction boom of the late 1990s, for example, even the carpenters' union — long known as a "traditional bastion of white men, a world where a coveted union card was handed down from father to son" — began openly encouraging women, blacks, and Hispanics to join its internship program. At least in the workplace, jobs chasing people obviously does more to promote a fluid society than people chasing jobs.

① simplifies the hiring process
② increases wage discrimination
③ helps break down social barriers
④ improves the productivity of a company

지문 분석

It is not hard to see that a strong economy, …… , ______________.

…… 튼튼한 경제는 __________라는 것을 이해하기는 어렵지 않다.

글의 첫 문장은 '튼튼한 경제'의 성질이 곧 빈칸이라고 설명하고 있다. 빈칸이 글의 전반부에 위치하고 있고 보기 문항의 길이가 길기 때문에 빈칸의 내용이 곧 글 전체의 주제에 해당할 것이라고 유추할 수 있다.

In the American construction boom of the late 1990s, **for example**, even the carpenters' union …… began openly encouraging women, blacks, and Hispanics to join its internship program.

예를 들어, 1990년대 후반 미국의 건설 호황기에 …… 목수 노조조차도 여성, 흑인, 그리고 히스패닉에게 그들의 인턴 프로그램에 참가하라고 공개적으로 장려하기 시작했다.

연결사 for example을 이용하여 글의 주제에 대한 부연 설명을 이어가는 부분이다. 여성, 흑인, 히스패닉 등을 나열하여 소위 미국 내 사회적 약자에게 백인 남성의 전유물이었던 일자리가 장려되었음을 알 수 있다. 따라서 글의 주제는 사회적 약자에게 가로막혔던 일자리 제한이 완화되고 사라지는 것임을 알 수 있으며, 일자리가 풍부한 튼튼한 경제 사회에서는 기회 제공의 범위가 이전에 차별받던 사람들에게까지 넓어진다는 것을 유추할 수 있다.

정답 및 해석

정답 ③

해석 기회가 풍부하고 일자리를 원하는 사람이 없는 튼튼한 경제는 사회적 장벽을 무너뜨리는 데 도움이 된다는 것을 이해하기는 어렵지 않다. 편견을 가진 고용주들은 어떤 한 집단이나 혹은 다른 집단의 구성원을 고용하기를 여전히 싫어할 수도 있지만, 그 외에 아무도 구할 수 없을 때는, 차별은 대개 일을 수행해야만 한다는 기본적인 필요성에 자리를 내준다. 그것은 같이 일하고 싶은 사람과 같이 일하기 싫은 사람에 대한 편견을 가진 피고용자들에게 있어서도 마찬가지이다. 예를 들어, 1990년대 후반 미국의 건설 호황기에 '사람들의 부러움을 사는 노조 조합원 카드를 아버지에게서 아들에게로 물려주던 세계이자 백인 남성들의 전통적인 요새'로 오랫동안 알려져 온 목수 노조조차도 여성과 흑인 그리고 히스패닉에게 그들의 인턴 프로그램에 참가하라고 공개적으로 장려하기 시작했다. 최소한 업무 현장에서는 일자리가 사람을 쫓아다니는 것이 사람이 일자리를 쫓아다니는 것보다 유동적 사회를 촉진하는 데 분명히 더 많은 기여를 한다.

① 고용 과정을 단순화한다
② 급여 차별을 증가시킨다
③ 사회적 장벽을 무너뜨리는 데 도움이 된다
④ 기업의 생산성을 향상시킨다

어휘 plentiful 풍부한 go begging 원하는 사람이 없다, 구걸하고 다니다 biased 편향된 discrimination 차별 give way to 자리를 내주다 bastion 요새 coveted 부러움을 사는 hand down ~을 물려주다 obviously 명백히 fluid 유동적인

01 다음 글을 읽고, 빈칸에 들어갈 말로 가장 적절한 것은?

In a traditional theory, the poorer countries could catch up quickly because in those countries, ________________. For instance, a few roads in a poor country can open a whole new area for trade; in a rich country, a few more roads just relieve a little congestion. A little more education in a poor country can make all the difference; in a rich country, people with degrees often can't find a job. And of course, it should be easier to copy technology than for a rich country to invent it. When you look at some developing countries in the world, the theory of catch-up seems reasonable.

① public transportation is well organized
② new investments have far bigger rewards
③ people work hard to break the chain of poverty
④ wages are relatively lower than in rich countries

02 다음 글의 빈칸에 들어갈 말로 가장 적절한 것은?

Which is more important, good or bad? Regardless of which you consider to be the right answer, ________. For instance, the traffic jam that bogs down our day stays in our thoughts longer than the open road that sped us on our way. The rude clerk is memorable long after the nice clerk is forgotten. Remind yourself to see the good, to think about the good, and to remember the good. The good is out there just as much as the bad, but we are often prone to missing it.

① the open road is not always good
② we tend to choose the easy way
③ the bad is often a bigger part of our thoughts
④ the good plays a positive part in our life

03 주어진 글 다음에 이어질 글의 순서로 가장 적절한 것은?

Clearly, schematic knowledge helps you — guiding your understanding and enabling you to reconstruct things you cannot remember.

(A) Likewise, if there are things you can't recall, your schemata will fill in the gaps with knowledge about what's typical in that situation. As a result, a reliance on schemata will inevitably make the world seem more "normal" than it really is and will make the past seem more "regular" than it actually was.

(B) Any reliance on schematic knowledge, therefore, will be shaped by this information about what's "normal." Thus, if there are things you don't notice while viewing a situation or event, your schemata will lead you to fill in these "gaps" with knowledge about what's normally in place in that setting.

(C) But schematic knowledge can also hurt you, promoting errors in perception and memory. Moreover, the types of errors produced by schemata are quite predictable: Bear in mind that schemata summarize the broad pattern of your experience, and so they tell you, in essence, what's typical or ordinary in a given situation.

① (B) – (A) – (C)　　② (B) – (C) – (A)

③ (C) – (A) – (B)　　④ (C) – (B) – (A)

04 주어진 글 다음에 이어질 글의 순서로 가장 적절한 것은?

Bats are the primary predators of night-flying insects, playing a vital role in maintaining their balance in nature.

(A) The big-sized bats eat various moths and worms that are harmful to agriculture and forestry. The small-sized bats eat mosquitoes and other double-winged insects — carriers of diseases such as malaria.

(B) In addition, bats that eat fruit or flowers disperse seeds and pollinate flowers of more than 500 species of tropical trees and shrubs. If it were not for bats, the harvest of such tropical fruit as bananas and pineapples would decrease by 60%.

(C) One bat eats one-third of its body weight and is able to catch 600 mosquitoes in one hour. And different bat species hunt at different heights, preying on different kinds of insects.

① (A) – (C) – (B)　　② (B) – (C) – (A)

③ (C) – (A) – (B)　　④ (C) – (B) – (A)

05 다음 빈칸에 들어갈 말로 가장 적절한 것은?

When we claim that a certain fact is the cause of a certain other fact, there should be a real cause-and-effect relationship between the two facts. But it is not always an easy thing to see the relevance. For example, if a historian is investigating causes of the decline of the Roman Empire, should he learn the date when the Great Wall of China was built? Is this a relevant fact? On further investigation, we find that it is. There does appear to be a cause-and-effect relationship between the building of the Great Wall and the decline of the Roman Empire. The Chinese built the Great Wall to protect their borders. After it was built, the Huns couldn't advance on China. Unable to move east, they turned westward and finally reached the Roman area. There they contributed significantly to the fall of the Roman Empire. This shows that ______________________.

① the fall of the Roman Empire affected world history
② the relationship between two facts can easily be identified
③ historians should distinguish casual facts from inevitable results
④ apparently irrelevant facts may actually be more relevant than they seem

06 주어진 글 다음에 이어질 글의 순서로 가장 적절한 것은?

Most people probably associate coyotes with the American West. Indeed, these handsome and adaptable animals are native to that part of the world.

(A) Yet coyotes also prey on livestock. For this reason, some people seek to reduce their numbers or even eliminate them altogether. Ranchers in the western United States have long felt hostility toward coyotes because the animals kill hundreds of thousands of sheep each year.

(B) However, over the past hundred years, the species has greatly enlarged its territory. It has moved steadily eastward and into areas that are more densely populated. Today the melodious howls of coyotes can be heard throughout the United States and in parts of Canada and Central America.

(C) Why have coyotes been so successful? Their "omnivorous eating habits" have certainly helped them. They are known to eat just about anything, including insects, snakes, frogs, grass, apples, cactus fruit, and even watermelon.

① (B) – (A) – (C)　② (B) – (C) – (A)
③ (C) – (A) – (B)　④ (C) – (B) – (A)

Reading Skill 04

원인-결과 / 실험 구조
(Cause & Effect)

HOW TO SOLVE

영어지문에서 가장 많이 나오는 구조가 **원인-결과 구조**이다. 원인-결과 구조는 특별한 연결사나 구조 없이 나오는 경우가 대부분이므로 많은 연습이 필요하다. 또한 넓은 의미에서 보면 **문제점-해결책**도 **원인-결과 구조**이다.

실험 구조의 경우, 원서나 국내 대부분의 교재에 특별한 언급이 없지만, 시험뿐만 아니라 일반 글에도 자주 나오는 구조이기 때문에 알아둘 필요가 있다.

1 형태상 원인-결과(Cause & Effect)

so, thus, hence, therefore, accordingly, thereby, for these reasons, finally, consequently, as a result (따라서)
in short, in brief, in a word (요약해서)

❶ 앞 문장에는 원인, 뒤 문장에는 결과가 나온다.
❷ 이러한 연결사가 마지막 문장을 이끌면 그 마지막 문장이 대개 주제문이 된다. (요지 · 주장)

• A(원인) + [cause / bring about / lead to / give rise to / result in / produce / end in / contribute to] + B(결과)

cause	lead to	result in	end in
bring about	give rise to	produce	contribute to

❶ 주어가 원인, 목적어가 결과가 된다.
❷ 'A 해서 B가 된다'라고 해석한다.

• B(결과) + [result from / be produced by / arise from / be the consequence of / follow / be caused by / be the result of] + A(원인)

result from	arise from	follow	be caused by
be produced by	be the consequence of		be the result of

❶ 주어가 결과, 목적어가 원인이 된다.
❷ 'B는 A 때문이다'라고 해석한다.

• A(요인) +	have an influence[effect/impact] on affect　　influence　　play an important role in	+ B(대상)

❶ 주어가 요인, 목적어가 영향을 받는 대상이 된다.
❷ 'A가 B에 영향을 끼친다'라고 해석한다.

<u>원인</u> + This is why <u>결과</u>
<u>결과</u> + This is because <u>원인</u>

• **because**(~이므로)와 **why**(어째서, 왜)는 원인과 결과의 순서가 반대라는 것을 기억하자.

예 Mary works at the office for more than 12 hours. **This is why** she looks so tired.
Mary는 사무실에서 12시간 넘게 일한다. 이것이 그녀가 그렇게 피곤해 보이는 이유이다.

예 Tom got huffy. **That's because** Mary and Anna didn't take him to the zoo.
Tom은 삐쳤다. 그것은 Mary와 Anna가 그를 동물원에 데리고 가지 않았기 때문이다.

2 내용상 원인-결과(Cause & Effect)

특별한 연결사나 구조가 없기 때문에 가장 어려운 유형이다. 소재(Topic) 중심의 독해를 통하여 무엇이 원인이고 무엇이 결과인지를 파악하며 글을 읽어야 한다.

3 실험 구조

실험 구조는 두 가지만 제대로 알면 쉽게 답을 찾을 수 있다.
먼저 ❶ **실험군과 대조군**(원인)을 잡은 후에 ❷ **실험 결과**(결과)에 초점을 두고 글을 읽어 내려가면 어떤 유형(빈칸, 주제, 제목, 요지, 주장 …)의 문제도 쉽게 풀 수 있다.

❶ 실험군 vs 대조군

실험군과 대조군은 서로 **대조 구조**의 형태를 띠므로 **대조의 연결사, 특히 비교급 형태**가 많이 나온다.

- **실험군 및 대조군과 관련된 표현**
  some / others, one / the other, two / three, identical, subject
- **대조의 연결사**
  but, yet, however, in[by] contrast, on the contrary, on the other hand, while, whereas
- **비교급 표현**

❷ 실험 결과를 나타내는 표현

아래의 표현과 함께 실험 결과를 제시하는 경우가 많다.

research / experiment study / test / survey sociologist / researcher	+	show suggest discover	+	실험 결과 문두 : 소재 문중·미 : 주제

4 문제점과 해결책

문제점과 해결책 구조의 글은 크게 3가지 방향으로 전개된다.

문제점 ↓ 해결책 (주제)	문제점 ↓ (문제점이 주제)	문제점 ↓ 원인 ↓ 해결책 (주제)
Anna feels lonely. ↓ **She should find her Mr. Right.**	Every night, Mary goes to movie and goes shopping with friends. ↓ **She plays too much.**	Tom is a workaholic. ↓ He has never had a girlfriend before. ↓ **He should find his Miss. Right.**

해결책 제시 방법

- by RVing : ~함으로써
- the best way[solution] to RV : ~하기 위한 최고의 방법[해결책]
- to avoid[solve] the problem : 그 문제를 피하기[해결하기] 위해서는
- need to RV / the need[necessity] to RV[of 명사] : ~할 필요가 있다 / ~할 필요
- through A : A를 통해서
- if : 만약 ~한다면

SKILL EXAMPLE

01 다음 글의 빈칸에 들어갈 말로 가장 적절한 것은?

A new study suggests that kids might be at increased risk of getting the disease of the lungs depending on ____________________. Looking at more than 95,000 infants born from 1995 to 2000, researchers followed the children through 2005. What they found was those born in the autumn were nearly 30% more likely to get asthma. The researchers say it's because babies born in the fall months are much more likely to get common wintertime infections. At birth, infants have protection against certain diseases because antibodies have passed from the mother to her unborn baby. But the protection is temporary. So, as their immunities fade, babies become more subject to infections, especially on the winter months when all kinds of germs are swirling through air.

① where they live
② when they were born
③ what they usually eat
④ how healthy their parents are

지문 분석

A new study suggests that kids might be at increased risk of getting the disease of the lungs depending on ______________.

한 새로운 연구가 ______________에 따라 아이들이 폐병에 걸릴 위험이 높아질 수 있다고 밝힌다.

A new study, suggests로 보아 이 글이 실험 구조의 글임을 알 수 있다. 이런 문장은 실험 구조의 가장 전형적인 표현이다.

What they found was those born in the autumn were nearly 30% more likely to get asthma.

그들이 발견한 것은 가을에 태어난 아기들이 (다른 계절에 태어난 아기들보다) 천식에 걸릴 확률이 거의 30%나 더 높다는 것이었다.

'What they found'를 통해 뒤에 실험 결과가 이어진다고 예측할 수 있다. '가을에 태어난 아기(실험군)'와 '다른 계절에 태어난 아기(대조군)'를 비교함으로써 빈칸에 들어갈 내용을 찾을 수 있다.

정답 및 해석

정답 ②

해석 한 새로운 연구는 아이들이 언제 태어났는지에 따라 그 아이들이 폐 질환에 걸릴 위험이 높아질 수 있다는 것을 시사한다. 연구원들은 1995년에서 2000년 사이에 태어난 95,000명 이상의 유아들을 관찰하면서 2005년까지 그 아이들을 추적하였다. 그들이 발견한 것은 가을에 태어난 아이들이 천식에 걸릴 확률이 거의 30%나 높았다는 것이다. 연구원들은 그 이유가 가을철에 태어난 아기들이 흔한 겨울철 질병에 걸릴 가능성이 훨씬 더 크기 때문이라고 말한다. 출생 시에 유아들은 항체가 어머니로부터 태아에게 전달되기 때문에 특정한 질병에 대한 방어력이 있다. 그러나 그 방어력은 일시적이다. 그래서 그들의 면역력이 사라져감에 따라 아기들은 더 질병에 걸리기 쉬워지는데, 온갖 종류의 세균들이 공기 중에 들끓는 겨울철에 특히 그러하다.

① 아이들이 어디에 사는지
② 아이들이 언제 태어났는지
③ 아이들이 보통 무엇을 먹는지
④ 아이들의 부모가 얼마나 건강한지

어휘 lung 폐 asthma 천식 infection 질병 antibody 항체 unborn baby 태아 temporary 일시적인 immunity 면역성 subject to ~에 걸리기 쉬운 germ 세균 swirl 소용돌이치다

정답 및 해설 08P

01 다음 빈칸에 들어갈 말로 가장 적절한 것은?

The sun is slowly getting brighter as its core contracts and heats up. In a billion years it will be about 10 percent brighter than today, heating the planet to an uncomfortable degree. Water evaporating from the oceans may set off a runaway greenhouse effect that turns Earth into a damp version of Venus, wrapped permanently in a thick, white blanket of cloud. Or the transformation may take some time and be more gentle, with an increasingly hot and cloudy atmosphere able to shelter microbial life for some time. Either way, water will escape into the stratosphere and be broken down by UV light into oxygen and hydrogen. Oxygen will be left in the stratosphere — perhaps misleading aliens into thinking the planet is still inhabited — while the hydrogen is light enough to escape into space. So our water will gradually ___________.

① leak away
② be frozen
③ flow over
④ accumulate

02 다음 빈칸에 들어갈 말로 가장 적절한 것은?

Dreams are a natural part of sleep, and everybody has them, whether they remember them or not. But ________ depends on who they are and how old they are. For instance, marriage has an effect on dreaming. One study showed that unmarried women dream more than married ones. Men dream less than women, whether they are married or not. Younger people tend to dream quite a lot. On the other hand, by the time they reach retirement age, people dream a lot less often.

① why people dream
② how much people dream
③ what dreams mean
④ what dreams people have

03 다음 빈칸에 들어갈 말로 가장 적절한 것은?

In Chinese food, the idea is that it should be boiling hot, because that is crucial to its flavor, embodied in the phrase *wok hei*, which means the 'breath' or essence of the combination of tastes added by a hot wok. In 2005 Belgian researchers at Leuven University confirmed just how the link between temperature and taste works. They identified microscopic channels in our taste buds, which seem to respond differently at different temperatures. Apparently, the higher the temperature, the more intense the flavor. This is why ____________________, which is why ice cream makers add stacks of sugar — as you can tell all too clearly when ice cream melts. In a similar way, some bitter tastes, like tea, taste better when hot because they are more intense.

*wok: 중국 요리용 냄비

① ice cream tastes better when tea flavors are added
② ice cream does not taste that sweet straight from the fridge
③ it is not recommended to eat ice cream while drinking hot tea
④ ice cream tastes sweeter especially in the winter time

04 주어진 글 다음에 이어질 글의 순서로 가장 적절한 것은?

An extraordinary successful and economical example of weed control can be found in Australia. Around 1787, a man brought the prickly pear, a kind of cactus, into Australia.

(A) To eliminate them, Australian scientists were sent to North and South America to study enemies of the prickly pears. After trials of several species, three billion eggs of an Argentine moth were spread in Australia.

(B) Some of the prickly pears escaped from his garden. Having no natural controls in this new territory, they spread immensely, eventually occupying about sixty million acres.

(C) Seven years later, the dense growth of the prickly pear had been destroyed and the once uninhabitable areas reopened to settlement and grazing. The whole operation had cost less than a penny per acre.

① (A) – (C) – (B)　　② (B) – (A) – (C)
③ (B) – (C) – (A)　　④ (C) – (A) – (B)

05 다음 글의 빈칸에 들어갈 말로 가장 적절한 것은?

When drawing human figures, children often make the head too large for the rest of the body. A recent study offers some insight into this common disproportion in children's drawings. As part of the study, researchers asked children between four and seven years old to make several drawings of adults. When they drew frontal views of the adults, the size of the heads was markedly enlarged. However, when the children drew rear views of the adults, the size of the heads was not nearly so exaggerated. The researchers suggest that children draw bigger heads when they know that they must leave room for facial details. They say the distorted head size in children's drawing is ______________________________.

① a form of planning ahead
② evidence of poor drawing skills
③ an indication of a poor sense of scale
④ an expression of their hope to grow up

06 다음 빈칸에 들어갈 말로 가장 적절한 것은?

Researchers asked college student volunteers to think through a fantasy version of an experience (looking attractive in a pair of high-heeled shoes, winning an essay contest, or getting an A on a test) and then evaluated the fantasy's effect on the subjects and on how things unfolded in reality. When participants envisioned the most positive outcome, their energy levels, as measured by blood pressure, dropped, and they reported having a worse experience with the actual event than those who had conjured more realistic or even negative visions. To assess subjects' real life experiences, the researchers compared lists of goals that subjects had set for themselves against what they had actually accomplished and also relied on self-reports. "When we fantasize about it — especially when you fantasize something very positive — it's almost like you are actually living it," says one of the study's co-authors. That ________________________________, draining the incentive to "get energized to go and get it," she explains. Subjects may be better off imagining how to surmount obstacles instead of ignoring them.

① prompts you into assessing the real life as it is
② turns a rosy dream into an actual accomplishment
③ tricks the mind into thinking the goal has been achieved
④ makes you believe that obstacles are insurmountable

Reading Skill

05

필자의 강조 · 지시 형용사

HOW TO SOLVE

1 필자의 강조

모든 필자는 글을 쓸 때 자신이 주장하고자 하는 부분을 더 강조하기 마련이다. 이때 필자가 주장을 강조하기 위해 쓰는 장치들을 알아두면 더 쉽고 빠르게 답을 찾아낼 수 있다.

❶ 의문문 + 그 대답 / 인용문

의문문이나 인용문 모두 필자가 자신의 주장을 강조하기 위한 장치이다. 특히 문단 중간이나 끝에 있는 '의문문 + 그 대답'과 '인용문'은 대개 주제문이 된다.

❷ 필자의 주장 강조

'~해야 한다'라는 당위성을 지닌 표현은 대개 주제나 중요한 정보를 제시한다.

must should need to	important	The most(최상급) The best way	It is time ~	명령문(RV)

- Mary **should[must, needs to]** take a rest. Mary는 휴식을 취해야만 한다.
- It's **important** for Julia to make a trip regularly. Julia가 정기적으로 여행을 하는 것은 중요하다.
- **The best way** to lose your weight is to eat less and less. 체중을 줄이는 최선의 방법은 점점 덜 먹는 것이다.
- Tom always says that **it's time** to go to have lunch. Tom은 언제나 점심을 먹으러 갈 시간이라고 말한다.

❸ B를 강조하는 표현들 (B > A)

not A but B	Instead of A, B	Although A, B	not only A but also B (= B as well as A)

- Instead of attending her friend's wedding, **Jessica decided to work this evening.**
  친구의 결혼식에 참석하는 대신, Jessica는 오늘 밤 일을 하기로 결심했다.

2 지시 형용사

❶ this[these] + 명 / that[those] + 명 / such + 명

이 경우, 명사에 대한 설명은 **반드시 앞**에 언급된다.

❷ another(또 다른) + 명

이 경우, 앞에 어떤 명사에 대한 설명이 나오고, 뒤에는 또 다른 명사에 대한 설명이 나온다. 나열 구조가 올 수도 있다.

❸ a + 명 / the + 명

'a + 명사'와 'the + 명사' 중 'a + 명사'가 먼저 언급된다.

3 비교급 · 원급

비교 대상 A		비교 대상 B
동명사 / 명사 + 관계사 사람 / 장소	more[-er] than as ~ as	동명사 / 명사 + 관계사 사람 / 장소

비교급이 나온 경우, 비교되는 두 대상을 잡으면 글의 주제나 요지, 빈칸에 들어갈 내용 등을 쉽게 파악할 수 있다.
이때 **비교 대상 B의 위치는 than 뒤 혹은 두 번째 as 뒤이다.**
따라서 B를 먼저 잡고, 그와 비슷한 구조를 띠는 것을 찾으면 그것이 **비교 대상 A가 된다.**
비교 대상 A와 B는 서로 대조(대칭)의 구조를 띤다.

• **My beauty** is more attractive than **that of Julia**.

• **Mary** is as cute and lovely as **Julia**.

4 유사의 연결사

유사의 연결사가 나온 문장은 주제나 중요 정보가 될 수 있다.

that is that is to say namely as it were so to speak in other words	즉, 다시 말해서	Diana plays the piano and studies very well. She also can sometimes bake some bread and cookies. Besides, she can make a computer program very well. Finally she can speak English fluently. **Namely**, she is a genius.

SKILL EXAMPLE

01 다음 글의 요지로 가장 적절한 것은?

You see the world as one big contest, where everyone is competing against everybody else. You feel that there is a set amount of good and bad fortune out there. You believe that there is no way that everyone can have everything. When other people fail, you feel there's a better chance for you to succeed. However, there is not a limited supply of resources out there. When one person wins, everyone wins. Every victory one person makes is a breakthrough for all. Whenever an Olympic swimmer sets a new world record, it inspires others to bring out the best within them and go beyond that achievement to set new records of human performance. Whenever a geneticist unlocks new secrets of the DNA molecule, it adds to our knowledge base and enables us to better the human condition. Remember that life is a game where there are multiple winners.

① Competitive mind is the driving force to break a record.
② Those who succeed have a distinct achievement motivation.
③ Competition is inevitable in the world with limited resources.
④ One's victory eventually leads to the victory of all.

지문 분석

You see the world as one big contest, where everyone is competing against everybody else.
당신은 세상을 모든 사람이 다른 모든 사람과 경쟁하는 하나의 큰 경기로 여긴다.

첫 문장에서 소재가 경쟁과 경기에 관련된 것을 알 수 있다.

You feel that there is a set amount of good and bad fortune out there. You believe that there is no way that everyone can have everything. When other people fail, you feel there's a better chance for you to succeed.
당신은 저 바깥에는 정해진 양의 행운과 불운이 있다고 생각한다. 당신은 모든 사람이 모든 것을 가질 수 있는 방법은 없다고 믿는다. 다른 사람들이 실패할 때, 당신은 당신이 성공할 확률이 높아진다고 생각한다.

정해진 양의 행운과 불행이 있다고 믿는 통념에 대한 이야기가 서술된다.

However, there is not a limited supply of resources out there. When one person wins, everyone wins. Every victory one person makes is a breakthrough for all. Whenever an Olympic swimmer sets a new world record, it inspires others to bring out the best within them and go beyond that achievement to set new records of human performance. Whenever a geneticist unlocks new secrets of the DNA molecule, it adds to our knowledge base and enables us to better the human condition. Remember that life is a game where there are multiple winners.

그러나 저 밖에는 한정된 공급량의 자원이 있는 것이 아니다. 한 사람이 이길 때, 모든 사람이 이긴다. 한 사람이 만드는 모든 승리는 모두에게 획기적인 약진이다. 한 명의 올림픽 수영 선수가 세계 신기록을 세울 때마다, 그것은 다른 사람들 안에 있는 최고의 것을 불러내어 인간의 성과의 새로운 기록을 세우기 위해서 그 성취를 뛰어넘도록 고취한다. 한 유전학자가 DNA 분자의 새로운 비밀을 알아낼 때마다, 그것은 우리 지식의 기반에 더해져서 우리로 하여금 인간의 상황을 더 좋게 만들 수 있게 한다. 인생은 다수의 승리자가 있는 경기임을 명심하라.

역접의 연결사 However 이후 한 사람이 이길 때 모든 사람이 이길 수 있다는 글의 요지가 드러난다. 또한 마지막 문장은 명령문으로 필자의 주장을 한번 더 부연해주고 있다.

정답 및 해석

정답 ④

해석 당신은 세상을 모든 사람이 다른 모든 사람과 경쟁하는 하나의 큰 경기로 여긴다. 당신은 저 바깥에는 정해진 양의 행운과 불운이 있다고 생각한다. 당신은 모든 사람이 모든 것을 가질 수 있는 방법은 없다고 믿는다. 다른 사람들이 실패할 때, 당신은 당신이 성공할 확률이 높아진다고 생각한다. 그러나 저 밖에는 한정된 공급량의 자원이 있는 것이 아니다. 한 사람이 이길 때, 모든 사람이 이긴다. 한 사람이 만드는 모든 승리는 모두에게 획기적인 약진이다. 한 명의 올림픽 수영 선수가 세계 신기록을 세울 때마다, 그것은 다른 사람들 안에 있는 최고의 것을 불러내어 인간의 성과의 새로운 기록을 세우기 위해서 그 성취를 뛰어넘도록 고취한다. 한 유전학자가 DNA 분자의 새로운 비밀을 알아낼 때마다, 그것은 우리 지식의 기반에 더해져서 우리로 하여금 인간의 상황을 더 좋게 만들 수 있게 한다. 인생은 다수의 승리자가 있는 경기임을 명심하라.

① 경쟁심이 기록을 깨는 원동력이다.
② 성공하는 사람은 뚜렷한 성취 동기를 가지고 있다.
③ 한정된 자원을 가진 세계에서 경쟁은 불가피하다.
④ 한 사람의 승리는 결국 모두의 승리로 이어진다.

어휘 compete 경쟁하다 breakthrough 약진 inspire 고취하다 geneticist 유전학자 unlock (비밀 등을) 알아내다 molecule 분자 better 개선시키다 driving force 원동력

01 다음 글에서 필자가 주장하는 바로 가장 적절한 것은?

Patients often ask me, "Why is everything I enjoy bad for me?" Well, that's not necessarily true, although it often seems that way. For example, you may eat all the chocolate you like as long as your body can stand the extra calories. Do you like eggs? If your cholesterol level is normal, you may have three, four or even five eggs a week. People react differently to cholesterol in the diet. In some, it raises the blood levels, while in others, it does not. So, if you love eggs and chocolate, eat some. Just don't go overboard.

① 자신의 체질에 맞는 음식은 즐겨라.
② 청소년기에는 열량이 높은 음식을 섭취하라.
③ 건강에 나쁘다고 알려진 음식은 멀리하라.
④ 콜레스테롤이 많은 음식은 피하라.

02 글의 흐름으로 보아, 주어진 문장이 들어가기에 가장 적절한 곳은?

> Despite such evidence of favoritism toward handsome politicians, follow-up research demonstrated that voters did not realize their bias.

Research has shown that we automatically assign to good-looking individuals such favorable traits as talent, kindness, honesty, and intelligence. Furthermore, we make these judgements without being aware that physical attractiveness plays a role in the process. (①) Some consequences of this unconscious assumption that "good-looking equals good" scare me. (②) For example, a study of the 1974 Canadian federal elections found that attractive candidates received more than two and a half times as many votes as unattractive candidates. (③) In fact, 73 percent of Canadian voters surveyed denied in the strongest possible terms that their votes had been influenced by physical appearance; only 14 percent even allowed for the possibility of such influence. (④) Voters can deny the impact of attractiveness on electability all they want, but evidence has continued to confirm its troubling presence.

03 다음 글의 제목으로 가장 적절한 것은?

Processing a TV message is much more like the all-at-once processing of the ear than the linear processing of the eye reading a printed page. According to McLuhan, television is fundamentally an acoustic medium. To make this point clear, he invited people to try a simple experiment. First, turn the sound down on the TV set for one minute during your favorite program. Now, for another minute, adjust the TV set so that you can hear the sound but you can't see any picture. Which condition was more frustrating? Which condition gave you less information? McLuhan believed that people who tried this little exercise would invariably report more frustration in the condition where the picture was visible but the sound was inaudible.

① TV Messages: More Visual or Acoustic?
② Surveys of Favorite TV Programs
③ TV as Efficient Equipment for the Deaf
④ More Frustrating Conditions: Invisible Situations

04 글의 흐름으로 보아, 주어진 문장이 들어가기에 가장 적절한 곳은?

> Due to this trade, the plant variety became widespread in a region.

For thousands of years, farmers at harvest time have selected seeds, cuttings, or tubers from superior plants to save for the next planting. Farmers often protected the stored seeds from insects or animals by sealing them in clay pots or burying them in baskets covered with ash. (①) They also often stored tubers in cold areas and either replanted cuttings immediately or kept them dry until the next planting time. (②) Farmers thus saved their genetic stocks from season to season. (③) They could exchange remaining stocks with neighbors or exchange them in the local market. (④) Organized seed production, however, did not begin until the early 1900s.

05 다음 빈칸에 들어갈 말로 가장 적절한 것은?

Globalization, accessibility to an overwhelming array of products and information, and technological innovation are already rapidly changing the marketplace in significant ways. As a result, consumers are changing the way they buy, and businesses need to change the way they compete. We need to rethink the habits that have made us successful in the past, and challenge the conventional wisdom and industry models that have defined our world. In the words of marketing expert Seth Godin, "Industries are being built every day. The revolution is in full swing, and an entire generation is eager to change everything because of it." To thrive in this new era, organizations and institutions, executives and entrepreneurs need to ______________________.

① learn to think and act unconventionally
② destroy old habits that made themselves fail
③ change their ways of thinking about success
④ be reluctant to take new and innovative ideas

06 글의 흐름으로 보아 주어진 문장이 들어가기에 가장 적절한 곳은?

Moreover, the swamps provided perfect breeding grounds for mosquitos, which brought deadly malaria with them.

In the eastern Mediterranean, Ephesus once was the most important seaport of the Roman Empire. But within 600 years of Roman occupation, Ephesus became a ghost town. The Romans upset the balance of Nature, which led to the downfall of the city. The Romans cleared a massive area of forest located around the city to make way for more crops, which eventually cut off the city of Ephesus from the sea forever. (①) With the rainfall not being broken by the forest, water brought away the fertile topsoil with it, and it dumped the soil near the coast. (②) As more and more of this sediment built up, the city was cut off from the sea, which was a disaster for the seaport. (③) Now, there were only massive swamps where once seawater had come in freely. (④) As huge numbers of Ephesians died of the disease, the Empire couldn't hold the land, so it abandoned the city, leaving all the great temples and monuments behind.

구조별 주요 연결사

1 비평 · 대조

접속사	but yet	그러나
	while whereas	~에 반하여
접속부사	however	그러나
	nevertheless nonetheless and yet still even so	그럼에도 불구하고
	in contrast by contrast on the contrary	대조적으로
	on the other hand	반면에

2 예시

접속부사	for example for instance	예를 들면

3 유사

접속부사	that is that is to say namely as it were so to speak in other words	다시 말해서

4 열거

접속부사	also	또한
	moreover furthermore besides in addition what is more	게다가
	at the same time	동시에
	similarly likewise	마찬가지로

5 원인 · 결과

접속사	so	따라서
	because	~때문에
접속부사	thus hence therefore accordingly thereby	따라서
	for these reasons	이러한 이유로
	finally	결국
	consequently as a result	그 결과
	in short in brief in a word	요컨대
	this is why	이것이 ~인 이유이다
	this is because	이는 ~때문이다

Part 02

글의 중심 내용 파악하기

Reading Skill 06

주제 · 제목 추론

HOW TO SOLVE

주제 · 제목 추론 유형은 매해 최소 1문제씩 출제되고 있으며, 특히 제목 추론 유형은 해마다 1~2문제씩 출제되고 있다. 글의 중심 내용이 곧 주제이며, 주제문을 다른 표현으로 바꾼 것이 정답이 된다. 주제를 간단명료하게 표현한 것이 제목이다.

▶ 주제 : 필자가 글을 통해 나타내려는 중심 내용
▶ 제목 : 글의 주제나 요지를 압축적, 상징적으로 표현한 것

전체 글이 한 단락인 경우에는 그 단락에 해당하는 주제만 찾으면 되지만, 단락이 두 개 이상인 경우에는 각 단락의 주제를 먼저 찾은 다음 전체 주제를 찾아야 한다.

최근 공무원 시험 독해 지문의 길이가 점차 길어지고 있으며 다양한 소재와 성격의 지문이 출제되고 있다. 지문이 길어 글을 읽다가 앞에 나온 내용이 뒤로 갈수록 기억이 나지 않아 글을 다 읽고 나서 다시 처음부터 읽어 본 경험이 있을 것이다. 이러한 일을 되풀이하지 않으려면, 먼저 글의 중심 내용을 잘 파악한 후, 글이 어떤 흐름으로 전개되는지를 분석해야 한다.

1 주제 · 제목 추론

주제 · 제목은 세세한 독해력보다는 필자가 글 전체를 통해 어떤 내용을 나타내려고 하는지를 파악하는 것이 중요하다. 즉, 정확하게 해석만 하는 것보다는 글을 크게 볼 수 있는 독해 능력을 기르는 것이 더 중요하다. 따라서 먼저 그 글의 소재를 파악한 후, 해당 소재에 대해 필자가 무슨 말을 하고자 하는지를 이해해야 한다. 그러기 위해서는 항상 '이 글은 무엇에 대한 이야기이지?'라는 생각으로 글을 읽어 내려가면서 연결사를 통한 글의 흐름 변화에 주의해야 한다.

❶ 소재 잡기

앞에 한두 문장을 읽으면서 소재, 즉 무엇에 대한 이야기인지를 파악해야 한다.

A series of high-profile cases involving the loss of computer discs by Government departments has left many police forces having to rethink the way they carry confidential information.

정부 부서에 의한 컴퓨터 디스크의 손실을 포함한 일련의 이목을 끈 사건들은 많은 경찰들로 하여금 그들이 기밀 정보를 운반하는 방법을 다시 생각하게 만들었다.

'경찰들의 기밀 정보(confidential information)를 운반하는 방법에 대한 고찰'이 이 글의 소재이다.

❷ 어느 정도 글이 잡히면 보기 문항을 미리 보면서 '소재와 초점 / 필자의 견해'에 대해 파악하기 (단, 꼼꼼한 보기 해석이 가능해야 한다.)

① Technology developed by police forces (경찰력에 의해 발전된 기술)

② Technology designed for accessing information (정보에 접근하기 위해 만들어진 기술)

③ Technology used in the fight against crime (범죄에 대항하여 싸우는 데 이용된 기술)

④ Technology for protecting confidential information (기밀 정보를 보호하기 위한 기술)

❸ 마지막 2~3줄에서 답 찾기

보통 마지막 2~3줄 정도에 주제가 정리되어 있다. 그곳에서 답이 안 나오는 경우엔 나머지 부분의 독해를 적절히 해야 한다.

오답을 피하는 법

[1] 보기 해석의 중요성

주제 · 제목의 경우 오히려 본문보다 보기 문항 때문에 문제 풀이가 어려운 경우가 많다. 본문은 소재 중심으로 대략적인 전체 내용을 잡아내면 된다. 이에 비해 보기 문항은 정확한 해석과 3가지 오답의 원리에 따라 정확하게 처리해야 한다.

※ 오답의 원리

① too narrow / too wide (소재 중심)

일단 소재를 중심으로 답이 아닌 것을 지워라. 대개 보기 중 1~2개는 답이 되지 않는다.

② contrary(⊕ / ⊖)로 나누기

바로 지워지지 않는 것은 전체 소재를 생각하면서 글 맥락에 대해 ⊕(긍정적인 것)와 ⊖(부정적인 것)로 나누어라.

③ 역추론

그래도 답이 안 나오는 경우, 반대로 해당 보기가 답이 되려면 본문에 어떤 내용이 나와야 할까를 역으로 생각하라.

[2] 소재 중심의 독해: 같은 소재 다른 표현

소재에 대한 표현이 바뀌어도 그 바뀐 표현들을 알아차릴 수 있어야 한다. 그러기 위해서는 첫 문장을 통해 어느 정도 **소재를 미리 파악**해야 한다.

2 주제문을 암시하는 다양한 표현

❶ 필자의 생각 / 의견을 나타내는 어구

- I think[believe, find, guess, insist, mean, prefer, report, say, suppose]
- in my opinion[view, eyes] (내 생각에는, 내가 보기에는)
- As far as I'm concerned (나로서는)
- I'm convinced[sure, certain] that ~ (나는 ~라고 확신한다)

❷ 필자의 판단에 대한 근거를 나타내는 어구

Research Study Survey Scientists	+	find believe discover say show	+	that ~

❸ 중요 / 필요 / 당위성을 나타내는 어구

- must, have to, need to, be required to + RV
- should, ought to, had better, would rather + RV
- It's important[necessary, essential, vital] that S + V ~
- It ~ that 강조 구문

❹ 역접 / 대조를 나타내는 어구

but, yet, however, nevertheless, in contrast, on the contrary, on the other hand, while, although, otherwise 등

❺ 원인 / 결과를 나타내는 어구

because, cause, lead to, result in, end in, bring about, give rise to, result from, be caused by 등

❻ 결론을 유도하는 어구

so, thus, therefore, accordingly, finally, consequently, as a result, after all, in short, in fact 등

SKILL EXAMPLE

01 다음 글의 제목으로 가장 적절한 것은?

As a system for transmitting specific factual information without any distortion or ambiguity, the sign system of honey-bees would probably win easily over human language every time. However, language offers something more valuable than mere information exchange. Because the meanings of words are not invariable and because understanding always involves interpretation, the act of communicating is always a joint, creative effort. Words can carry meanings beyond those consciously intended by speakers or writers because listeners or readers bring their own perspectives to the language they encounter. Ideas expressed imprecisely may be more intellectually stimulating for listeners or readers than simple facts. The fact that language is not always reliable for causing precise meanings to be generated in someone else's mind is a reflection of its powerful strength as a medium for creating new understanding. It is the inherent ambiguity and adaptability of language as a meaning-making system that makes the relationship between language and thinking so special.

① Erase Ambiguity in Language Production!
② Not Creative but Simple: The Way Language Works
③ Communication as a Universal Goal in Language Use
④ What in Language Creates Varied Understanding?

지문 분석

As a system for transmitting specific factual information without any distortion or ambiguity, the sign system of honey-bees would probably win easily over human language every time. **However**, language offers something more valuable than mere information exchange.

아무런 왜곡이나 모호성 없이 특정한 사실적 정보를 전송하기 위한 체계로서, 꿀벌들의 신호 체계는 아마도 인간의 언어를 언제든지 쉽게 이길 것이다. 그러나 언어는 단순한 정보 교환을 넘어서 좀 더 가치 있는 것을 제공한다.

꿀벌들의 신호 체계를 언급하면서 인간 언어의 특징을 설명하려 하고 있다. 연결사 However 뒤에서 언어는 단순한 정보 교환 이상의 가치 있는 것을 제공한다고 했으므로, 언어가 가지는 특징이 이 글의 소재임을 알 수 있다.

It is the inherent ambiguity and adaptability of language as a meaning-making system **that** makes the relationship between language and thinking so special.

언어와 사고의 관계를 특별하게 만드는 것은 바로 의미 생성 체계로서 언어에 내재하는 모호성과 적응성이다.

It ~ that 강조 구문을 통해 언어가 가지는 '모호성'과 '적응성'이 의미 생성 체계로서 언어와 사고의 관계를 특별하게 만든다고 하면서 주제를 암시하고 있다.

그래서 글의 첫 부분에 나온 소재와 종합해보면, 언어가 가지는 특징인 모호성과 적응성이 언어로 하여금 단순한 정보 교환 이상의 가치 있는 것을 제공하게 해주고, 언어와 사고의 관계를 특별하게 만든다는 것을 알 수 있다. 따라서 글의 제목으로 가장 적절한 것은 ④ '언어에서 무엇이 다양한 이해를 만들어 내는가?'이다.

정답 및 해석

정답 ④

해석 아무런 왜곡이나 모호성 없이 특정한 사실적 정보를 전송하기 위한 체계로서, 꿀벌들의 신호 체계는 아마도 인간의 언어를 언제든지 쉽게 이길 것이다. 그러나 언어는 단순한 정보 교환을 넘어서 좀 더 가치 있는 것을 제공한다. 단어들의 의미가 변함없는 것이 아니고 이해는 언제나 해석을 수반하기 때문에, 의사소통 행위는 항상 공동의 창의적인 노력이다. 단어들은 화자들이나 작가들에 의해 의식적으로 의도된 것을 넘어서는 의미들을 수반할 수 있는데, 왜냐하면 청자들이나 독자들은 자신들이 접하는 언어에 자신들의 관점을 가져오기 때문이다. 부정확하게 표현된 개념들은 단순한 사실들보다 청자들이나 독자들에게 더 지적으로 자극적일 수 있다. 언어가 어떤 사람의 정신 속에 정확한 의미가 형성되도록 하는 데 있어서 항상 신뢰할 만한 것은 아니라는 사실은 새로운 이해를 만들기 위한 수단으로서의 언어의 강력한 힘을 반영하는 것이다. 언어와 사고의 관계를 특별하게 만드는 것은 바로 의미 생성 체계로서 언어에 내재하는 모호성과 적응성이다.

① 언어의 생산에 있어서 모호성을 제거하라!
② 창의적이지 않고 단순하다: 언어가 작용하는 방식
③ 언어 사용에서 보편적 목표인 의사소통
④ 언어에서 무엇이 다양한 이해를 만들어 내는가?

어휘 transmit 전송하다 ambiguity 모호(성) invariable 변함없는, 불변의 interpretation 해석 joint 공동의 consciously 의식적으로 perspective 관점, 시각 imprecisely 부정확하게 stimulating 자극적인 reliable 신뢰할 만한 reflection 반영, 투영 inherent 내재된 adaptability 적응성

01 다음 글의 제목으로 가장 적절한 것은? (2022, 지방직 9급)

> One of the areas where efficiency can be optimized is the work force, through increasing individual productivity — defined as the amount of work (products produced, customers served) an employee handles in a given time. In addition to making sure you have invested in the right equipment, environment, and training to ensure optimal performance, you can increase productivity by encouraging staffers to put an end to a modern-day energy drain: multitasking. Studies show it takes 25 to 40 percent longer to get a job done when you're simultaneously trying to work on other projects. To be more productive, says Andrew Deutscher, vice president of business development at consulting firm The Energy Project, "do one thing, uninterrupted, for a sustained period of time."

① How to Create More Options in Life
② How to Enhance Daily Physical Performance
③ Multitasking is the Answer for Better Efficiency
④ Do One Thing at a Time for Greater Efficiency

02 다음 글의 제목으로 가장 적절한 것은? (2022, 국가직 9급)

Lasers are possible because of the way light interacts with electrons. Electrons exist at specific energy levels or states characteristic of that particular atom or molecule. The energy levels can be imagined as rings or orbits around a nucleus. Electrons in outer rings are at higher energy levels than those in inner rings. Electrons can be bumped up to higher energy levels by the injection of energy — for example, by a flash of light. When an electron drops from an outer to an inner level, "excess" energy is given off as light. The wavelength or color of the emitted light is precisely related to the amount of energy released. Depending on the particular lasing material being used, specific wavelengths of light are absorbed (to energize or excite the electrons) and specific wavelengths are emitted (when the electrons fall back to their initial level).

① How Is Laser Produced?
② When Was Laser Invented?
③ What Electrons Does Laser Emit?
④ Why Do Electrons Reflect Light?

03 다음 글의 제목으로 가장 적절한 것은? (2022, 국가직 9급)

Do people from different cultures view the world differently? A psychologist presented realistic animated scenes of fish and other underwater objects to Japanese and American students and asked them to report what they had seen. Americans and Japanese made about an equal number of references to the focal fish, but the Japanese made more than 60 percent more references to background elements, including the water, rocks, bubbles, and inert plants and animals. In addition, whereas Japanese and American participants made about equal numbers of references to movement involving active animals, the Japanese participants made almost twice as many references to relationships involving inert, background objects. Perhaps most tellingly, the very first sentence from the Japanese participants was likely to be one referring to the environment, whereas the first sentence from Americans was three times as likely to be one referring to the focal fish.

① Language Barrier Between Japanese and Americans
② Associations of Objects and Backgrounds in the Brain
③ Cultural Differences in Perception
④ Superiority of Detail-oriented People

04 다음 글의 제목으로 가장 적절한 것은? (2021, 국가직 9급)

Warming temperatures and loss of oxygen in the sea will shrink hundreds of fish species — from tunas and groupers to salmon, thresher sharks, haddock and cod — even more than previously thought, a new study concludes. Because warmer seas speed up their metabolisms, fish, squid and other water-breathing creatures will need to draw more oxygen from the ocean. At the same time, warming seas are already reducing the availability of oxygen in many parts of the sea. A pair of University of British Columbia scientists argue that since the bodies of fish grow faster than their gills, these animals eventually will reach a point where they can't get enough oxygen to sustain normal growth. "What we found was that the body size of fish decreases by 20 to 30 percent for every 1 degree Celsius increase in water temperature," says author William Cheung.

① Fish Now Grow Faster than Ever
② Oxygen's Impact on Ocean Temperatures
③ Climate Change May Shrink the World's Fish
④ How Sea Creatures Survive with Low Metabolism

05 다음 글의 주제로 가장 적절한 것은? (2021, 국가직 9급)

During the late twentieth century socialism was on the retreat both in the West and in large areas of the developing world. During this new phase in the evolution of market capitalism, global trading patterns became increasingly interlinked, and advances in information technology meant that deregulated financial markets could shift massive flows of capital across national boundaries within seconds. 'Globalization' boosted trade, encouraged productivity gains and lowered prices, but critics alleged that it exploited the low-paid, was indifferent to environmental concerns and subjected the Third World to a monopolistic form of capitalism. Many radicals within Western societies who wished to protest against this process joined voluntary bodies, charities and other non-governmental organizations, rather than the marginalized political parties of the left. The environmental movement itself grew out of the recognition that the world was interconnected, and an angry, if diffuse, international coalition of interests emerged.

① The affirmative phenomena of globalization in the developing world in the past
② The decline of socialism and the emergence of capitalism in the twentieth century
③ The conflict between the global capital market and the political organizations of the left
④ The exploitative characteristics of global capitalism and diverse social reactions against it

06 다음 글의 제목으로 가장 적절한 것은? (2020, 국가직 9급)

The future may be uncertain, but some things are undeniable: climate change, shifting demographics, geopolitics. The only guarantee is that there will be changes, both wonderful and terrible. It's worth considering how artists will respond to these changes, as well as what purpose art serves, now and in the future. Reports suggest that by 2040 the impacts of human-caused climate change will be inescapable, making it the big issue at the centre of art and life in 20 years' time. Artists in the future will wrestle with the possibilities of the post-human and post-Anthropocene — artificial intelligence, human colonies in outer space and potential doom. The identity politics seen in art around the #MeToo and Black Lives Matter movements will grow as environmentalism, border politics and migration come even more sharply into focus. Art will become increasingly diverse and might not 'look like art' as we expect. In the future, once we've become weary of our lives being visible online for all to see and our privacy has been all but lost, anonymity may be more desirable than fame. Instead of thousands, or millions, of likes and followers, we will be starved for authenticity and connection. Art could, in turn, become more collective and experiential, rather than individual.

① What will art look like in the future?
② How will global warming affect our lives?
③ How will artificial intelligence influence the environment?
④ What changes will be made because of political movements?

07 다음 글의 주제로 가장 적절한 것은? (2020, 지방직 9급)

> The e-book applications available on tablet computers employ touchscreen technology. Some touchscreens feature a glass panel covering two electronically-charged metallic surfaces lying face-to-face. When the screen is touched, the two metallic surfaces feel the pressure and make contact. This pressure sends an electrical signal to the computer, which translates the touch into a command. This version of the touchscreen is known as a resistive screen because the screen reacts to pressure from the finger. Other tablet computers feature a single electrified metallic layer under the glass panel. When the user touches the screen, some of the current passes through the glass into the user's finger. When the charge is transferred, the computer interprets the loss in power as a command and carries out the function the user desires. This type of screen is known as a capacitive screen.

① how users learn new technology
② how e-books work on tablet computers
③ how touchscreen technology works
④ how touchscreens have evolved

08 다음 글의 제목으로 가장 적절한 것은? (2019, 국가직 9급)

Mapping technologies are being used in many new applications. Biological researchers are exploring the molecular structure of DNA("mapping the genome"), geophysicists are mapping the structure of the Earth's core, and oceanographers are mapping the ocean floor. Computer games have various imaginary "lands" or levels where rules, hazards, and rewards change. Computerization now challenges reality with "virtual reality", artificial environments that stimulate special situations, which may be useful in training and entertainment. Mapping techniques are being used also in the realm of ideas. For example, relationships between ideas can be shown using what are called concept maps. Starting from a general or "central" idea, related ideas can be connected, building a web around the main concept. This is not a map by any traditional definition, but the tools and techniques of cartography are employed to produce it, and in some ways it resembles a map.

① Computerized Maps vs. Traditional Maps
② Where Does Cartography Begin?
③ Finding Ways to DNA Secrets
④ Mapping New Frontiers

09 다음 글의 제목으로 가장 적절한 것은? (2018, 지방직 9급)

With the help of the scientist, the commercial fishing industry has found out that its fishing must be done scientifically if it is to be continued. With no fishing pressure on a fish population, the number of fish will reach a predictable level of abundance and stay there. The only fluctuation would be due to natural environmental factors, such as availability of food, proper temperature, and the like. If a fishery is developed to take these fish, their population can be maintained if the fishing harvest is small. The mackerel of the North Sea is a good example. If we increase the fishery and take more fish each year, we must be careful not to reduce the population below the ideal point where it can replace all of the fish we take out each year. If we fish at this level, called the *maximum sustainable yield*, we can maintain the greatest possible yield, year after year. If we catch too many, the number of fish will decrease each year until we fish ourselves out of a job. Examples of severely overfished animals are the blue whale of the Antarctic and the halibut of the North Atlantic. Fishing just the correct amount to maintain a maximum annual yield is both a science and an art. Research is constantly being done to help us better understand the fish population and how to utilize it to the maximum without depleting the population.

① Say No to Commercial Fishing
② Sea Farming Seen As a Fishy Business
③ Why Does the Fishing Industry Need Science?
④ Overfished Animals: Cases of Illegal Fishing

10 다음 글의 주제로 가장 적절한 것은? (2017, 지방직 하반기 9급)

It is easy to look at the diverse things people produce and to describe their differences. Obviously a poem is not a mathematical formula, and a novel is not an experiment in genetics. Composers clearly use a different language from that of visual artists, and chemists combine very different things than do playwrights. To characterize people by the different things they make, however, is to miss the universality of how they create. For at the level of the creative process, scientists, artists, mathematicians, composers, writers, and sculptors use a common set of what we call "tools for thinking," including emotional feelings, visual images, bodily sensations, reproducible patterns, and analogies. And all imaginative thinkers learn to translate ideas generated by these subjective thinking tools into public languages to express their insights, which can then give rise to new ideas in others' minds.

① obstacles to imaginative thinking
② the difference between art and science
③ the commonality of the creative process
④ distinctive features of various professions

Reading Skill

07 요지·주장 추론

HOW TO SOLVE

요지 · 주장 추론 유형은 대개 설명문보다는 논설문의 성격을 띤다. 따라서 글을 읽으면서 소재(Topic)나 필자가 제기하는 이슈를 잡고, 나아가 그에 대한 필자의 견해를 파악해야 한다.

이렇게 하면 정답률도 높이면서 문제를 빨리 풀 수 있는 능력까지 길러진다. 주제문이 앞쪽에 제시되는 두괄식 형태가 가장 많으며, 그다음으로 글 뒤쪽에 제시되는 미괄식 형태가 많다. 간혹 주제문이 글 중간에 오는 경우와 주제가 명확하게 드러나지 않는 글도 있는데, 이 경우에는 논리적인 추론을 통해 필자의 견해를 파악해야 한다.

유의할 점은 글의 전반부에서 잡은 소재를 생각하면서 글을 읽어 내려가야 한다는 점이다. 만약 글의 첫 부분과 마지막 부분만 읽게 된다면 오답을 고를 수도 있으므로 유의해야 한다.

1 처음 2~3줄에서 소재 찾기

요지 · 주장 유형의 지문에서는 특히 글의 뒷부분이 중요하다. 하지만 글의 뒷부분만 읽어서는 절대 답을 쉽게 찾을 수 없다. 오히려 글의 앞부분을 통해 필자가 말하고자 하는 소재를 정확하게 파악해야 빠르고 쉽게 나온다.

2 소재를 찾고 난 후에는 글의 마지막 2~3줄 정도를 읽어 필자의 견해 파악하기

마지막 2~3줄 정도에 필자의 견해가 있다. 특히 주장 문제의 경우, 마지막 문장이 답인 경우가 95% 이상이므로 꼭 명심해야 한다.

3 보기를 읽고 답을 찾기

보기 문항이 문장으로 되어 있으므로 보기 문항 문장의 주어와 동사에 유의하여 핵심을 정확하게 파악하면 생각보다 쉽게 답이 나온다. 처음 2~3줄을 통해 소재를 찾은 후 바로 보기를 읽고 답을 찾아도 문제를 풀 수 있다.

4 답을 찾을 수 없는 경우 ⇒ 밑에서부터 또는 위에서부터

답을 찾을 수 없었지만 거의 답에 근접했다는 판단이 들면, 마지막에 읽은 부분 바로 앞부터 다시 읽는 것도 좋은 전략이다.

SKILL EXAMPLE

01 다음 글의 요지로 가장 적절한 것은?

How on earth will it help the poor if governments try to strangle globalization by stemming the flow of trade, information, and capital — the three components of the global economy? That disparities between rich and poor are still too great is undeniable. But it is just not true that economic growth benefits only the rich and leaves out the poor, as the opponents of globalization and the market economy would have us believe. A recent World Bank study entitled "Growth Is Good for the Poor" reveals a one-for-one relationship between income of the bottom fifth of the population and per capita GDP. In other words, incomes of all sectors grow proportionately at the same rate. The study notes that openness to foreign trade benefits the poor to the same extent that it benefits the whole economy.

① Globalization deepens conflicts between rich and poor.
② The global economy grows at the expense of the poor.
③ Globalization can be beneficial regardless of one's economic status.
④ Governments must control the flow of trade to revive the economy.

지문 분석

Ⅰ 처음 2~3줄을 읽고 소재를 파악해라.

How on earth will it help the poor if governments try to strangle globalization by stemming the flow of trade, information, and capital — the three components of the global economy? That disparities between rich and poor are still too great is undeniable. But it is just not true that economic growth benefits only the rich and leaves out the poor, as the opponents of globalization and the market economy would have us believe.

정부가 세계 경제의 세 요소인 무역, 정보, 자본의 흐름을 막아서 세계화를 억압하려 할 경우, 도대체 그것이 가난한 사람들에게 어떻게 도움이 될 것인가? 빈부 격차가 여전히 지나치게 크다는 것은 부정할 수 없다. 그러나 세계화와 시장 경제의 반대자들이 우리를 믿게 하려고 하듯, 경제 성장이 부유한 사람들에게만 득이 되고 가난한 사람들은 배제한다는 것은 진실이 아니다.

첫 문장에서 세계화를 억압하는 것이 가난한 사람들에게 도대체 어떤 도움이 된다는 것인지 의문을 제기하고 있다. 또한 역접 연결사와 함께 경제 성장이 가난한 사람들을 배제한다는 것은 진실이 아니라고 강조하는 것을 보아, 이어질 내용에는 세계화와 경제 성장이 오히려 가난한 사람들에게 도움이 된다는 내용이 전개될 것임을 짐작할 수 있다.

② **마지막 두세 문장을 읽어보면 필자의 견해가 확실하게 드러난다.**

In other words, incomes of all sectors grow proportionately at the same rate. The study notes that openness to foreign trade benefits the poor to the same extent that it benefits the whole economy.

다시 말해서, 모든 부문의 소득은 같은 비율로 비례하여 증가한다. 그 연구는 해외 무역에 대한 개방이 전체 경제에 득이 되는 것과 같은 정도로 가난한 사람들에게 득이 된다고 언급한다.

해외 무역에 대한 개방, 즉 세계화가 전체 경제와 가난한 사람들에게 같은 정도로 유익하다는 것이 바로 이 글의 핵심 내용이다.

보기 분석

보기 선택 시 지문에 언급된 단어, 특히 주제문에 사용된 단어가 보기 문항에 동일하게 사용된 경우 눈여겨보아야 한다. 주제문에 나온 단어들로 보기 문항을 만드는 경우, 매력적인 오답이 될 수 있으므로 주의해야 한다.

① Globalization deepens conflicts between rich and poor.
세계화가 빈부 갈등을 악화시킨다.

② The global economy grows at the expense of the poor.
세계 경제는 가난한 사람들의 희생으로 성장한다.

③ Globalization can be beneficial regardless of one's economic status.
세계화는 개인의 경제적 지위에 상관없이 유익할 수 있다.

④ Governments must control the flow of trade to revive the economy.
정부는 경제를 되살리기 위해 무역의 흐름을 통제해야 한다.

보통 보기 중 하나는 지문과 동떨어진 것이 제시되는데, ④가 그러한 경우다. '경제를 되살리기 위해 무역 흐름을 통제해야 한다'라는 내용은 언급되지 않았다. ①처럼 '세계화'라는 소재가 언급되었지만 지문에 언급된 내용은 아닌 경우도 있다. ②는 '세계 경제'와 '가난한 사람들'이라는 핵심 소재어가 포함되어 있으나, 지문의 처음과 끝부분에 명시된 '경제 성장이 가난한 사람들에게도 득이 된다'라는 내용과 반대로 그들을 희생시킨다고 했으므로 명백한 오답이다. 정답은 ③으로, 마지막 문장의 무역 시장 개방이 전체 경제와 가난한 사람들에게 '같은 정도로' 유익하다는 내용에서 세계화가 '경제적 지위에 상관없이' 유익하다는 것을 끌어낼 수 있다.

정답 및 해석

정답 ③

해석 정부가 세계 경제의 세 요소인 무역, 정보, 자본의 흐름을 막아서 세계화를 억압하려 할 경우, 도대체 그것이 가난한 사람들에게 어떻게 도움이 될 것인가? 빈부 격차가 여전히 지나치게 크다는 것은 부정할 수 없다. 그러나 세계화와 시장 경제의 반대자들이 우리를 믿게 하려고 하듯, 경제 성장이 부유한 사람들에게만 득이 되고 가난한 사람들은 배제한다는 것은 진실이 아니다. 최근 세계은행이 실시한 "(경제) 성장은 가난한 사람들에게 이롭다"라는 제목의 연구는 인구의 하위 20%의 소득과 1인당 국내 총생산의 일대일 대응 관계를 밝힌다. 다시 말해서, 모든 부문의 소득은 같은 비율로 비례하여 증가한다. 그 연구는 해외 무역에 대한 개방이 전체 경제에 득이 되는 것과 같은 정도로 가난한 사람들에게 득이 된다고 언급한다.
① 세계화가 빈부 갈등을 악화시킨다.
② 세계 경제는 가난한 사람들의 희생으로 성장한다.
③ 세계화는 개인의 경제적 지위에 상관없이 유익할 수 있다.
④ 정부는 경제를 되살리기 위해 무역의 흐름을 통제해야 한다.

어휘 on earth 도대체 strangle 억압하다 stem (흐름을) 막다 disparity 차이 undeniable 부정할 수 없는 opponent 반대자 entitle 제목을 붙이다 per capita 1인당 proportionately 비례해서 at the expense of ~의 희생으로 revive 되살리다

정답 및 해설 14P

01 다음 글의 요지로 가장 적절한 것은? (2022, 지방직 9급)

In one study, done in the early 1970s when young people tended to dress in either "hippie" or "straight" fashion, experimenters donned hippie or straight attire and asked college students on campus for a dime to make a phone call. When the experimenter was dressed in the same way as the student, the request was granted in more than two-thirds of the instances; when the student and requester were dissimilarly dressed, the dime was provided less than half the time. Another experiment showed how automatic our positive response to similar others can be. Marchers in an antiwar demonstration were found to be more likely to sign the petition of a similarly dressed requester and to do so without bothering to read it first.

① People are more likely to help those who dress like themselves.
② Dressing up formally increases the chance of signing the petition.
③ Making a phone call is an efficient way to socialize with other students.
④ Some college students in the early 1970s were admired for their unique fashion.

02 다음 글의 요지로 가장 적절한 것은? (2022, 국가직 9급)

If someone makes you an offer and you're legitimately concerned about parts of it, you're usually better off proposing all your changes at once. Don't say, "The salary is a bit low. Could you do something about it?" and then, once she's worked on it, come back with "Thanks. Now here are two other things I'd like..." If you ask for only one thing initially, she may assume that getting it will make you ready to accept the offer (or at least to make a decision). If you keep saying "and one more thing...," she is unlikely to remain in a generous or understanding mood. Furthermore, if you have more than one request, don't simply mention all the things you want — A, B, C, and D; also signal the relative importance of each to you. Otherwise, she may pick the two things you value least, because they're pretty easy to give you, and feel she's met you halfway.

① Negotiate multiple issues simultaneously, not serially.
② Avoid sensitive topics for a successful negotiation.
③ Choose the right time for your negotiation.
④ Don't be too direct when negotiating salary.

03 다음 글의 요지로 가장 적절한 것은? (2020, 국가직 9급)

Listening to somebody else's ideas is the one way to know whether the story you believe about the world — as well as about yourself and your place in it — remains intact. We all need to examine our beliefs, air them out and let them breathe. Hearing what other people have to say, especially about concepts we regard as foundational, is like opening a window in our minds and in our hearts. Speaking up is important. Yet to speak up without listening is like banging pots and pans together: even if it gets you attention, it's not going to get you respect. There are three prerequisites for conversation to be meaningful: 1. You have to know what you're talking about, meaning that you have an original point and are not echoing a worn-out, hand-me-down or pre-fab argument; 2. You respect the people with whom you're speaking and are authentically willing to treat them courteously even if you disagree with their positions; 3. You have to be both smart and informed enough to listen to what the opposition says while handling your own perspective on the topic with uninterrupted good humor and discernment.

① We should be more determined to persuade others.
② We need to listen and speak up in order to communicate well.
③ We are reluctant to change our beliefs about the world we see.
④ We hear only what we choose and attempt to ignore different opinions.

04 다음 글의 요지로 가장 적절한 것은? (2019, 국가직 9급)

When giving performance feedback, you should consider the recipient's past performance and your estimate of his or her future potential in designing its frequency, amount, and content. For high performers with potential for growth, feedback should be frequent enough to prod them into taking corrective action, but not so frequent that it is experienced as controlling and saps their initiative. For adequate performers who have settled into their jobs and have limited potential for advancement, very little feedback is needed because they have displayed reliable and steady behavior in the past, knowing their tasks and realizing what needs to be done. For poor performers — that is, people who will need to be removed from their jobs if their performance doesn't improve — feedback should be frequent and very specific, and the connection between acting on the feedback and negative sanctions such as being laid off or fired should be made explicit.

① Time your feedback well.
② Customize negative feedback.
③ Tailor feedback to the person.
④ Avoid goal-oriented feedback.

05 다음 글의 요지로 가장 적절한 것은? (2018, 지방직 9급)

My students often believe that if they simply meet more important people, their work will improve. But it's remarkably hard to engage with those people unless you've already put something valuable out into the world. That's what piques the curiosity of advisers and sponsors. Achievements show you have something to give, not just something to take. In life, it certainly helps to know the right people. But how hard they go to bat for you, how far they stick their necks out for you, depends on what you have to offer. Building a powerful network doesn't require you to be an expert at networking. It just requires you to be an expert at something. If you make great connections, they might advance your career. If you do great work, those connections will be easier to make. Let your insights and your outputs — not your business cards — do the talking.

① Sponsorship is necessary for a successful career.
② Building a good network starts from your accomplishments.
③ A powerful network is a prerequisite for your achievement.
④ Your insights and outputs grow as you become an expert at networking.

06 다음 글의 요지로 가장 적절한 것은? (2017, 지방직 9급)

Novelty-induced time expansion is a well-characterized phenomenon which can be investigated under laboratory conditions. Simply asking people to estimate the length of time they are exposed to a train of stimuli shows that novel stimuli simply seem to last longer than repetitive or unremarkable ones. In fact, just being the first stimulus in a moderately repetitive series appears to be sufficient to induce subjective time expansion. Of course, it is easy to think of reasons why our brain has evolved to work like this — presumably novel and exotic stimuli require more thought and consideration than familiar ones, so it makes sense for the brain to allocate them more subjective time.

① Response to stimuli is an important by-product of brain training.
② The intensity of stimuli increases with their repetition.
③ Our physical response to stimuli influences our thoughts.
④ New stimuli give rise to subjective time expansion.

Part 03

글의 논리 전개 파악하기

Reading Skill

08

빈칸 완성

HOW TO SOLVE

빈칸 완성은 매년 2~4문제씩 출제되고 있고 대부분의 수험생들이 가장 어려워하는 유형이다. 실제로 중위권 수험생들이 상위권 점수대로 넘어갈 때 가장 힘들어하는 유형이기도 하다.

빈칸 완성 문제를 잘 풀기 위해서는 **정확한 독해 능력**을 가지고 있어야 한다. 최근 공무원 영어에서는 어려운 단어와 복잡한 구문을 포함한, 내용 자체가 어려운 지문이 출제되기 때문에 언어적 능력과 전략적인 독해 능력이 부족한 수험생들은 상당히 힘들어한다.

빈칸에 들어갈 말들은 대체적으로 그 글의 소재나 주제와 관련이 있다. 다만 선택지를 구성할 때 본문에 사용된 단어를 그대로 사용하기보다는 비슷한 단어로 약간 뒤틀어 표현하기 때문에 글 자체를 이해하는 능력뿐만 아니라 필자가 말하고자 하는 바를 정확하게 이해하는 능력도 필요하다.

1 빈칸의 위치에 따른 출제 유형

❶ 빈칸이 맨 앞이나 맨 뒤에 위치한 경우

→ 주제 추론(소재 + 내용)을 한 후 보기 분석을 하라!

빈칸이 맨 처음이나 맨 끝에 위치한 경우 대부분 그 글의 전체 내용을 이해하면 답이 보인다. 따라서 빈칸보다도 글 전체의 주제나 필자의 요지에 초점을 맞춰서 글을 읽어야 한다. 이때 **빈칸 앞 문장이 특히 중요하다**는 점을 꼭 기억해야 한다.

글의 주제를 생각한 후 보기를 정확하게 분석하면 문제가 쉽게 풀린다. 특히 보기가 긴 경우에는 핵심 내용이 무엇인지를 정확하게 파악하는 것이 중요하다.

❷ 빈칸이 중간에 있는 경우

→ 연결사를 확인한 후 빈칸과 빈칸 주변을 살펴라!

빈칸이 중간에 있는 경우, 빈칸 주변에 연결사가 나오는 경우가 많다. 따라서 **연결사를 먼저 확인**한 후, 그 연결사를 활용해서 문제를 푼다. 하지만 연결사가 없는 경우에는 빈칸과 빈칸 주변이 중요하다. 특히 빈칸이 지문의 앞쪽에 있을수록 빈칸 뒷부분이 중요하고, 빈칸이 지문의 뒤쪽에 있을수록 빈칸이 포함된 문장과 그 앞뒤 문장이 중요하다.

It derives from the prevalent belief that all of us are similar bio-mechanical units that rolled off the same assembly line — a most imperfect conception of human beings that limits conventional medicine's effectiveness. The doctor of the future, **however**, needs to practice medicine in fundamentally different ways.

그것은 우리 모두가 동일한 조립라인에서 출고된 유사한 생체 역학적인 집단들이라는 만연한 믿음에서 유래한다. (이것은) 전통적인 의학의 유효성을 제한하는 인간에 대한 매우 불완전한 개념이다. 하지만 미래의 의사는 근본적으로 다른 방법들로 의술을 행할 필요가 있다.

연결사 'however'를 중심으로 상반되는 내용이 전개된다는 것을 파악해야 한다.

❸ 빈칸 다음에 마지막 문장이 있는 경우

→ 빈칸 다음의 마지막 문장은 매우 중요하다!

빈칸 다음에 마지막 문장이 나온다면, 당연히 그 마지막 문장은 빈칸과 관련하여 중요한 정보를 가질 수밖에 없다. 따라서 그 마지막 부분을 잘 읽으면 정답을 쉽게 찾을 수 있다.

If you see things through your camera lens that distract from what you are trying to say, get rid of them. So when you photograph people, remember to get closer to them to exclude unwanted objects.

만약 당신이 당신의 카메라 렌즈를 통해서 당신이 말하고자 애쓰고 있는 것으로부터 주의를 딴 데로 돌리는 것들을 본다면 그것들을 없애라. 그러므로 당신이 사람들을 찍을 때 불필요한 사물들을 제외하기 위해서는 그들에게 더 가까이 다가갈 것을 기억해라.

마지막 문장에서 사진에서 원하지 않는 부분을 제외시키기 위해 피사체에 다가가라고 하고 있다. 그러므로 당신이 찍고 싶은 것을 방해하는 주변 물체는 프레임에서 제외시키라는 내용이 빈칸에 들어갈 것임을 알 수 있다.

2 빈칸의 길이에 따른 출제 유형

❶ 빈칸의 길이가 긴 경우

→ 주제 추론(소재 + 내용)을 한 후 보기 분석을 하라!

빈칸의 길이가 긴 경우에는 빈칸의 위치와 관계없이 전체 주제나 필자의 요지가 무엇인지를 찾아야 한다. 빈칸의 길이가 긴 경우 단락 구조가 생각보다 단순하다. 따라서 빈칸에 집중하기보다는, 그 글이 전체적으로 무엇을 말하는지부터 잡아내야 한다. 그런 다음 보기 분석을 하는데, 이때 긴 보기의 핵심이 무엇인지를 잘 파악해야 한다.

1. 주제 추론

Sometimes one way to find a peaceful solution is to ______________________.

때때로 평화로운 해결책을 찾는 한 방법은 ______________하는 것이다.

제시문은 평화로운 해결책을 찾는 방법에 대한 내용이다. 문제점과 해결책 구조로 되어 있다. 빈칸에 들어갈 내용이 해결책이다.

2. 보기 분석

① try very hard to impress the other person
② respond quickly to the other person's request
③ let the other person experience things in your shoes
④ set a good example to the other person instead of making excuses

보기의 핵심을 파악하면,

① 깊은 인상을 주라는 건지
② 타인의 요청을 들어주라는 건지
③ 당신의 입장을 경험하게 하라는 건지
④ 좋은 본보기를 보이라는 건지

각각 다른 것을 주장하고 있음을 알 수 있다. 따라서 보기의 핵심을 파악하면 본문에서 대략적인 핵심 내용만 잡아도 빈칸에 들어갈 내용을 쉽게 찾을 수 있다.

❷ 빈칸의 길이가 짧은 경우

→ 빈칸이 포함된 문장을 분석하는 것이 매우 중요하다!

빈칸이 짧은 경우, 빈칸이 있는 문장을 먼저 정확하게 분석한다.

From this period the roles of mathematicians and architects were seen as ____________ in a way that did not happen in the seventeenth century.

① distinct ② similar ③ excellent ④ trivial

이때부터 수학자와 건축가의 역할은, 17세기에는 일어나지 않았던 방식으로 ________ 것으로 간주됐다.

빈칸이 있는 문장을 정확하게 분석하면 수학자와 건축가의 역할이 '어떠한지'를 파악하면 된다는 것을 알 수 있다. 그 역할이 '다른지', '비슷한지', '훌륭한지', '사소한지'만 파악하면 쉽게 답을 찾을 수 있다. 또한 'a way that did not happen in the seventeenth century'에서 시간상의 대조를 이루는 구조의 글임을 알 수 있다.

❸ 빈칸이 있는 문장 자체가 긴 경우

→ 빈칸이 있는 문장 분석이 가장 중요하다!

빈칸의 길이와 상관없이 빈칸이 있는 문장의 길이가 긴 경우, 그 문장 자체가 가장 중요하다. 해당 문장만 잘 분석을 해도 답이 쉽게 보이는 경우가 있다.

SHIMSON'S TIP

모든 빈칸 완성 유형의 풀이 방법

① 빈칸이 맨 앞이나 맨 끝에 있는 경우: 주제 추론 (소재 + 내용)

② 빈칸이 중간에 있는 경우: 전체 소재를 생각하고 빈칸과 빈칸의 앞뒤를 특히 정확히 해석

SHIMSON'S TIP

보기 분석 3법칙

빈칸 완성 유형을 풀이하는 핵심은 보기 분석 능력이다. 출제자는 본문에 자주 등장하거나 인상적인 단어를 사용하여 오답 보기 문항을 구성하므로 보기 분석법을 이용하여 오답을 제거하는 연습이 필요하다.

① 소재 제거법	지문의 첫 문장 또는 도입부의 내용을 통해 소재를 파악하고, 제시된 보기 문항 중 소재와 관련이 없는 보기 제거하기
② [⊕/⊖] 단순화	지문에서 화자가 말하고자 하는 내용과 보기 문항의 내용을 비교하여, 맥락에 따라 [⊕/⊖]로 단순화한 후 헷갈리는 보기 제거하기
③ 역추론	소재 제거법과 [⊕/⊖] 단순화로 정답이 아닌 것을 제외한 후, 남은 보기를 지문의 빈칸 위치에 역으로 대입하여 글의 흐름이 자연스러운지 생각하기

<보기에 자주 나오는 [⊕/⊖] 빈칸 어휘>

다른			같은	
diverse	다양한		same	같은
different	다른		common	일반적인
unusual	이상한		general	일반적인
distinctive	특징적인		universal	보편적인
uncommon	보기 드문	↔	widespread	널리 퍼진
rare	드문		similar	비슷한
extraordinary	비범한		uncontroversial	논란의 여지가 없는
special	특별한			
specific	독특한, 구체적인			
exceptional	예외적인			

변하는			변하지 않는	
changeable	변하기 쉬운		unchangeable	변하지 않는
new	새로운		conventional	인습적인
innovative	혁신적인		old	오래된
flexible	유연한		absolute	절대적인
relative	상대적인		constant	변치 않는
temporary	일시적인		steady	꾸준한
unpredictable	예측할 수 없는	↔	invariable	변치 않는
unmeasurable	측정할 수 없는		faithful	충실한
			loyal	충실한
			predictable	예측 가능한
			measurable	측정할 수 있는
			permanent	영구적인
			perpetual	영구적인

영향력이 있는			영향력이 없는	
influential	영향을 미치는	↔	inferior	열등한
dominant	지배적인		secondary	이류의
significant	중요한		humble	겸손한, 비천한
superior	우수한		vulnerable	취약한

SKILL EXAMPLE

01 다음 글의 빈칸에 들어갈 말로 가장 적절한 것은?

In an orchestra, brass players are often told that ________________________. Brass instruments are made of yards of tubing, coiled up like snakes. If you unrolled all the tubing in a typical french horn, for example, it would be seventeen feet in length. That's as long as three adults of average height standing on each other's shoulders! As you blow into a brass instrument, your air enters the tubing, snakes all the way through its length, deposits some spit on the inside of the instrument, and emerges as a sound at the other end. That's bound to take some time. No wonder the sound comes out a bit late. Good brass players often find that they need to compensate for this time lag to avoid playing behind the other musicians.

① their instruments need to be replaced more often
② they should play earlier than the other players
③ their instruments resemble animal shapes
④ they should not avoid the other players

지문 분석

빈칸의 길이가 길고 빈칸이 맨 처음 문장에 위치하는 경우 주제를 추론하는 것이 중요하다.

In an orchestra, brass players are often told that ________________.

오케스트라에서, 금관악기 연주자들은 ____________라는 말을 종종 듣는다.

As you blow into a brass instrument, your air enters the tubing, snakes all the way through its length, deposits some spit on the inside of the instrument, and emerges as a sound at the other end. That's bound to take some time. No wonder the sound comes out a bit late.

금관악기를 불면 당신의 숨이 관 속으로 들어가 그것의 길이를 모두 지나고, 악기 안에 침을 조금 남기고 나서야 소리가 되어 다른 끝으로 나온다. 이것은 시간이 조금 걸릴 수밖에 없다. 소리가 조금 늦게 나는 것은 당연하다.

금관악기를 불 때 왜 소리가 조금씩 늦게 나오는지를 설명하고 있다.

Good brass players often find that they need to compensate for this time lag to avoid playing behind the other musicians.

종종 실력 있는 금관악기 연주자들은 다른 연주자들보다 뒤처져서 연주하지 않기 위해서는 이 시차를 보완해야 하는 것을 안다.

실력 있는 금관악기 연주자들은 다른 악기들과의 시차를 보완한다는 것을 말하고 있다. 금관악기를 불 때 왜 소리가 조금씩 늦게 나는지, 그러므로 금관악기를 어떻게 연주해야 하는지에 관한 글임을 알 수 있다.

보기 분석

① their instruments need to be replaced more often

➲ 언급된 바 없다.

② they should play earlier than the other players

③ their instruments resemble animal shapes

➲ 글의 주제와 관련이 없다.

④ they should not avoid the other players

➲ 언급된 바 없다. 마지막 문장의 avoid를 활용한 오답이다.

금관악기는 다른 악기들보다 소리가 늦게 난다고 하였으므로, 그 시차를 보완하기 위해 다른 악기들보다 먼저 연주해야 한다는 내용이 빈칸에 들어가야 함을 알 수 있다. 그러므로 정답은 ② '다른 연주자들보다 먼저 연주해야 한다'이다.

정답 및 해석

정답 ②

해석 오케스트라에서 금관악기 연주자들은 종종 다른 연주자들보다 먼저 연주해야 한다는 얘기를 듣는다. 금관악기들은 몇 야드의 관으로 만들어지며, 뱀과 같이 감겨있다. 예를 들어, 만약 당신이 전형적인 프렌치 호른의 모든 관을 푼다면 그 길이는 17피트가 될 것이다. 그것은 평균 키의 성인 세 명이 서로의 어깨에 올라가 있는 높이만큼이나 길다! 금관악기를 불 때 당신의 숨이 관 속으로 들어가서 그것의 길이를 모두 지나고, 그 악기 안에 약간의 침을 남기고 다른 쪽 끝에서 소리로 나온다. 이것은 시간이 좀 걸릴 수밖에 없다. 소리가 조금 늦게 나는 것은 당연하다. 종종 뛰어난 금관악기 연주자들은 다른 음악가들보다 뒤처져서 연주하는 것을 피하기 위해서는 이러한 시차를 보완해야 할 필요가 있음을 안다.

① 그들의 악기가 더 자주 교체되어야 한다

② 다른 연주자들보다 먼저 연주해야 한다

③ 그들의 악기가 동물 모양을 닮았다

④ 그들이 다른 연주자들을 피해서는 안 된다

어휘 orchestra 관현악단 brass 금관악기 instrument 악기 tubing 관 coil 감다 unroll 풀다 snake 굽이치며 가다 deposit 두다 spit 침 emerge 나오다 be bound to ~할 수밖에 없다 compensate 보완하다 replace 교체하다

02 다음 글의 빈칸에 들어갈 말로 가장 적절한 것은?

> The goal of medicine as it is currently practiced is to develop procedures and drugs that work equally well on all patients, regardless of gender, age, or genetics. It derives from the prevalent belief that all of us are similar bio-mechanical units that rolled off the same assembly line — a most imperfect conception of human beings that limits conventional medicine's effectiveness. The doctor of the future, however, needs to practice medicine in fundamentally different ways. One of the most important shifts will be an increased recognition of ____________________, a concept now largely ignored. Instead of treating different patients that display similar symptoms with the same drugs, doctors should identify root causes of disease to come up with a personalized treatment.

① wonder drugs
② patient individuality
③ medical technology
④ doctors' qualifications

지문 분석

첫 문장을 통해 글의 주제 또는 소재를 파악한다.

> The goal of medicine as it is currently practiced is to develop procedures and drugs that work equally well on all patients, regardless of gender, age, or genetics.
> 현재 행해지고 있는 것처럼 의학의 목표는 성, 나이, 유전적 특질과 상관없이 모든 환자에게 다 잘 듣는 수술과 약을 만들어 내는 것이다.

이 글은 '의학의 목표'에 대해 전개될 것이라고 예측할 수 있다.

빈칸이 중간에 있는 경우 먼저 빈칸 주변의 연결사를 찾는다.

> The doctor of the future, **however**, needs to practice medicine in fundamentally different ways.
> 그러나 미래의 의사는 의술을 근본적으로 다른 방법으로 행해야 한다.

중간에 however가 있는 것으로 보아, 이 문장을 기준으로 내용이 반전될 것임에 유의하여 풀어야 한다.

빈칸 다음에 마지막 문장이 있으므로, 마지막 문장에서 정답의 근거를 찾는다.

One of the most important shifts will be an increased recognition of ______________, a concept now largely ignored. Instead of treating different patients that display similar symptoms with the same drugs, doctors should identify root causes of disease to come up with a personalized treatment.

가장 중요한 변화들 중 하나는 지금은 크게 무시당하고 있는 개념인 ______________을 더 많이 인정하는 것이 될 것이다. 비슷한 증세를 호소하는 서로 다른 환자들을 똑같은 약으로 치료하는 대신, 의사들은 병들의 근본 원인들을 알아내어 개별화된 치료법을 찾아야만 한다.

마지막 문장에서 다양한 환자를 똑같은 약으로 치료하지 말고 개별화된 치료를 제공해야 한다고 하였으므로, 빈칸에 들어갈 말로 가장 적절한 것은 ② '환자의 개별성'이다.

정답 및 해석

정답 ②

해석 현재 실행되고 있는 것처럼 의학의 목적은 성, 나이, 또는 유전적 특질과 관계없이 모든 환자에게 똑같이 잘 듣는 수술과 약을 개발하는 것이다. 그것은 우리들 모두가 똑같은 조립라인에서 출고된 유사한 생체 역학적인 집단이라는 널리 알려진 믿음으로부터 유래하는데, 그것은 전통 의학의 효력을 제한하는 인간에 대한 매우 불완전한 개념이다. 그러나 미래의 의사는 근본적으로 다른 방식으로 의학을 실천할 필요가 있다. 가장 중요한 변화 중의 하나는, 현재 대체로 무시당하고 있는 개념인 환자의 개별성에 대한 인식의 증가가 될 것이다. 유사한 증상을 나타내는 다양한 환자를 똑같은 약으로 치료하는 것 대신 의사들은 병의 근본 원인을 밝혀내어 개별화된 치료를 제시해야 한다.

① 특효약
② 환자의 개별성
③ 의학 기술
④ 의사의 자격

어휘 medicine 의학 procedure 절차, 수술 regardless of ~와 관계없이 genetics 유전적 특징, 유전학 derive from ~에서 유래하다 prevalent 널리 알려진 bio-mechanical 생체 역학적인 assembly line 조립라인 imperfect 불완전한 conventional 기존의 effectiveness 효력 fundamentally 근본적으로 shift 변화 recognition 인식 ignore 무시하다 display 나타내다 symptom 증상 personalized 개별화된 individuality 개별성 qualification 자격

01 밑줄 친 부분에 들어갈 말로 가장 적절한 것은? (2022, 지방직 9급)

One of the most frequently used propaganda techniques is to convince the public that the propagandist's views reflect those of the common person and that he or she is working in their best interests. A politician speaking to a blue-collar audience may roll up his sleeves, undo his tie, and attempt to use the specific idioms of the crowd. He may even use language incorrectly on purpose to give the impression that he is "just one of the folks." This technique usually also employs the use of glittering generalities to give the impression that the politician's views are the same as those of the crowd being addressed. Labor leaders, businesspeople, ministers, educators, and advertisers have used this technique to win our confidence by appearing to be ______________________.

① beyond glittering generalities
② just plain folks like ourselves
③ something different from others
④ better educated than the crowd

02 밑줄 친 부분에 들어갈 말로 가장 적절한 것은? (2022, 국가직 9급)

Scientists have long known that higher air temperatures are contributing to the surface melting on Greenland's ice sheet. But a new study has found another threat that has begun attacking the ice from below: Warm ocean water moving underneath the vast glaciers is causing them to melt even more quickly. The findings were published in the journal Nature Geoscience by researchers who studied one of the many "ice tongues" of the Nioghalvfjerdsfjorden Glacier in northeast Greenland. An ice tongue is a strip of ice that floats on the water without breaking off from the ice on land. The massive one these scientists studied is nearly 50 miles long. The survey revealed an underwater current more than a mile wide where warm water from the Atlantic Ocean is able to flow directly towards the glacier, bringing large amounts of heat into contact with the ice and __________ the glacier's melting.

① separating ② delaying

③ preventing ④ accelerating

03 밑줄 친 부분에 들어갈 말로 가장 적절한 것은? (2021, 국가직 9급)

Social media, magazines and shop windows bombard people daily with things to buy, and British consumers are buying more clothes and shoes than ever before. Online shopping means it is easy for customers to buy without thinking, while major brands offer such cheap clothes that they can be treated like disposable items — worn two or three times and then thrown away. In Britain, the average person spends more than ￡1,000 on new clothes a year, which is around four percent of their income. That might not sound like much, but that figure hides two far more worrying trends for society and for the environment. First, a lot of that consumer spending is via credit cards. British people currently owe approximately ￡670 per adult to credit card companies. That's 66 percent of the average wardrobe budget. Also, not only are people spending money they don't have, they're using it to buy things ____________________. Britain throws away 300,000 tons of clothing a year, most of which goes into landfill sites.

① they don't need
② that are daily necessities
③ that will be soon recycled
④ they can hand down to others

04 밑줄 친 부분에 들어갈 말로 가장 적절한 것은? (2021, 국가직 9급)

Excellence is the absolute prerequisite in fine dining because the prices charged are necessarily high. An operator may do everything possible to make the restaurant efficient, but the guests still expect careful, personal service: food prepared to order by highly skilled chefs and delivered by expert servers. Because this service is, quite literally, manual labor, only marginal improvements in productivity are possible. For example, a cook, server, or bartender can move only so much faster before she or he reaches the limits of human performance. Thus, only moderate savings are possible through improved efficiency, which makes an escalation of prices ___________. (It is an axiom of economics that as prices rise, consumers become more discriminating.) Thus, the clientele of the fine-dining restaurant expects, demands, and is willing to pay for excellence.

① ludicrous ② inevitable
③ preposterous ④ inconceivable

05 밑줄 친 부분에 들어갈 말로 가장 적절한 것은? (2021, 지방직 9급)

As more and more leaders work remotely or with teams scattered around the nation or the globe, as well as with consultants and freelancers, you'll have to give them more ___________. The more trust you bestow, the more others trust you. I am convinced that there is a direct correlation between job satisfaction and how empowered people are to fully execute their job without someone shadowing them every step of the way. Giving away responsibility to those you trust can not only make your organization run more smoothly but also free up more of your time so you can focus on larger issues.

① work
② rewards
③ restrictions
④ autonomy

06 밑줄 친 부분에 들어갈 말로 가장 적절한 것은? (2019, 지방직 9급)

> Language proper is itself double-layered. Single noises are only occasionally meaningful: mostly, the various speech sounds convey coherent messages only when combined into an overlapping chain, like different colours of ice-cream melting into one another. In birdsong also, ______________________; the sequence is what matters. In both humans and birds, control of this specialized sound-system is exercised by one half of the brain, usually the left half, and the system is learned relatively early in life. And just as many human languages have dialects, so do some bird species: In California, the white-crowned sparrow has songs so different from area to area that Californians can supposedly tell where they are in the state by listening to these sparrows.

① individual notes are often of little value
② rhythmic sounds are important
③ dialects play a critical role
④ no sound-system exists

07 밑줄 친 부분에 들어갈 말로 가장 적절한 것은? (2019, 지방직 9급)

Nobel Prize-winning psychologist Daniel Kahneman changed the way the world thinks about economics, upending the notion that human beings are rational decision-makers. Along the way, his discipline-crossing influence has altered the way physicians make medical decisions, and investors evaluate risk on Wall Street. In a paper, Kahneman and his colleagues outline a process for making big strategic decisions. Their suggested approach, labeled as "Mediating Assessments Protocol," or MAP, has a simple goal: To put off gut-based decision-making until a choice can be informed by a number of separate factors. "One of the essential purposes of MAP is basically to ____________ intuition," Kahneman said in a recent interview with *The Post*. The structured process calls for analyzing a decision based on six to seven previously chosen attributes, discussing each of them separately and assigning them a relative percentile score, and finally, using those scores to make a holistic judgment.

① improve ② delay
③ possess ④ facilitate

08 다음 빈칸에 들어갈 말로 가장 알맞은 것은? (2017, 지방직 하반기 9급)

In a famous essay on Tolstoy, the liberal philosopher Sir Isaiah Berlin distinguished between two kinds of thinkers by harking back to an ancient saying attributed to the Greek lyric poet Archilochus (seventh century BC): "The fox knows many things, but the hedgehog knows one big thing." Hedgehogs have one central idea and see the world exclusively through the prism of that idea. They overlook complications and exceptions, or mold them to fit into their world view. There is one true answer that fits at all times and all circumstances. Foxes, for whom Berlin had greater sympathy, have a variegated take on the world, which prevents them from ____________________. They are skeptical of grand theories as they feel the world's complexity prevents generalizations. Berlin thought Dante was a hedgehog while Shakespeare was a fox.

① behaving rationally
② finding multiple solutions
③ articulating one big slogan
④ grasping the complications of the world

09 밑줄 친 부분에 들어갈 말로 가장 적절한 것은? (2016, 국가직 9급)

There's a knock at your door. Standing in front of you is a young man who needs help. He's injured and is bleeding. You take him in and help him, make him feel comfortable and safe and phone for an ambulance. This is clearly the right thing to do. But if you help him just because you feel sorry for him, according to Immanuel Kant, ______________________________. Your sympathy is irrelevant to the morality of your action. That's part of your character, but nothing to do with right and wrong. Morality for Kant wasn't just about what you do, but about why you do it. Those who do the right thing don't do it simply because of how they feel: the decision has to be based on reason, reason that tells you what your duty is, regardless of how you happen to feel.

① that wouldn't be a moral action at all
② your action is founded on reason
③ then you're exhibiting ethical behavior
④ you're encouraging him to be an honest person

10 밑줄 친 부분에 가장 적절한 것은? (2015, 국가직 9급)

Language is saturated with implicit metaphors like "Events are objects and time is space." Indeed, space turns out to be a conceptual vehicle not just for time but for many kinds of states and circumstances. Just as a meeting can be moved from 3:00 to 4:00, a traffic light can go from green to red, a person can go from flipping burgers to running a corporation, and the economy can go from bad to worse. Metaphor is so widespread in language that it's hard to find expressions for abstract ideas that are not metaphorical. Does it imply that even our wispiest concepts are represented in the mind as hunks of matter that we move around on a mental stage? Does it say that rival claims about the world can never be true or false but can only be ________________? Few things in life cannot be characterized in terms of variables and the causation of changes in them.

① proven to be always true in all circumstances
② irreversible and established truths that cannot be disputed
③ subject to scientific testings for their authenticity and clarity
④ alternative metaphors that frame a situation in different ways

11 밑줄 친 부분에 가장 적절한 것은? (2014, 국가직 9급)

The emphasis on decoding, translated mainly as phonemic awareness and knowledge of the alphabetic principle, has led schools to search for packaged or commercially produced reading programs that help students master the skills of decoding. According to the teachers we work with, this highly scripted approach to reading instruction has produced many students who know how to sound out words, but that is where the process of reading ends for them. While the students can decode and even become fluent oral readers, they do not truly comprehend the material; they cannot read between the lines, infer meaning, or detect the author's bias, among other things. Reading ____________________.

① is basically decoding since phonemic and alphabetical knowledge is added to the general decoding process

② is much more complex than simply mastering phonemic awareness and alphabet recognition

③ can be more efficiently learned together with peers than either alone or with teachers

④ can be mastered when learners know how to sound out words fluently

12 다음 글의 빈칸에 들어갈 말로 가장 적절한 것은?

> The spread of prosperity, the single-family home, the invention of television and computers have all made it possible for us to live private lives unimaginable to previous generations. We no longer live in close quarters with our neighbors, we can move about without crowding into buses or trains; we do not have to go to theaters or share our tastes with our neighbors. However, the same technologies that help separate us from the crowds also make it possible to monitor and record our behaviors. Although fewer people have intimate knowledge of our lives, many people — mostly unknown to us — know something about us. The very technology that was supposed to free us from mass society has turned out to be as much a fishbowl as an information highway. In modern society, we have discovered that ______________________________.

① being free often means also being naked
② cooperating with people leads to wrong conclusions
③ more people become indifferent to the spread of prosperity
④ technology makes us independent from natural environments

Reading Skill

09

연결사 추론

HOW TO SOLVE

연결사 추론 문제는 문장과 문장 간의 연결 고리에 대해 묻는 유형이므로 연결되는 두 문장을 정확하게 해석할 수 있는 능력과 두 문장 간의 논리성을 파악하는 사고력을 모두 갖추고 있어야 한다. 수험생 스스로가 해석 능력이 좋지 않거나 논리성이 약하다고 생각한다면 어려울 수 있는 유형이지만 풀이 전략을 익히고 연습을 한다면 생각보다 쉽게 풀이할 수 있다.

※ 접속부사 : 접속사 역할을 하는 부사

※ 접속부사를 묻는 문제가 나오면 그 접속부사가 포함된 문장과 그 앞 문장 간의 관계를 묻는 것이다. 즉, 문장과 문장 간의 관계를 나타내는 것으로 이때 접속부사는 문장의 중간이나 끝에 나올 수도 있다는 점에 유의해야 한다.

SHIMSON'S TIP

주의해야 할 접속부사 (p.064 참고)

비평 · 대조	however, nevertheless, nonetheless, and yet, still, even so, in contrast, by contrast, on the contrary, on the other hand
예시	for example, for instance
유사	that is, that is to say, namely, as it were, so to speak, in other words
열거	also, moreover, furthermore, besides, in addition, what is more, at the same time, similarly, likewise
결과	thus, hence, therefore, accordingly, thereby, for these reasons, finally, consequently, as a result, in short, in brief, in a word

1 비평 · 대조와 예시의 연결사를 먼저 생각하자!

무조건 답을 찾기보다는 비교적 쉬운 유형의 보기부터 대입해 본다. 연결사 중에서 비평 · 대조와 예시가 특히 쉬우므로 보기에 비평 · 대조나 예시가 나오면 해당 보기가 답으로 적절한지 먼저 파악한다.
비평 · 대조 → 예시 → 유사 → 열거 → 원인 · 결과 순서로 확인하도록 한다.

2 역추론 후 뒤 문장을 읽도록 하자!

빈칸 앞 문장을 읽은 후 바로 뒤 문장을 읽지 말고, 비평 · 대조의 연결사가 답이라면 뒤에 어떤 내용이 나올지, 예시의 연결사가 답이라면 뒤에 어떤 내용이 나올지 역추론을 한 후 뒤 문장을 읽으면 훨씬 답을 쉽게 찾을 수 있다.

When the students watched the film with an authority figure present, their faces showed only the slightest hints of reaction. ______________, when they thought they were alone (though they were being taped by a secret camera) their faces twisted into vivid mixes of uncomfortable feelings.

학생들이 권위 있는 인물과 함께 영화를 봤을 때, 그들의 얼굴은 단지 최소한의 반응의 기색만을 보였다. ______________, (비록 그들은 비밀 카메라로 촬영되는 중이었지만) 그들이 혼자 있다고 생각했을 때에는 그들의 얼굴은 불편한 감정이 생생하게 뒤범벅이 되어 뒤틀려 있었다.

빈칸 앞에 나온 내용은 with an authority figure present, (권위 있는 인물과 함께 참석한 상태)
their faces showed only the slightest hints of reaction.
(그들의 얼굴은 단지 최소한의 반응의 기색만을 보였다.)

반대로 빈칸 뒤에 나온 내용은 they were alone (혼자 있는 상태)
their faces twisted into vivid mixes of uncomfortable feelings.
(그들의 얼굴은 불편한 감정이 생생하게 뒤범벅이 되어 뒤틀려 있었다.)

즉, 빈칸의 앞과 뒤는 서로 반대되는 상황이므로, 대조를 나타내는 연결사 However가 들어가야 한다.

오답을 피하는 법

1 접속부사가 문장 중간에 나오는 경우 조심해야 한다.

접속부사는 문장 앞부분뿐만 아니라, 문장 중간 또는 끝에도 위치할 수 있다. 접속부사가 문장 중간에 나오는 경우, 빈칸 앞과 빈칸 뒤가 아니라 빈칸 앞 문장과 빈칸이 있는 문장 간의 관계를 살펴야 하고, 전치사 및 접속사는 한 문장 안에서의 관계를 살펴야 한다.

2 비평 · 대조의 경우 전체 문맥 속에서 ⊕/⊖를 나누어야 한다.

비평 · 대조의 경우 반드시 전체 문맥 속에서 ⊕/⊖를 나누어야 한다.

3 문장이 긴 경우, 핵심 내용을 압축하도록 한다.

접속부사의 경우, 앞 문장과 뒤 문장이 긴 경우가 많다. 이 경우 해석도 중요하지만, 해석 후 핵심을 압축하여 두 문장 간의 관계를 파악해야 한다.

SKILL EXAMPLE

01 밑줄 친 (A), (B)에 들어갈 말로 가장 적절한 것은?

> Assertive behavior involves standing up for your rights and expressing your thoughts and feelings in a direct, appropriate way that does not violate the rights of others. It is a matter of getting the other person to understand your viewpoint. People who exhibit assertive behavior skills are able to handle conflict situations with ease and assurance while maintaining good interpersonal relations. ___(A)___, aggressive behavior involves expressing your thoughts and feelings and defending your rights in a way that openly violates the rights of others. Those exhibiting aggressive behavior seem to believe that the rights of others must be subservient to theirs. ___(B)___, they have a difficult time maintaining good interpersonal relations. They are likely to interrupt, talk fast, ignore others, and use sarcasm or other forms of verbal abuse to maintain control.

	(A)	(B)
①	In contrast	Thus
②	Similarly	Moreover
③	However	On one hand
④	Accordingly	On the other hand

지문 분석

1 비평·대조와 예시의 연결사를 먼저 생각한다.

보기에 있는 비평·대조의 연결사 In contrast와 However를 먼저 (A)에 대입해보도록 한다.

2 역추론 후 뒤 문장을 읽는다.

People who exhibit assertive behavior skills are able to handle conflict situations with ease and assurance while maintaining good interpersonal relations. ___(A)___, aggressive behavior involves expressing your thoughts and feelings and defending your rights in a way that openly violates the rights of others.

적극적 행동 기술을 보이는 사람들은 좋은 대인관계를 유지하면서 갈등 상황을 쉽고 확실하게 처리할 수 있다. ___(A)___, 공격적 행동은 타인의 권리를 공공연히 침해하는 방식으로 당신의 생각과 감정을 표현하고 당신의 권리를 지키는 것을 수반한다.

빈칸 앞은 assertive behavior에 관한 내용으로 '좋은 대인관계를 유지', '갈등 상황을 쉽고 확실하게 처리'와 같은 긍정적인 표현이 쓰이고 있다. In contrast나 However가 답이라면 뒤에 앞의 내용과 반대되는 부정적인 표현이 나올 것이라고 추론할 수 있다. 실제로 빈칸 뒤엔 aggressive behavior라는 새로운 소재가 등장하며 '타인의 권리를 공공연히 침해'와 같은 부정적인 표현이 쓰이고 있다. 즉, 빈칸 앞뒤로 assertive behavior(⊕)와 aggressive behavior(⊖) 두 대상이 대조되고 있으므로, (A)에는 대조의 연결사 In contrast가 적절하다.

Those exhibiting aggressive behavior seem to believe that the rights of others must be subservient to theirs. ___(B)___, they have a difficult time maintaining good interpersonal relations.

공격적 행동을 보이는 사람들은 타인의 권리가 자신의 권리보다 부차적이어야 한다고 믿는 것처럼 보인다. ___(B)___, 그들은 좋은 대인관계를 유지하는 데 어려움을 겪는다.

빈칸 앞의 핵심 내용은 앞서 부정적인 논조로 묘사된 aggressive behavior를 보이는 사람들이 타인의 권리를 자신의 것보다 아래로 본다는 것이다. 그리고 빈칸 뒤는 그들이 좋은 대인관계를 유지하기 어렵다는, 부정적인 내용이 이어지고 있다. 즉, 타인의 권리를 무시하여 대인관계에서 어려움을 겪는다는 인과관계가 성립되므로, (B)에는 결과의 연결사 Thus가 들어가야 한다.

정답 및 해석

정답 ①

해석 적극적 행동은 타인의 권리를 침해하지 않는 직접적이고 적절한 방식으로 당신의 권리를 옹호하고 당신의 생각과 감정을 표현하는 것을 수반한다. 그것은 상대방이 당신의 관점을 이해하게 하는 문제이다. 적극적 행동 기술을 보이는 사람들은 좋은 대인관계를 유지하면서 갈등 상황을 쉽고 확실하게 처리할 수 있다. 그에 반해서, 공격적 행동은 타인의 권리를 공공연히 침해하는 방식으로 당신의 생각과 감정을 표현하고 당신의 권리를 지키는 것을 수반한다. 공격적 행동을 보이는 사람들은 타인의 권리가 자신의 권리보다 부차적이어야 한다고 믿는 것처럼 보인다. 따라서, 그들은 좋은 대인관계를 유지하는 데 어려움을 겪는다. 그들은 지배력을 유지하기 위해 담화를 방해하고, 빠르게 말하고, 타인을 무시하며, 빈정대는 말이나 다른 형태의 언어폭력을 사용하기 쉽다.

어휘 assertive 적극적인, 확신에 찬 stand up for ~을 옹호하다, 지지하다 appropriate 적절한 assurance 확신 aggressive 공격적인 subservient 부차적인, 종속하는 sarcasm 빈정댐, 비꼼 verbal abuse 언어폭력, 폭언

01 (A)와 (B)에 들어갈 말로 가장 적절한 것은? (2022, 지방직 9급)

Duration shares an inverse relationship with frequency. If you see a friend frequently, then the duration of the encounter will be shorter. Conversely, if you don't see your friend very often, the duration of your visit will typically increase significantly. ___(A)___, if you see a friend every day, the duration of your visits can be low because you can keep up with what's going on as events unfold. If, however, you only see your friend twice a year, the duration of your visits will be greater. Think back to a time when you had dinner in a restaurant with a friend you hadn't seen for a long period of time. You probably spent several hours catching up on each other's lives. The duration of the same dinner would be considerably shorter if you saw the person on a regular basis. ___(B)___, in romantic relationships the frequency and duration are very high because couples, especially newly minted ones, want to spend as much time with each other as possible. The intensity of the relationship will also be very high.

(A)	(B)
① For example	Conversely
② Nonetheless	Furthermore
③ Therefore	As a result
④ In the same way	Thus

02 밑줄 친 (A), (B)에 들어갈 말로 가장 적절한 것은? (2022, 국가직 9급)

Beliefs about maintaining ties with those who have died vary from culture to culture. For example, maintaining ties with the deceased is accepted and sustained in the religious rituals of Japan. Yet among the Hopi Indians of Arizona, the deceased are forgotten as quickly as possible and life goes on as usual. ___(A)___, the Hopi funeral ritual concludes with a break-off between mortals and spirits. The diversity of grieving is nowhere clearer than in two Muslim societies — one in Egypt, the other in Bali. Among Muslims in Egypt, the bereaved are encouraged to dwell at length on their grief, surrounded by others who relate to similarly tragic accounts and express their sorrow. ___(B)___, in Bali, bereaved Muslims are encouraged to laugh and be joyful rather than be sad.

	(A)	(B)
①	However	Similarly
②	In fact	By contrast
③	Therefore	For example
④	Likewise	Consequently

03 (A)와 (B)에 들어갈 말로 가장 적절한 것은? (2021, 지방직 9급)

Ancient philosophers and spiritual teachers understood the need to balance the positive with the negative, optimism with pessimism, a striving for success and security with an openness to failure and uncertainty. The Stoics recommended "the premeditation of evils," or deliberately visualizing the worst-case scenario. This tends to reduce anxiety about the future: when you soberly picture how badly things could go in reality, you usually conclude that you could cope. ___(A)___, they noted, imagining that you might lose the relationships and possessions you currently enjoy increases your gratitude for having them now. Positive thinking, ___(B)___, always leans into the future, ignoring present pleasures.

	(A)	(B)
①	Nevertheless	in addition
②	Furthermore	for example
③	Besides	by contrast
④	However	in conclusion

04 밑줄 친 (A), (B)에 들어갈 말로 가장 적절한 것은? (2020, 국가직 9급)

Advocates of homeschooling believe that children learn better when they are in a secure, loving environment. Many psychologists see the home as the most natural learning environment, and originally the home was the classroom, long before schools were established. Parents who homeschool argue that they can monitor their children's education and give them the attention that is lacking in a traditional school setting. Students can also pick and choose what to study and when to study, thus enabling them to learn at their own pace. ___(A)___, critics of homeschooling say that children who are not in the classroom miss out on learning important social skills because they have little interaction with their peers. Several studies, though, have shown that the home-educated children appear to do just as well in terms of social and emotional development as other students, having spent more time in the comfort and security of their home, with guidance from parents who care about their welfare. ___(B)___, many critics of homeschooling have raised concerns about the ability of parents to teach their kids effectively.

(A)	(B)
① Therefore	Nevertheless
② In contrast	In spite of this
③ Therefore	Contrary to that
④ In contrast	Furthermore

05 밑줄 친 (A), (B)에 들어갈 말로 가장 적절한 것은? (2019, 지방직 9급)

Today the technology to create the visual component of virtual-reality (VR) experiences is well on its way to becoming widely accessible and affordable. But to work powerfully, virtual reality needs to be about more than visuals. ___(A)___ what you are hearing convincingly matches the visuals, the virtual experience breaks apart. Take a basketball game. If the players, the coaches, the announcers, and the crowd all sound like they're sitting midcourt, you may as well watch the game on television — you'll get just as much of a sense that you are "there." ___(B)___, today's audio equipment and our widely used recording and reproduction formats are simply inadequate to the task of re-creating convincingly the sound of a battlefield on a distant planet, a basketball game at courtside, or a symphony as heard from the first row of a great concert hall.

	(A)	(B)
①	If	By contrast
②	Unless	Consequently
③	If	Similarly
④	Unless	Unfortunately

06 다음 글의 빈칸 (A), (B)에 들어갈 말로 가장 적절한 것은?

At certain times in history, cultures have taken it for granted that a person was not fully human unless he or she learned to master thoughts and feelings. In ancient Sparta, in Republican Rome, and among the British upper classes of the Victorian era, ______(A)______, people were held responsible for keeping control of their emotions. Anyone who lost his or her temper too easily was deprived of the right to be accepted as a member of the community. In other historical periods such as the one in which we are now living, ______(B)______, the ability to control oneself is not always highly respected. People who attempt it are often thought to be odd.

	(A)	(B)
①	for example	therefore
②	for example	however
③	in addition	moreover
④	in addition	similarly

Reading Skill 10

순서 배열

HOW TO SOLVE

순서 배열 문제는 최근 중요해지는 추세이며 매번 1문제씩 출제되고 있다. 이 유형은 독해력보다는 사고력을 묻는 문제인데, 독해에 의존해서 문제를 풀려고 하다 보니 그리 어려운 유형이 아님에도 불구하고 정답률이 낮다. 제시된 풀이법대로 논리에 초점을 맞춰 순서 배열 문제를 풀면 쉽게 맞출 수 있을 것이다.

1 (A), (B), (C) 본문에서 Signal 찾기 ⇨ 독해 전략 세우기

(A), (B), (C)에서 Signal을 잡으면 이 글을 어떤 식으로 읽어야 하고, 어떤 개념을 잡아야 하는지가 보인다. 참고로 Signal이란 글의 단락 구조를 알 수 있는 단서로 연결사보다 큰 개념이다. 연결사뿐만 아니라 대명사, 지시형용사도 넓은 의미에서 Signal에 해당한다.

2 제시된 Box에서 글의 소재 찾기

제시된 Box는 큰 의미가 없다. 다만 글의 소재가 무엇인지 정도만 파악하면 된다.

3 본문을 읽으면서 답 찾기: Signal이 있는 것부터 해석

Box를 읽었다면 Signal이 있는 문장을 읽어가면서, Grouping(분류)의 기준을 잡아야 한다.

※ (A), (B), (C) 본문이 긴 경우, 핵심 내용을 압축하라.

(A), (B), (C) 본문이 긴 경우, 해석을 한 후에 각각의 핵심 내용을 압축하는 것이 특히 중요하다.
(A), (B), (C) 각 문단의 핵심 내용만 잡아내면 생각보다 순서 배열이 쉽게 풀린다.
(A), (B), (C) 각 문단이 긴 경우, 연결되는 문단을 찾으려면 각 문단의 첫 문장과 마지막 문장의 의미를 정확하게 이해하는 것이 중요하다.

오답을 피하는 법

[1] 비평 · 대조의 Signal이 나왔다면 전체 소재를 기준으로 ⊕/⊖를 구별해야 한다.

단순히 좋은 내용이라고 해서 ⊕, 나쁜 내용이라고 해서 ⊖인 것이 아니다. 전체적인 틀(또는 소재) 속에서 ⊕인지 ⊖인지를 잡아야 한다.

[2] 만약 Signal이 주어지지 않았다면, 의미 파악을 통해서 문제를 푼다.

① 소재(큰 개념 → 작은 개념)
② process와 실험 구조 및 문제점과 해결책 구조도 자주 나온다.

순서 배열 문제에 Signal을 주지 않았다는 것은 결국 내용으로 파악하라는 의미다. 따라서 내용 파악, 특히 소재를 잘 보면 쉽게 답이 나온다. 또한 Signal이 없을 경우 특별한 단락 구조가 없는 글일 수도 있지만, process와 실험 구조의 글일 수도 있다는 점에 유의해야 한다.

SHIMSON'S TIP

문단 순서 배열은 특히 Grouping이 중요(소재 중심)

- **대조** Signal의 경우 : ⊕ vs ⊖
- **예시** Signal의 경우 : 큰(추상) vs 작은(구체)
- **나열** Signal의 경우 : 내용으로 A or B

SKILL EXAMPLE

01 주어진 글 다음에 이어질 글의 순서로 가장 적절한 것은?

> Depression afflicts more than 19 million people in the United States at any given time, and almost one in five over the course of a lifetime.

> (A) The tendency for men to tough it out rather than ask for help is just one of several reasons why experts believe the oft-quoted statistics are artificially low.
>
> (B) According to statistics, approximately 20 percent of all women suffer from depression and about 10 percent of men.
>
> (C) But some researchers question the latter number. "Men are less likely than women to seek mental-health treatment in general," says Michael Addis, an assistant professor of psychology at Clark University.

① (B)−(A)−(C)　　② (B)−(C)−(A)
③ (C)−(A)−(B)　　④ (C)−(B)−(A)

지문 분석

> Depression afflicts more than 19 million people in the United States at any given time, and almost one in five over the course of a lifetime.
>
> 우울증은 미국에 사는 1,900만 명 이상의 사람들을 언제든지 괴롭히고, 거의 5명 중 1명을 평생에 걸쳐 괴롭힌다.

글의 소재는 우울증 환자의 수임을 알 수 있다.

> (A) The tendency for men to tough it out rather than ask for help is just one of several reasons why experts believe the oft-quoted statistics are artificially low.
>
> 남자들이 도움을 구하기보다는 어려움을 참고 견디는 성향은 전문가들이 자주 인용되는 통계 수치가 부자연스럽게 낮은 것이라고 믿는 여러 가지 이유 중의 하나일 뿐이다.

핵심 내용: 남자들은 도움을 구하기보다 견뎌내려는 경향이 있는데 이 경향은 바로 전문가들이 통계 수치가 부자연스럽게 낮다고 생각하는 이유이다.

(B) According to statistics, approximately 20 percent of all women suffer from depression and about 10 percent of men.

통계에 따르면, 모든 여성의 대략 20%가 우울증으로 고생하고 있으며, 남자는 약 10%가 그렇다.

핵심 내용: 남성보다 여성의 우울증 발병 비율이 더 높다.

(C) But some researchers question the latter number. "Men are less likely than women to seek mental-health treatment in general," says Michael Addis, an assistant professor of psychology at Clark University.

하지만 일부 연구자들은 후자의 숫자에 대하여 이의를 제기한다. "일반적으로 남자는 여자보다 정신 건강 치료를 받을 가능성이 작다."라고 Clark 대학의 심리학 조교수인 Michael Addis는 말한다.

핵심 내용: 남자는 여자보다 정신과 치료를 덜 찾기 때문에 통계 수치를 신뢰할 수 없다.

the latter number를 보고 (C)가 (B) 다음에 오는 내용임을 알 수 있다. "Men are ~ in general"은 (A)에서 '남자들이 도움을 구하기보다는 어려움을 참고 견디는 성향'이라고 부연 설명되므로 글의 순서는 (B)-(C)-(A)이다.

정답 및 해석

정답 ②

해석 우울증은 미국에 사는 1,900만 명 이상의 사람들을 언제든지 괴롭히고, 거의 5명 중 1명을 평생에 걸쳐 괴롭힌다. (B) 통계에 따르면, 모든 여성의 대략 20%가 우울증으로 고생하고 있으며, 남자는 약 10%가 그렇다. (C) 하지만 몇몇의 연구자들은 후자의 숫자에 대하여 이의를 제기한다. "일반적으로 남자는 여자보다 정신 건강 치료를 받을 가능성이 작다."라고 Clark 대학의 심리학 조교수인 Michael Addis는 말한다. (A) 남자들이 도움을 구하기보다는 어려움을 참고 견디는 성향은 전문가들이 자주 인용되는 통계 수치가 부자연스럽게 낮은 것이라고 믿는 여러 가지 이유 중 하나일 뿐이다.

어휘 depression 우울증 afflict 괴롭히다 tough it out 어려움을 참고 견디다 oft-quoted 자주 인용되는 statistics 통계 artificially 부자연스럽게 approximately 대략 latter 후자의 assistant professor 조교수

01 주어진 글 다음에 이어질 글의 순서로 가장 적절한 것은? (2022, 지방직 9급)

For people who are blind, everyday tasks such as sorting through the mail or doing a load of laundry present a challenge.

(A) That's the thinking behind Aira, a new service that enables its thousands of users to stream live video of their surroundings to an on-demand agent, using either a smartphone or Aira's proprietary glasses.
(B) But what if they could "borrow" the eyes of someone who could see?
(C) The Aira agents, who are available 24/7, can then answer questions, describe objects or guide users through a location.

① (A)−(B)−(C)
② (A)−(C)−(B)
③ (B)−(A)−(C)
④ (C)−(A)−(B)

02 주어진 글 다음에 이어질 글의 순서로 가장 적절한 것은? (2022, 국가직 9급)

Today, Lamarck is unfairly remembered in large part for his mistaken explanation of how adaptations evolve. He proposed that by using or not using certain body parts, an organism develops certain characteristics.

(A) There is no evidence that this happens. Still, it is important to note that Lamarck proposed that evolution occurs when organisms adapt to their environments. This idea helped set the stage for Darwin.

(B) Lamarck thought that these characteristics would be passed on to the offspring. Lamarck called this idea *inheritance of acquired characteristics*.

(C) For example, Lamarck might explain that a kangaroo's powerful hind legs were the result of ancestors strengthening their legs by jumping and then passing that acquired leg strength on to the offspring. However, an acquired characteristic would have to somehow modify the DNA of specific genes in order to be inherited.

① (A)－(C)－(B) ② (B)－(A)－(C)
③ (B)－(C)－(A) ④ (C)－(A)－(B)

03 주어진 글 다음에 이어질 글의 순서로 가장 적절한 것은? (2021, 국가직 9급)

> To be sure, human language stands out from the decidedly restricted vocalizations of monkeys and apes. Moreover, it exhibits a degree of sophistication that far exceeds any other form of animal communication.

(A) That said, many species, while falling far short of human language, do nevertheless exhibit impressively complex communication systems in natural settings.

(B) And they can be taught far more complex systems in artificial contexts, as when raised alongside humans.

(C) Even our closest primate cousins seem incapable of acquiring anything more than a rudimentary communicative system, even after intensive training over several years. The complexity that is language is surely a species-specific trait.

① (A)－(B)－(C)　　② (B)－(C)－(A)
③ (C)－(A)－(B)　　④ (C)－(B)－(A)

04 주어진 글 다음에 이어질 글의 순서로 가장 적절한 것은? (2021, 지방직 9급)

Growing concern about global climate change has motivated activists to organize not only campaigns against fossil fuel extraction consumption, but also campaigns to support renewable energy.

(A) This solar cooperative produces enough energy to power 1,400 homes, making it the first large-scale solar farm cooperative in the country and, in the words of its members, a visible reminder that solar power represents "a new era of sustainable and 'democratic' energy supply that enables ordinary people to produce clean power, not only on their rooftops, but also at utility scale."

(B) Similarly, renewable energy enthusiasts from the United States have founded the Clean Energy Collective, a company that has pioneered "the model of delivering clean power-generation through medium-scale facilities that are collectively owned by participating utility customers."

(C) Environmental activists frustrated with the UK government's inability to rapidly accelerate the growth of renewable energy industries have formed the Westmill Wind Farm Co-operative, a community-owned organization with more than 2,000 members who own an onshore wind farm estimated to produce as much electricity in a year as that used by 2,500 homes. The Westmill Wind Farm Co-operative has inspired local citizens to form the Westmill Solar Co-operative.

① (C)－(A)－(B) ② (A)－(C)－(B)
③ (B)－(C)－(A) ④ (C)－(B)－(A)

05 주어진 글 다음에 이어질 글의 순서로 가장 적절한 것은? (2020, 국가직 9급)

Past research has shown that experiencing frequent psychological stress can be a significant risk factor for cardiovascular disease, a condition that affects almost half of those aged 20 years and older in the United States.

(A) Does this mean, though, that people who drive on a daily basis are set to develop heart problems, or is there a simple way of easing the stress of driving?

(B) According to a new study, there is. The researchers noted that listening to music while driving helps relieve the stress that affects heart health.

(C) One source of frequent stress is driving, either due to the stressors associated with heavy traffic or the anxiety that often accompanies inexperienced drivers.

① (A)−(C)−(B) ② (B)−(A)−(C)
③ (C)−(A)−(B) ④ (C)−(B)−(A)

06 주어진 글 다음에 이어질 글의 순서로 가장 적절한 것은? (2020, 지방직 9급)

Nowadays the clock dominates our lives so much that it is hard to imagine life without it. Before industrialization, most societies used the sun or the moon to tell the time.

(A) For the growing network of railroads, the fact that there were no time standards was a disaster. Often, stations just some miles apart set their clocks at different times. There was a lot of confusion for travelers.

(B) When mechanical clocks first appeared, they were immediately popular. It was fashionable to have a clock or a watch. People invented the expression "of the clock" or "o'clock" to refer to this new way to tell the time.

(C) These clocks were decorative, but not always useful. This was because towns, provinces, and even neighboring villages had different ways to tell the time. Travelers had to reset their clocks repeatedly when they moved from one place to another. In the United States, there were about 70 different time zones in the 1860s.

① (A)－(B)－(C) ② (B)－(A)－(C)

③ (B)－(C)－(A) ④ (C)－(A)－(B)

07 주어진 문장 다음에 이어질 글의 순서로 가장 적절한 것은? (2018. 국가직 9급)

> A technique that enables an individual to gain some voluntary control over autonomic, or involuntary, body functions by observing electronic measurements of those functions is known as biofeedback.

(A) When such a variable moves in the desired direction (for example, blood pressure down), it triggers visual or audible displays — feedback on equipment such as television sets, gauges, or lights.

(B) Electronic sensors are attached to various parts of the body to measure such variables as heart rate, blood pressure, and skin temperature.

(C) Biofeedback training teaches one to produce a desired response by reproducing thought patterns or actions that triggered the displays.

① (A)－(B)－(C)　　② (B)－(C)－(A)

③ (B)－(A)－(C)　　④ (C)－(A)－(B)

08 주어진 글 다음에 이어질 글의 순서로 가장 적절한 것은? (2017, 국가직 9급)

The most innovative of the group therapy approaches was psychodrama, the brainchild of Jacob L. Moreno. Psychodrama as a form of group therapy started with premises that were quite alien to the Freudian worldview that mental illness essentially occurs within the psyche or mind.

(A) But he also believed that creativity is rarely a solitary process but something brought out by social interactions. He relied heavily on theatrical techniques, including role-playing and improvisation, as a means to promote creativity and general social trust.

(B) Despite his theoretical difference from the mainstream viewpoint, Moreno's influence in shaping psychological consciousness in the twentieth century was considerable. He believed that the nature of human beings is to be creative and that living a creative life is the key to human health and well-being.

(C) His most important theatrical tool was what he called role reversal — asking participants to take on another's persona. The act of pretending "as if" one were in another's skin was designed to help bring out the empathic impulse and to develop it to higher levels of expression.

① (A)－(C)－(B) ② (B)－(A)－(C)

③ (B)－(C)－(A) ④ (C)－(B)－(A)

09 주어진 글 다음에 이어질 글의 순서로 가장 적절한 것은? (2016, 국가직 9급)

All animals have the same kind of brain activation during sleep as humans. Whether or not they dream is another question, which can be answered only by posing another one: Do animals have consciousness?

(A) These are three of the key aspects of consciousness, and they could be experienced whether or not an animal had verbal language as we do. When the animal's brain is activated during sleep, why not assume that the animal has some sort of perceptual, emotional, and memory experience?

(B) Many scientists today feel that animals probably do have a limited form of consciousness, quite different from ours in that it lacks language and the capacity for propositional or symbolic thought.

(C) Animals certainly can't report dreams even if they do have them. But which pet owner would doubt that his or her favourite animal friend has perception, memory, and emotion?

① (A)−(B)−(C)　② (A)−(C)−(B)
③ (B)−(C)−(A)　④ (C)−(B)−(A)

10 주어진 글 다음에 이어질 글의 순서로 가장 적절한 것은? (2015, 국가직 9급)

Thunderstorms are extremely common in many parts of the world, for example, throughout most of North America. Updrafts of warm air set off these storms.

(A) This more buoyant air then rises and carries water vapor to higher altitudes. The air cools as it rises, and the water vapor condenses and starts to drop as rain. As the rain falls, it pulls air along with it and turns part of the draft downward.

(B) An updraft may start over ground that is more intensely heated by the sun than the land surrounding the area. Bare, rocky, or paved areas, for example, usually have updrafts above them. The air in contact with the ground heats up and thus becomes lighter, more buoyant, than the air surrounding it.

(C) The draft may turn upward again and send the rain churning around in the cloud. Some of it may freeze to hail. Sooner or later, the water droplets grow heavy enough to resist the updrafts and fall to the ground, pulling air in the form of downdrafts with them.

① (A)－(C)－(B) ② (B)－(A)－(C)
③ (B)－(C)－(A) ④ (C)－(A)－(B)

Reading Skill

11 문장 삽입

HOW TO SOLVE

문장 삽입 유형은 독해력보다는 사고력을 요구하는 유형이다. 따라서 아래 제시된 Skill대로 논리에 초점을 맞춰 문제를 풀면 누구나 쉽게 맞출 수 있다.

1 본문에서 연결사를 찾아라.

미리 본문에서 연결사를 찾아두면 단락 전개를 예상할 수 있기 때문에 문제 풀이가 쉬워진다.

2 본문에서 첫 번째와 두 번째 문장을 읽는다.

제시된 Box부터 읽는 것은 절대 좋은 방법이라고 할 수 없다. 일단 처음 두 문장을 통해 무엇에 관한 내용인지를 파악한 후 Box를 읽어야 한다.

다음 문장을 읽고 어떤 내용이 나올 것인지 예상해보자.

> Why is it that if you tickle yourself, it doesn't tickle, but if someone else tickles you, you cannot stand it?
>
> 왜 당신이 당신 자신을 간지럽히면 간지럽지 않고, 다른 사람이 간지럼을 태우면 참기가 힘든 것인가?

왜 자신이 스스로를 간지럽힐 때는 간지럽지 않고, 다른 사람이 간지럼을 태우면 간지러운지 그 이유에 관한 글일 것이다.

3 Box에서 Signal을 잡고 앞뒤 내용을 유추한다.

Box 분석이 가장 중요하다. Signal을 잡은 후 Box를 읽고 앞에 나올 내용과 뒤에 나올 내용을 각각 유추해야 한다. 앞에 나올 내용을 유추하는 것은 이미 처음 두 문장을 읽었기 때문에 쉽다. 뒤에 나올 내용은 Box와 유사한 내용이거나 Box 내용 다음 단계일 것이다.

※ 연결사, 지시대명사, 대명사 ⊂ Signal

> **However**, when you try to tickle yourself, you are in complete control of the situation.
>
> 그러나, 당신이 당신 자신을 간지럼 태울 때, 당신은 완전히 상황을 통제하는 상태에 있다.

However로 보아, 앞 문장에는 자신이 스스로를 간지럽히는 것이 아닌, 다른 사람이 자신을 간지럽히는 내용이 올 것이라 예상할 수 있다.

4 Box 내용을 염두에 두고 본문을 읽어나간다.

본문을 읽으면서 그 내용이 Box 앞에 있을 내용인지 뒤에 있을 내용인지를 파악한다.

> The tension is due to physical contact, the lack of control, and the fear of whether it will tickle or hurt. (④) There is no need to get tense and **therefore**, no reaction.
>
> 긴장은 신체적인 접촉, 통제 부족, 그리고 간지러울 것인지 아니면 아플 것인지에 대한 두려움에서 발생한다. (④) 긴장할 필요도 없으므로 반응도 없다.

therefore로 자연스럽게 연결되지 않는다고 느껴야 한다. 그러면 box 내용이 ④에 들어가야 한다고 추측해 볼 수 있다.

❶ 특정 문장과 문장이 바로 연결됨을 알려 주는 단어 및 어구

지시어	this, that, these, those, the same, the 명사
대명사	it, they, his, her, their

❷ 문장 간 배열 순서를 알려 주는 단어 및 어구

연결어	문장과 문장을 연결	however, and, but, thus, then 등
시간 · 순서	시간의 순서를 나타냄	first, second, formerly, later, before, after, then, finally, last
대조	앞의 내용은 상반된 내용	while, on the other hand, however, but, yet, still
결과	앞의 내용은 이에 대한 원인	therefore, thus, so, hence, as a result
예시	앞의 내용은 이를 포괄하는 내용	for example, for instance
비교	앞의 내용은 유사한 내용	likewise, similarly, in the same way, in like manner
첨가	앞의 내용은 같은 내용	also, besides, furthermore, moreover, likewise, what is more, as well, in addition
열거	앞의 내용은 이를 포괄하는 내용	first, first of all, second, third, lastly, finally

SKILL EXAMPLE

01 글의 흐름으로 보아, 주어진 문장이 들어가기에 가장 적절한 곳은?

> Older workers, in contrast, more often have skills that are quite specific to the industry or firm in which they are currently employed.

Younger workers tend to have more general skills and are less certain about where their skills might be put to their best uses. Hence, they tend to move between jobs on a regular basis. (①) But when they leave their old job, they have little trouble finding a new one. (②) They already know their best employment option and are not inclined to move around between jobs. (③) When they do leave work, however, finding a position that matches well with their precise skills is often difficult and time-consuming. (④) Thus, unemployment that is a nuisance for a younger worker can be a damaging and financially draining experience for a mature worker.

지문 분석

Ⅰ 본문의 연결사를 미리 찾아 단락 전개를 예상한다.

Hence, they tend to move between jobs on a regular basis.

그러므로 그들은 정기적으로 이직하는 경향이 있다.

... 중략 ...

But when they leave their old job, they have little trouble finding a new one.

그러나 그들이 이전 직업을 떠날 때, 그들은 새 직업을 찾는 데 거의 어려움을 겪지 않는다.

... 중략 ...

Thus, unemployment that is a nuisance for a younger worker can be a damaging and financially draining experience for a mature worker.

그래서 젊은 노동자에게는 성가신 일인 실직이 숙련 노동자에게는 타격을 주고 재정적으로 고갈시키는 경험이 될 수 있다.

이 글의 소재는 노동자의 이직임을 알 수 있으며, 본문에는 크게 세 개의 연결사가 제시되어 있다. 결과의 연결사 Hence와 Thus, 역접의 연결사 But이 쓰였음을 파악하여 글의 흐름을 예측할 수 있다.

[2] Younger workers vs Older workers 구도임을 파악한 뒤, 각각의 특징을 찾아낸다.

Younger workers tend to have more general skills and are less certain about where their skills might be put to their best uses. Hence, they tend to move between jobs on a regular basis. (①) But when they leave their old job, they have little trouble finding a new one.

젊은 노동자들은 좀 더 보편적 기술을 가지고 있어서 그들의 기술을 가장 잘 이용할 방식에 대해서는 확신이 덜한 경향이 있다. 그러므로 그들은 정기적으로 이직하는 경향이 있다. 그러나 그들이 이전 직업을 떠날 때, 그들은 새 직업을 찾는 데 거의 어려움을 겪지 않는다.

Younger workers는 tend to move between jobs, have little trouble finding a new one이라는 특징을 갖고 있다. 그렇다면 Older workers는 그 반대의 경향이 있을 것이라고 예측할 수 있다.

(②) They already know their best employment option and are not inclined to move around between jobs.

그들은 이미 최선의 고용 조건을 알고 있으며, 직업을 전전하려 하지 않는다.

not inclined to move around between jobs라는 표현을 통해 ②에서 Older workers에 관한 이야기로 화제가 전환되었음을 알 수 있다.

(③) When they do leave work, however, finding a position that matches well with their precise skills is often difficult and time-consuming.

그러나 그들이 이직을 하려 하더라도 그들의 정밀한 기술과 잘 어울리는 직책을 찾기가 종종 어렵고 시간이 든다.

① 뒤 문장의 'little trouble'과 ③ 뒤 문장의 'difficult and time-consuming'이 대조를 이루고 있으며, Older workers에 관한 내용이 계속 이어지고 있다. 따라서 답을 ②로 확정지을 수 있다.

정답 및 해석

정답 ②

해석 젊은 노동자들은 좀 더 보편적 기술을 가지고 있어서 그들의 기술을 가장 잘 이용할 방식에 대해서는 확신이 덜한 경향이 있다. 그러므로 그들은 정기적으로 이직하는 경향이 있다. 그러나 그들이 이전 직업을 떠날 때, 그들은 새 직업을 찾는 데 거의 어려움을 겪지 않는다. 대조적으로, 나이 든 노동자들은 좀 더 자주 그들이 현재 고용되어 있는 산업이나 회사에 맞는 매우 특수한 기술들을 가지고 있다. 그들은 이미 최선의 고용 조건을 알고 있으며, 직업을 전전하려 하지 않는다. 그러나 그들이 이직을 하려 하더라도 그들의 정밀한 기술과 잘 어울리는 직책을 찾기가 종종 어렵고 시간이 든다. 그래서, 젊은 노동자에게는 성가신 일인 실직이 숙련 노동자에게는 타격을 주고 재정적으로 고갈시키는 경험이 될 수 있다.

어휘 specific 특수한 industry 산업 employ 고용하다 general 일반적인 put A to use A를 이용하다 on a regular basis 정기적으로 be inclined to ~할 의향이 있다 precise 정밀한 unemployment 실업 nuisance 성가신 일 financially 재정적으로 drain 고갈시키다 mature 숙련된

정답 및 해설 23P

01 주어진 문장이 들어갈 위치로 가장 적절한 곳은? (2022, 지방직 9급)

> The comparison of the heart to a pump, however, is a genuine analogy.

An analogy is a figure of speech in which two things are asserted to be alike in many respects that are quite fundamental. Their structure, the relationships of their parts, or the essential purposes they serve are similar, although the two things are also greatly dissimilar. Roses and carnations are not analogous. (①) They both have stems and leaves and may both be red in color. (②) But they exhibit these qualities in the same way; they are of the same genus. (③) These are disparate things, but they share important qualities: mechanical apparatus, possession of valves, ability to increase and decrease pressures, and capacity to move fluids. (④) And the heart and the pump exhibit these qualities in different ways and in different contexts.

02 주어진 문장이 들어갈 위치로 가장 적절한 곳은? (2022, 국가직 9급)

> Thus, blood, and life-giving oxygen, are easier for the heart to circulate to the brain.

People can be exposed to gravitational force, or g-force, in different ways. It can be localized, affecting only a portion of the body, as in getting slapped on the back. It can also be momentary, such as hard forces endured in a car crash. A third type of g-force is sustained, or lasting for at least several seconds. (①) Sustained, body-wide g-forces are the most dangerous to people. (②) The body usually withstands localized or momentary g-force better than sustained g-force, which can be deadly because blood is forced into the legs, depriving the rest of the body of oxygen. (③) Sustained g-force applied while the body is horizontal, or lying down, instead of sitting or standing tends to be more tolerable to people, because blood pools in the back and not the legs. (④) Some people, such as astronauts and fighter jet pilots, undergo special training exercises to increase their bodies' resistance to g-force.

03 주어진 문장이 들어갈 위치로 가장 적절한 것은? (2021, 국가직 9급)

> For example, the state archives of New Jersey hold more than 30,000 cubic feet of paper and 25,000 reels of microfilm.

Archives are a treasure trove of material: from audio to video to newspapers, magazines and printed material — which makes them indispensable to any History Detective investigation. While libraries and archives may appear the same, the differences are important. (①) An archive collection is almost always made up of primary sources, while a library contains secondary sources. (②) To learn more about the Korean War, you'd go to a library for a history book. If you wanted to read the government papers, or letters written by Korean War soldiers, you'd go to an archive. (③) If you're searching for information, chances are there's an archive out there for you. Many state and local archives store public records — which are an amazing, diverse resource. (④) An online search of your state's archives will quickly show you they contain much more than just the minutes of the legislature — there are detailed land grant information to be found, old town maps, criminal records and oddities such as peddler license applications.

*treasure trove: 귀중한 발굴물(수집물)
*land grant: (대학·철도 등을 위해) 정부가 주는 땅

04 주어진 문장이 들어갈 위치로 가장 적절한 것은? (2021, 지방직 9급)

And working offers more than financial security.

Why do workaholics enjoy their jobs so much? Mostly because working offers some important advantages. (①) It provides people with paychecks — a way to earn a living. (②) It provides people with self-confidence; they have a feeling of satisfaction when they've produced a challenging piece of work and are able to say, "I made that". (③) Psychologists claim that work also gives people an identity; they work so that they can get a sense of self and individualism. (④) In addition, most jobs provide people with a socially acceptable way to meet others. It could be said that working is a positive addiction; maybe workaholics are compulsive about their work, but their addiction seems to be a safe — even an advantageous — one.

05 주어진 문장이 들어갈 위치로 가장 적절한 것은? (2020, 국가직 9급)

> It was then he remembered his experience with the glass flask, and just as quickly, he imagined that a special coating might be applied to a glass windshield to keep it from shattering.

In 1903 the French chemist, Edouard Benedictus, dropped a glass flask one day on a hard floor and broke it. (①) However, to the astonishment of the chemist, the flask did not shatter, but still retained most of its original shape. (②) When he examined the flask he found that it contained a film coating inside, a residue remaining from a solution of collodion that the flask had contained. (③) He made a note of this unusual phenomenon, but thought no more of it until several weeks later when he read stories in the newspapers about people in automobile accidents who were badly hurt by flying windshield glass. (④) Not long thereafter, he succeeded in producing the world's first sheet of safety glass.

06 주어진 문장이 들어갈 위치로 가장 적절한 것은? (2020, 지방직 9급)

> But there is also clear evidence that millennials, born between 1981 and 1996, are saving more aggressively for retirement than Generation X did at the same ages, 22~37.

Millennials are often labeled the poorest, most financially burdened generation in modern times. Many of them graduated from college into one of the worst labor markets the United States has ever seen, with a staggering load of student debt to boot. (①) Not surprisingly, millennials have accumulated less wealth than Generation X did at a similar stage in life, primarily because fewer of them own homes. (②) But newly available data providing the most detailed picture to date about what Americans of different generations save complicates that assessment. (③) Yes, Gen Xers, those born between 1965 and 1980, have a higher net worth. (④) And that might put them in better financial shape than many assume.

07 글의 흐름으로 보아, 주어진 문장이 들어가기에 가장 적절한 곳은?

> But were we to give the ballplayers a paper-and-pencil test on the principles of physical, they probably would not score as well.

Our understanding of media differences sheds light on the interrelation between the type of skill or knowledge being measured and the medium in which it is being assessed. (①) For example, consider what the members of the Chicago Cubs could demonstrate about their knowledge of physics if they were given a practical test in the ball park. (②) Their ability to catch a baseball at the precise place where it falls to earth would clearly demonstrate that they understand things like velocity and trajectory. (③) The written test is so appropriate to assess how properly the physics theory is comprehended. (④) However, to assess the Cub's hands-on knowledge, the field test would be a much fairer and more accurate measure of their understanding.

08 글의 흐름으로 보아, 주어진 문장이 들어가기에 가장 적절한 곳은?

But for the translator or interpreter a higher consideration than money or continued employability is professional pride, professional integrity, and professional self-esteem.

It is significant for users to be able to rely on translation — on the text as well as on the translator, and generally on the entire translation process. Because this is important to the people who pay the bills, it will be important to the translator as well. (①) The pragmatic considerations of keeping your job (for inhouse people) or continuing to get offered jobs (for freelancers) will mandate a willingness to satisfy an employer's or client's needs. (②) They all want to feel that the job they are doing is important, that they do it well, and that the people they do it for appreciate their work. (③) Most people, in fact, would rather take professional pride in a job that pays less than get rich doing things they don't believe in. (④) The areas in and through which translators typically take professional pride are reliability, involvement in the profession, and ethics.

Reading Skill

12 문단의 일관성

HOW TO SOLVE

문단의 일관성 문제는 최근 몇 년간 매번 1문제씩 출제되고 있다. 이 유형에는 글의 전체 흐름과 무관한 문장을 고르는 유형이 있고 큰 흐름에서 벗어나진 않지만 연결사의 쓰임이 잘못되어 있는 유형이 있다.

* 전체 흐름 + 연결사
문제 자체가 글에서 '전체 흐름'과 관계없는 문장을 고르라는 것이다. 바꿔서 말하면, 이 단락을 관통하는 전체 흐름이 존재한다는 것이고, 그 전체 흐름과 관계가 없는 문장 하나를 반드시 제시한다는 것이다. 따라서 글의 전체 흐름을 파악하는 것이 가장 중요하다.

1 처음 한두 문장에서 전체 흐름을 잡아라!

문단의 일관성 문제의 95% 이상은 처음 한두 문장에서 전체 흐름을 제시해 준다. 전체 흐름은 '소재 + 초점'까지를 함께 잡아야 한다.

2 전체적인 흐름(특히 초점과 ⊕/⊖)을 생각하며 본문을 읽어라!

나머지 문장을 읽으면서도 항상 '이 글의 전체 흐름은 무엇일까?'라는 생각을 하면서 글을 읽어야 한다. 흐름상 이상한 내용이라고 생각하더라도 바로 답으로 고르지 말고, 반드시 다 읽은 후 전체 흐름 속에서 답을 찾아야 한다. 예를 들어 ③이 이상하다고 바로 답을 체크하는 것이 아니라, 나머지 ④까지 모두 읽고 글 전체 흐름이 무엇인지를 생각하면서 답을 찾는다.

3 연결사의 쓰임새를 체크하라!

문단에 연결사가 나오면 그 쓰임새가 제대로 되었는지 확인해야 한다.

오답을 피하는 법

연결사가 나온 경우, 특히 그다음 문장을 조심한다.

고난도 문제에서는 연결사로 흐름을 한번 바꿔준 다음, 그다음 문장에 전체 흐름과 관계없는 문장을 집어넣는 경우가 있다. 이런 경우에는 상당히 어려운 문제지만, 전체 흐름과 관련해서 글을 읽는다면 쉽게 함정에 빠지지 않을 것이다.

SKILL EXAMPLE

01 다음 글에서 전체 흐름과 관계가 없는 문장은?

There are some areas of mathematics where long, unpleasant but basically routine calculations have to be done, and there are some good computer programs for doing them. Thus, computers can be very useful time-saving devices, sometimes so much so that they enable mathematicians to discover results that they could not have discovered on their own. ① Nevertheless, the kind of help that computers can provide is very limited. ② One point that deserves to be made is that the lack of women in mathematics is another statistical phenomenon. ③ If it happens that your problem, or more usually sub-problem, is one of the small minority that can be solved by a long and repetitive search, then well and good. ④ If, on the other hand, you are stuck and need a bright idea, then, in the present state of technology, a computer will not help whatsoever.

지문 분석

1 첫 번째 또는 두 번째 문장에서 흐름을 잡는다.

There are some areas of mathematics where long, unpleasant but basically routine calculations have to be done, and there are some good computer programs for doing them. Thus, computers can be very useful time-saving devices, sometimes so much so that they enable mathematicians to discover results that they could not have discovered on their own.

수학에는 길고 하기 싫지만 기본적으로 늘 계산을 해야만 하는 분야가 있고, 그것을 해내는 몇몇 좋은 컴퓨터 프로그램들이 있다. 그러므로 컴퓨터는 아주 유용한 시간 절약 장치가 될 수 있으며, 때때로 대단히 유용해서 수학자들이 스스로는 발견하지 못했을 결과를 발견하도록 해주기도 한다.

전체적으로 컴퓨터의 편리함에 대한 글일 것이라고 추측할 수 있다.

2 전체적인 흐름을 생각하며 나머지 부분을 읽는다.

① Nevertheless, the kind of help that computers can provide is very limited.

그럼에도 불구하고 컴퓨터가 제공해줄 수 있는 도움의 유형은 아주 제한적이다.

Nevertheless로 보아 ①을 기점으로 앞부분과는 상반된 내용이 전개될 것임을 추측할 수 있다.

② One point that deserves to be made is that the lack of women in mathematics is another statistical phenomenon.

지적할 만한 가치가 있는 한 가지 요점은 수학에서의 여성 부족은 또 하나의 통계적 현상이라는 것이다.

앞서 언급된 수학자와 관련된 내용이라고 생각할 수 있지만, 컴퓨터의 편리함이라는 글 전체의 소재와는 관계없이 수학에서 여성의 비중에 대해 이야기하고 있다.

③ If it happens that your problem, or more usually sub-problem, is one of the small minority that can be solved by a long and repetitive search, then well and good.

만약 당신의 문제 또는 보다 일반적으로 하위 문제가 오랜 시간 반복적인 탐색으로 풀릴 수 있는 소수의 문제들 중 하나라면, 별로 문제가 되지 않는다.

③만으로는 내용 파악이 쉽지 않지만 ②를 제외하고 읽으면 앞 문장과 이어진다는 것을 알 수 있다.

④ If, on the other hand, you are stuck and need a bright idea, then, in the present state of technology, a computer will not help whatsoever.

반면에 당신이 궁지에 빠져서 훌륭한 아이디어가 필요하다면, 현재 기술의 상태에서는 컴퓨터가 전혀 도움이 되지 못할 것이다.

①의 Nevertheless에서 짐작했듯이 컴퓨터의 한계가 나와 있다.

정답 및 해석

정답 ②

해석 수학에는 길고 하기 싫지만 기본적으로 늘 계산을 해야만 하는 분야가 있고, 그것을 해내는 몇몇 좋은 컴퓨터 프로그램들이 있다. 그러므로 컴퓨터는 아주 유용한 시간 절약 장치가 될 수 있으며, 때때로 대단히 유용해서 수학자들이 스스로는 발견하지 못했을 결과를 발견하도록 해주기도 한다. 그럼에도 불구하고 컴퓨터가 제공해줄 수 있는 도움의 유형은 아주 제한적이다. (지적할 만한 가치가 있는 한 가지 요점은 수학에서의 여성 부족은 또 하나의 통계적 현상이라는 것이다.) 만약 당신의 문제 또는 보다 일반적으로 하위 문제가 오랜 시간 반복적인 탐색으로 풀릴 수 있는 소수의 문제들 중 하나라면, 별로 문제가 되지 않는다. 반면에 당신이 궁지에 빠져서 훌륭한 아이디어가 필요하다면, 현재 기술의 상태에서는 컴퓨터가 전혀 도움이 되지 못할 것이다.

어휘 mathematics 수학 routine 틀에 박힌 calculation 계산 deserve ~할 가치가 있다 statistical 통계적인 phenomenon 현상 repetitive 반복적인 stuck 막힌 whatsoever 전혀

01 글의 흐름상 가장 어색한 문장은? (2022, 지방직 9급)

The skill to have a good argument is critical in life. But it's one that few parents teach to their children. ① We want to give kids a stable home, so we stop siblings from quarreling and we have our own arguments behind closed doors. ② Yet if kids never get exposed to disagreement, we may eventually limit their creativity. ③ Children are most creative when they are free to brainstorm with lots of praise and encouragement in a peaceful environment. ④ It turns out that highly creative people often grow up in families full of tension. They are not surrounded by fistfights or personal insults, but real disagreements. When adults in their early 30s were asked to write imaginative stories, the most creative ones came from those whose parents had the most conflict a quarter-century earlier.

02 다음 글의 흐름상 가장 어색한 문장은? (2022, 국가직 9급)

Markets in water rights are likely to evolve as a rising population leads to shortages and climate change causes drought and famine. ① But they will be based on regional and ethical trading practices and will differ from the bulk of commodity trade. ② Detractors argue trading water is unethical or even a breach of human rights, but already water rights are bought and sold in arid areas of the globe from Oman to Australia. ③ Drinking distilled water can be beneficial, but may not be the best choice for everyone, especially if the minerals are not supplemented by another source. ④ "We strongly believe that water is in fact turning into the new gold for this decade and beyond," said Ziad Abdelnour. "No wonder smart money is aggressively moving in this direction."

03 다음 글의 흐름상 가장 어색한 문장은? (2021, 국가직 9급)

The term burnout refers to a "wearing out" from the pressures of work. Burnout is a chronic condition that results as daily work stressors take their toll on employees. ① The most widely adopted conceptualization of burnout has been developed by Maslach and her colleagues in their studies of human service workers. Maslach sees burnout as consisting of three interrelated dimensions. The first dimension — emotional exhaustion — is really the core of the burnout phenomenon. ② Workers suffer from emotional exhaustion when they feel fatigued, frustrated, used up, or unable to face another day on the job. The second dimension of burnout is a lack of personal accomplishment. ③ This aspect of the burnout phenomenon refers to workers who see themselves as failures incapable of effectively accomplishing job requirements. ④ Emotional labor workers enter their occupation highly motivated although they are physically exhausted. The third dimension of burnout is depersonalization. This dimension is relevant only to workers who must communicate interpersonally with others (eg. clients, patients, students) as part of the job.

04 다음 글의 흐름상 적절하지 않은 문장은?

(2021, 지방직 9급)

There was no divide between science, philosophy, and magic in the 15th century. All three came under the general heading of 'natural philosophy'. ① Central to the development of natural philosophy was the recovery of classical authors, most importantly the work of Aristotle. ② Humanists quickly realized the power of the printing press for spreading their knowledge. ③ At the beginning of the 15th century Aristotle remained the basis for all scholastic speculation on philosophy and science. ④ Kept alive in the Arabic translations and commentaries of Averroes and Avicenna, Aristotle provided a systematic perspective on mankind's relationship with the natural world. Surviving texts like his Physics, Metaphysics, and Meteorology provided scholars with the logical tools to understand the forces that created the natural world.

05 다음 글의 흐름상 가장 어색한 문장은? (2020, 국가직 9급)

When the brain perceives a threat in the immediate surroundings, it initiates a complex string of events in the body. It sends electrical messages to various glands, organs that release chemical hormones into the bloodstream. Blood quickly carries these hormones to other organs that are then prompted to do various things. ① The adrenal glands above the kidneys, for example, pump out adrenaline, the body's stress hormone. ② Adrenaline travels all over the body doing things such as widening the eyes to be on the lookout for signs of danger, pumping the heart faster to keep blood and extra hormones flowing, and tensing the skeletal muscles so they are ready to lash out at or run from the threat. ③ The whole process is called the fight-or-flight response, because it prepares the body to either battle or run for its life. ④ Humans consciously control their glands to regulate the release of various hormones. Once the response is initiated, ignoring it is impossible, because hormones cannot be reasoned with.

06 글의 흐름상 가장 어색한 문장은? (2020, 지방직 9급)

Philosophers have not been as concerned with anthropology as anthropologists have with philosophy. ① Few influential contemporary philosophers take anthropological studies into account in their work. ② Those who specialize in philosophy of social science may consider or analyze examples from anthropological research, but do this mostly to illustrate conceptual points or epistemological distinctions or to criticize epistemological or ethical implications. ③ In fact, the great philosophers of our time often drew inspiration from other fields such as anthropology and psychology. ④ Philosophy students seldom study or show serious interest in anthropology. They may learn about experimental methods in science, but rarely about anthropological fieldwork.

Part

04

글의 세부 내용 파악하기

Reading Skill 13. 내용 일치 · 불일치

Reading Skill 13

내용 일치 · 불일치

HOW TO SOLVE

내용 일치 · 불일치 문제는 거의 매년 1~2문제씩 출제되다가 최근에는 3문제가 출제되는 경우도 있다. 최근에는 지문이 길어지고 보기 문항 또한 영어로 제시되는 경우가 많으므로 정확한 보기 분석 능력이 요구된다. 또한 다른 유형에 비해 고난도 어휘가 많이 나오는 경향이 있음에 유의해야 한다.

보기 문항은 대개 지문에 언급된 순서대로 제시되므로 이 점을 기억하면 문제를 더 빨리 풀이할 수 있다.

1 첫 문장에서 글의 소재를 찾아라.

첫 문장을 읽고 글의 소재, 즉 무엇에 관한 이야기인지 정도만 먼저 파악해 둔다.

2 보기 문항에서 핵심 단어(명사 중심)를 찾아라.

보기 문항은 대체로 본문에 언급된 순서대로 제시되기도 하지만, 그렇지 않은 경우 또한 많으므로 보기 문항을 먼저 보고 본문을 읽는 것이 좋다. 보기 문항을 볼 땐 본문에서 우리가 찾아야 할 핵심 어휘, 특히 명사를 살펴보아야 한다. 명사 중에서 특히 **고유명사**와 **숫자(연도)**는 눈에도 잘 띄고 본문에도 반드시 언급되기 때문에 우선적으로 봐야 한다.

3 본문의 전체 내용을 파악하라.

본문의 내용을 보기 문항에서 뒤트는 경우가 있다. 따라서 본문 전체의 내용 흐름에도 신경 써야 한다.

오답을 피하는 법

1 보기의 내용 중 일부분이 본문에 언급되었다고 해서 무조건 내용이 일치하는 것이 아니며 그 보기의 나머지 내용까지도 다 일치하는지 자세하게 살펴봐야 한다.

2 'A에 대해 일치하는/일치하지 않는' 것을 물을 때는 혹시 보기가 A가 아닌 다른 것에 대한 내용은 아닌지 확인해야 한다.

3 always(항상), usually(보통) 또는 both(둘 다), all/every(모두/모든), only(~뿐)과 같은 표현이 보기 문항에 쓰일 경우, 틀린 진술일 가능성이 크므로 조심해야 한다.

SKILL EXAMPLE

01 다음 글의 내용과 일치하지 않는 것은?

Scientists working in Central America have discovered ruins of one of the largest and most important palaces built by the ancient Mayan people at Cancuén, Guatemala. It was built about 1,300 years ago. Jungle plants have covered the ruins for hundreds of years, and the area looks like a huge hill covered by jungle. The palace has 170 rooms built around 11 open areas. The discovery of the ruins will certainly increase historians' understanding of the political life of the Mayan people, who were at the height of power in Central America and Mexico more than one thousand years ago. Writings on the newly found palace walls say it was built by King Tah ak Chaan, who ruled Cancuén for about fifty years beginning in the year 740 A.D.

① One of the largest and most important palaces was built about 1,300 years ago.
② The area looks like a huge hill covered by jungle.
③ The palace was built by a Mayan king in the 7th century.
④ The Mayan people were at the height of power in Central America and Mexico.

지문 분석

보기를 먼저 보고 본문에 관련된 내용이 언급되었는지 찾아본다.

① One of the largest and most important palaces was built about 1,300 years ago.

Scientists working in Central America have discovered ruins of one of the largest and most important palaces built by the ancient Mayan people at Cancuén, Guatemala. It was built about 1,300 years ago.

중앙아메리카에서 일하는 과학자들은 과테말라의 Cancuén에서 고대 마야인들에 의해 건설된 가장 거대하고 중요한 궁전들 중 하나의 폐허를 발견했다. 그것은 대략 1,300년 전에 지어진 것이었다.

② The area looks like a huge hill covered by jungle.

Jungle plants have covered the ruins for hundreds of years, and the area looks like a huge hill covered by jungle.

정글의 식물들이 수백 년간 그 폐허를 덮고 있었으며, 그 지역은 정글로 덮인 거대한 언덕처럼 보인다.

③ The palace was built by a Mayan king in the 7th century.

Writings on the newly found palace walls say it was built by King Tah ak Chaan, who ruled Cancuén for about fifty years beginning in the year 740 A.D.

새로이 발견된 궁전 벽에 대한 저술들은 그것이 서기 740년부터 시작해서 약 50년간 Cancuén을 통치했던 Tah ak Chaan 왕에 의해 건설되었다고 말하고 있다.

740 A.D.와 같은 구체적인 연도나, King Tah ak Chaan과 같은 고유명사에 유의하며 본문을 읽어야 한다. 'about fifty years beginning in the year 740 A.D.'에 근거하여 서기 740년도는 7세기가 아니라 8세기이므로 ③의 진술이 틀렸다는 것을 알 수 있다. 따라서 정답은 ③이다.

④ The Mayan people were at the height of power in Central America and Mexico.

The discovery of the ruins will certainly increase historians' understanding of the political life of the Mayan people, who were at the height of power in Central America and Mexico more than one thousand years ago.

그 폐허의 발견은 천 년 이상 전에 중앙아메리카와 멕시코에서 권력의 정점에 있었던 마야인들의 정치적 삶에 대한 역사가들의 이해를 확실히 증진시켜줄 것이다.

정답 및 해석

정답 ③

해석 중앙아메리카에서 일하는 과학자들은 과테말라의 Cancuén에서 고대 마야인들에 의해 건설된 가장 거대하고 중요한 궁전들 중 하나의 폐허를 발견했다. 그것은 대략 1,300년 전에 지어진 것이었다. 정글의 식물들이 수백 년간 그 폐허를 덮고 있었으며, 그 지역은 정글로 덮인 거대한 언덕처럼 보인다. 그 궁전은 11개의 개방된 지역 주변에 건설된 170개의 방을 가지고 있다. 그 폐허의 발견은 천 년 이상 전에 중앙아메리카와 멕시코에서 권력의 정점에 있었던 마야인들의 정치적 삶에 대한 역사가들의 이해를 확실히 증진시켜줄 것이다. 새로이 발견된 궁전 벽에 대한 저술들은 그것이 서기 740년부터 시작해서 약 50년간 Cancuén을 통치했던 Tah ak Chaan 왕에 의해 건설되었다고 말하고 있다.

① 가장 거대하고 중요한 궁전들 중의 하나가 약 1,300년 전에 지어졌다.
② 그 지역은 정글에 덮인 거대한 언덕처럼 보인다.
③ 그 궁전은 7세기에 한 마야의 왕에 의해 건설되었다.
④ 마야인들은 중앙아메리카와 멕시코에서 권력의 정점에 있었다.

어휘 ruins 폐허 historian 역사학자 political 정치적인 height 정점

01 다음 글의 내용과 일치하지 않는 것은? (2022, 지방직 9급)

Christopher Nolan is an Irish writer of some renown in the English language. Brain damaged since birth, Nolan has had little control over the muscles of his body, even to the extent of having difficulty in swallowing food. He must be strapped to his wheelchair because he cannot sit up by himself. Nolan cannot utter recognizable speech sounds. Fortunately, though, his brain damage was such that Nolan's intelligence was undamaged and his hearing was normal; as a result, he learned to understand speech as a young child. It was only many years later, though, after he had reached 10 years, and after he had learned to read, that he was given a means to express his first words. He did this by using a stick which was attached to his head to point to letters. It was in this 'unicorn' manner, letter-by-letter, that he produced an entire book of poems and short stories, *Dam-Burst of Dreams*, while still a teenager.

① Christopher Nolan은 뇌 손상을 갖고 태어났다.
② Christopher Nolan은 음식을 삼키는 것도 어려웠다.
③ Christopher Nolan은 청각 장애로 인해 들을 수 없었다.
④ Christopher Nolan은 10대일 때 책을 썼다.

02 다음 글의 내용과 일치하지 않는 것은? (2022, 지방직 9급)

In many Catholic countries, children are often named after saints; in fact, some priests will not allow parents to name their children after soap opera stars or football players. Protestant countries tend to be more free about this; however, in Norway, certain names such as Adolf are banned completely. In countries where infant mortality is very high, such as in Africa, tribes only name their children when they reach five years old, the age in which their chances of survival begin to increase. Until that time, they are referred to by the number of years they are. Many nations in the Far East give their children a unique name which in some way describes the circumstances of the child's birth or the parents' expectations and hopes for the child. Some Australian aborigines can keep changing their name throughout their life as the result of some important experience which has in some way proved their wisdom, creativity or determination. For example, if one day, one of them dances extremely well, he or she may decide to re-name him/herself 'supreme dancer' or 'light feet'.

① Children are frequently named after saints in many Catholic countries.

② Some African children are not named until they turn five years old.

③ Changing one's name is totally unacceptable in the culture of Australian aborigines.

④ Various cultures name their children in different ways.

03 다음 글의 내용과 일치하지 않는 것은? (2022, 국가직 9급)

Umberto Eco was an Italian novelist, cultural critic and philosopher. He is widely known for his 1980 novel *The Name of the Rose*, a historical mystery combining semiotics in fiction with biblical analysis, medieval studies and literary theory. He later wrote other novels, including *Foucault's Pendulum* and *The Island of the Day Before*. Eco was also a translator: he translated Raymond Queneau's book *Exercices de style* into Italian. He was the founder of the Department of Media Studies at the University of the Republic of San Marino. He died at his Milanese home of pancreatic cancer, from which he had been suffering for two years, on the night of February 19, 2016.

① *The Name of the Rose* is a historical novel.
② Eco translated a book into Italian.
③ Eco founded a university department.
④ Eco died in a hospital of cancer.

04 다음 글의 내용과 일치하는 것은? (2021, 국가직 9급)

The most notorious case of imported labor is of course the Atlantic slave trade, which brought as many as ten million enslaved Africans to the New World to work the plantations. But although the Europeans may have practiced slavery on the largest scale, they were by no means the only people to bring slaves into their communities: earlier, the ancient Egyptians used slave labor to build their pyramids, early Arab explorers were often also slave traders, and Arabic slavery continued into the twentieth century and indeed still continues in a few places. In the Americas some native tribes enslaved members of other tribes, and slavery was also an institution in many African nations, especially before the colonial period.

① African laborers voluntarily moved to the New World.
② Europeans were the first people to use slave labor.
③ Arabic slavery no longer exists in any form.
④ Slavery existed even in African countries.

05 다음 글의 내용과 일치하지 않는 것은? (2021, 국가직 9급)

Deserts cover more than one-fifth of the Earth's land area, and they are found on every continent. A place that receives less than 25 centimeters (10 inches) of rain per year is considered a desert. Deserts are part of a wider class of regions called drylands. These areas exist under a "moisture deficit," which means they can frequently lose more moisture through evaporation than they receive from annual precipitation. Despite the common conceptions of deserts as hot, there are cold deserts as well. The largest hot desert in the world, northern Africa's Sahara, reaches temperatures of up to 50 degrees Celsius (122 degrees Fahrenheit) during the day. But some deserts are always cold, like the Gobi Desert in Asia and the polar deserts of the Antarctic and Arctic, which are the world's largest. Others are mountainous. Only about 20 percent of deserts are covered by sand. The driest deserts, such as Chile's Atacama Desert, have parts that receive less than two millimeters (0.08 inches) of precipitation a year. Such environments are so harsh and otherworldly that scientists have even studied them for clues about life on Mars. On the other hand, every few years, an unusually rainy period can produce "super blooms," where even the Atacama becomes blanketed in wildflowers.

① There is at least one desert on each continent.
② The Sahara is the world's largest hot desert.
③ The Gobi Desert is categorized as a cold desert.
④ The Atacama Desert is one of the rainiest deserts.

06 다음 글의 내용과 일치하지 않는 것은? (2021, 지방직 9급)

Women are experts at gossiping, and they always talk about trivial things, or at least that's what men have always thought. However, some new research suggests that when women talk to women, their conversations are far from frivolous, and cover many more topics (up to 40 subjects) than when men talk to other men. Women's conversations range from health to their houses, from politics to fashion, from movies to family, from education to relationship problems, but sports are notably absent. Men tend to have a more limited range of subjects, the most popular being work, sports, jokes, cars, and women. According to Professor Petra Boynton, a psychologist who interviewed over 1,000 women, women also tend to move quickly from one subject to another in conversation, while men usually stick to one subject for longer periods of time. At work, this difference can be an advantage for men, as they can put other matters aside and concentrate fully on the topic being discussed. On the other hand, it also means that they sometimes find it hard to concentrate when several things have to be discussed at the same time in a meeting.

① 남성들은 여성들의 대화 주제가 항상 사소한 것들이라고 생각해 왔다.
② 여성들의 대화 주제는 건강에서 스포츠에 이르기까지 매우 다양하다.
③ 여성들은 대화하는 중에 주제의 변환을 빨리한다.
④ 남성들은 회의 중 여러 주제가 논의될 때 집중하기 어렵다.

07 다음 글의 내용과 일치하지 않는 것은? (2020, 국가직 9급)

The Second Amendment of the U.S. Constitution states: "A well-regulated Militia, being necessary to the security of a free State, the right of the people to keep and bear Arms, shall not be infringed." Supreme Court rulings, citing this amendment, have upheld the right of states to regulate firearms. However, in a 2008 decision confirming an individual right to keep and bear arms, the court struck down Washington, D.C. laws that banned handguns and required those in the home to be locked or disassembled. A number of gun advocates consider ownership a birthright and an essential part of the nation's heritage. The United States, with less than 5 percent of the world's population, has about 35~50 percent of the world's civilian-owned guns, according to a 2007 report by the Switzerland-based Small Arms Survey. It ranks number one in firearms per capita. The United States also has the highest homicide-by-firearm rate among the world's most developed nations. But many gun-rights proponents say these statistics do not indicate a cause-and-effect relationship and note that the rates of gun homicide and other gun crimes in the United States have dropped since highs in the early 1990's.

① In 2008, the U.S. Supreme Court overturned Washington, D.C. laws banning handguns.

② Many gun advocates claim that owning guns is a natural-born right.

③ Among the most developed nations, the U.S. has the highest rate of gun homicides.

④ Gun crimes in the U.S. have steadily increased over the last three decades.

08 다음 글의 내용과 일치하지 않는 것은? (2019. 국가직 9급)

> The earliest government food service programs began around 1900 in Europe. Programs in the United States date from the Great Depression, when the need to use surplus agricultural commodities was joined to concern for feeding the children of poor families. During and after World War II, the explosion in the number of working women fueled the need for a broader program. What was once a function of the family—providing lunch—was shifted to the school food service system. The National School Lunch Program is the result of these efforts. The program is designed to provide federally assisted meals to children of school age. From the end of World War II to the early 1980s, funding for school food service expanded steadily. Today it helps to feed children in almost 100,000 schools across the United States. Its first function is to provide a nutritious lunch to all students; the second is to provide nutritious food at both breakfast and lunch to underprivileged children. If anything, the role of school food service as a replacement for what was once a family function has been expanded.

① The increase in the number of working women boosted the expansion of food service programs.

② The US government began to feed poor children during the Great Depression despite the food shortage.

③ The US school food service system presently helps to feed children of poor families.

④ The function of providing lunch has been shifted from the family to schools.

Staff

Writer 심우철

Director 김지훈

Researcher 한은지 / 노윤기 / 정규리 / 장은영

Design 강현구

Manufacture 김승훈

Marketing 윤대규 / 장승재 / 황민순

발행일 2023년 1월 20일 (개정 6판 3쇄)

내용문의 http://cafe.naver.com/shimson2000

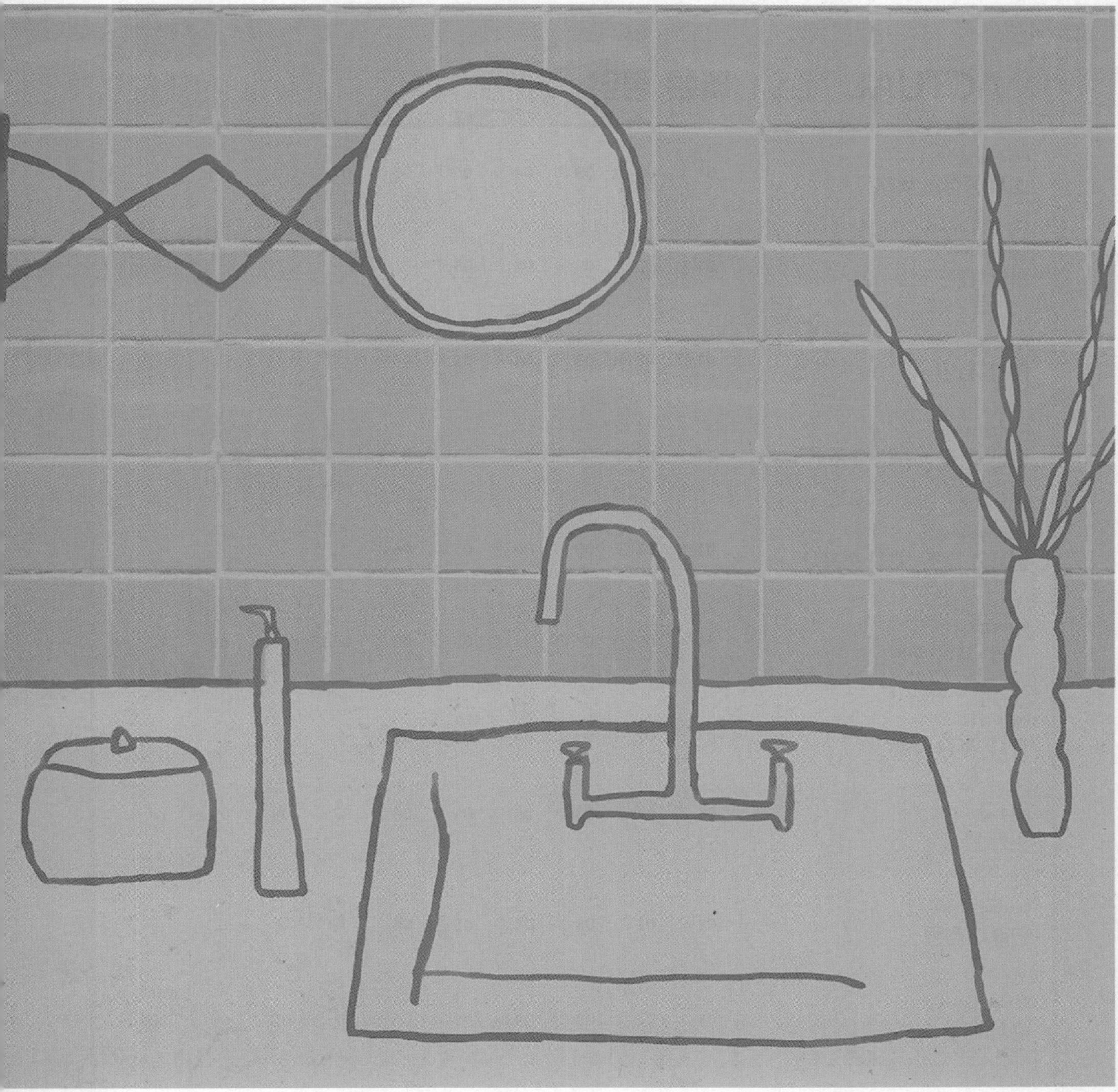

심우철 합격영어 3. 독해

공무원 영어 기본서

정답 및 해설

유형별 맞춤형 독해 전략을 통한 문제 풀이 시간 단축
수험생의 눈높이에 맞춘 올바른 정답 추론 과정 제시

심우철 지음

커넥츠 공단기
인터넷 강의
gong.conects.com

>> ACTUAL TEST 빠른 정답

Reading Skill 01 소재 중심의 독해	01 ① 02 ① 03 ② 04 ① 05 ① 06 ② 07 ①
Reading Skill 02 비평 · 대조 (연결사 중심의 독해)	01 ① 02 ① 03 ③ 04 ① 05 ②
Reading Skill 03 예시 · 나열	01 ② 02 ③ 03 ④ 04 ③ 05 ④ 06 ②
Reading Skill 04 원인-결과 / 실험 구조 (Cause & Effect)	01 ① 02 ② 03 ② 04 ② 05 ① 06 ③
Reading Skill 05 필자의 강조 · 지시 형용사	01 ① 02 ③ 03 ① 04 ④ 05 ① 06 ④
Reading Skill 06 주제 · 제목 추론	01 ④ 02 ① 03 ③ 04 ③ 05 ④ 06 ① 07 ③ 08 ④ 09 ③ 10 ③
Reading Skill 07 요지 · 주장 추론	01 ① 02 ① 03 ② 04 ③ 05 ② 06 ④
Reading Skill 08 빈칸 완성	01 ② 02 ④ 03 ① 04 ② 05 ④ 06 ① 07 ② 08 ③ 09 ① 10 ④ 11 ② 12 ①
Reading Skill 09 연결사 추론	01 ① 02 ② 03 ③ 04 ② 05 ④ 06 ②
Reading Skill 10 순서 배열	01 ③ 02 ③ 03 ③ 04 ① 05 ③ 06 ③ 07 ③ 08 ② 09 ③ 10 ②
Reading Skill 11 문장 삽입	01 ③ 02 ④ 03 ④ 04 ② 05 ④ 06 ④ 07 ③ 08 ②
Reading Skill 12 문단의 일관성	01 ③ 02 ③ 03 ④ 04 ② 05 ④ 06 ③
Reading Skill 13 내용 일치 · 불일치	01 ③ 02 ③ 03 ④ 04 ④ 05 ④ 06 ② 07 ④ 08 ②

Reading Skill 01 **소재 중심의 독해** ACTUAL TEST

01	①	02	①	03	②	04	①	05	①
06	②	07	①						

01 ①

해설 긍정적인 태도와 일에 대한 열정을 강조하는 글이다. Edward Simpson의 말을 인용하여 능력보다는 태도가 중요함을 강조하고 있으므로, 빈칸에 들어갈 말로 가장 적절한 것은 ① '능력보다는 열정'이다.

② 태도보다는 능력
③ 열정보다는 능력
④ 관심보다는 태도

해석 만약 당신이 긍정적이지 않다면, 당신은 일에서 생산적일 수 없다. "인생이란 90%의 태도와 10%의 능력이다. 자신을 어떻게 나타내고 무엇을 제공해야 하는가는 전적으로 당신의 태도에 속해 있는 것이다."라고 판매 책임자인 Edward Simpson은 말한다. "회사는 성공하기 위해 알 필요가 있는 것을 당신에게 가르쳐 줄 수는 있지만, 태도를 가르쳐 줄 수는 없다. 관심이 없는 아주 유능한 사람과 열정이 있는 덜 유능한 사람 사이에서 선택할 때, 나는 항상 능력보다는 열정을 선택한다."고 그는 덧붙여 말한다.

어휘

positive 긍정적인
representative 책임자
competent 유능한
productive 생산적인
purely 완전히
zeal 열정

02 ①

해설 르네상스 이전의 예술은 평면적이고 상징적이었지만, 르네상스 이후의 예술은 기하학을 이용하여 입체적이고 정확하며 사실적으로 표현했다고 설명한다. 따라서 빈칸에 들어갈 말로 가장 적절한 것은 ① '정확하게'이다.

② 전통적으로
③ 현실감 없이
④ 상징을 통해

해석 수학은 분명히 르네상스 예술에 영향을 주었다. 르네상스 예술은 중세의 예술과 여러 가지 면에서 달랐다. 르네상스 이전에는 그림에 있는 물체들이 외관상 사실적이라기보다는 평평하고 상징적이었다. 르네상스 시대의 예술가들은 그림을 개혁했다. 그들은 그림 속의 물체들이 정확하게 표현되기를 원했다. 수학은 인간의 눈에 보이는 것처럼 물체들의 본질적인 형태를 원근법으로 표현하기 위해 사용되었다. 르네상스 시대의 예술가들은 기하학을 사용하여 원근법을 성취했는데 이것은 실제 세계를 사실적이고 정확하고 3차원적으로 묘사하게 했다. 수학을 예술, 특히 그림에 응용한 것은 르네상스 예술의 주된 특징 중 하나였다.

어휘

mathematics 수학
flat 평평한
reform 개혁하다
portray 묘사하다
geometry 기하학
three-dimensional 3차원의
definitely 분명히
symbolic 상징적인
represent 표현하다
perspective 원근법
naturalistic 사실적인
application 응용

03 ②

해설 필자는 소설을 읽는 가장 좋은 방법이란 고전 소설과 현대 소설을 함께 읽는 것이라고 말하고 있다. 빈칸의 앞 문장에서 고전과 현대 소설 사이의 상충되는 점을 발견하지 못한다고 했으므로 빈칸에 들어갈 말로 가장 적절한 것은 ② '그것들은 상호 배타적이지 않다'이다.

① 고전 소설은 구하기 힘들다
③ 우리는 그것들 중 하나를 선택하는 것이 좋다
④ 지식은 고전에서 발견될 수 있다

해석 소설을 읽는 가장 좋은 방법은 과거를 희생하여 현재를 지지하지도 않고 현재를 희생하여 과거를 지지하지도 않으면서 독서를 혼합하는 것이다. 그리고 현대의 작품들이 과거의 위대한 작품들에 비해 얄팍하고 사소하게 보일 것이라고는 생각하지 마라. 그것이 반드시 그런 것은 절대 아니다. 전문적인 독자로서 나는 이전 시대의 소설에 대한 지식을 끊임없이 넓히고 깊게 하는 동시에 현대 소설도 옆에 두기 위해 노력해야만 한다. 나는 우리 시대의 가장 중요한 작품과 고전 소설을 계속 번갈아 가면서 읽고 있는데, 그것들 사이의 상충되는 점을 발견하지 못하고 있다. 다시 말해서 그것들은 상호 배타적이지 않다.

어휘

favor 지지하다
contemporary 현대의
trivial 사소한
opposition 대립, 대치
at the expense of ~을 희생하여
thin 얄팍한
vital 중요한
exclusive 배타적인

04 ①

해설 글의 전반부에서는 축구가 예상 밖의 승리가 많아 다른 스포츠보다 흥미롭다고 말했지만, however를 기점으로 강팀은 더 강해지고 예상 밖의 승리를 할 기회는 적어지고 있다고 말했다. 따라서 빈칸에 들어갈 말로 가장 적절한 것은 ① '재미가 덜하고 더 예측 가능하게'이다.

② 다른 팀 스포츠보다 더 스릴 있게
③ 선수들에게 너무 많은 돈을 지급하는 스포츠가
④ 훨씬 더 많은 예상 밖의 승리가 일어나는 스포츠가

해석 축구는 다른 어떤 최고의 팀 스포츠보다 더 재미있다. 이것은 한 팀의 과학자들의 연구에 따른 것이다. 그들은 1888년 이후에 행해진 300,000회가 넘는 경기의 결과를 분석했다. 그들은 경기에서 '예상 밖의 승리'가 일어날 수 있는 가능성이 재미를 측정하는 좋은 척도가 된다고 결론지었다. 예상 밖의 승리란 더 약한 팀이 더 강한 팀을 이길 때의 경기를 말한다. 그들은 축구 시합이 더 많은 예상 밖의 승리를 일으킨다는 것을 알아냈다. 그러나 조사 결과가 다른 팀 스포츠 애호가들에게 전적으로 나쁜 소식만은 아니다. 지난 50년 동안 축구는 재미가 덜하고 더 예측 가능하게 된 것처럼 보인다. 이것은 강팀은 더 강해지고 예상 밖의 승리를 할 기회는 적어진다는 것을 암시한다.

어휘

according to ~에 따르면
likelihood 가능성
survey 조사
analyze 분석하다
upset 예상 밖의 승리, 의외의 결과
enthusiast 애호가

05 ①

해설 메스티소들이 성형 수술을 받는 것은 하나의 유행일 뿐이지 그들의 외모를 가치 없게 여겨서가 아니라고 했다. 아프리카인들의 머리 모양을 한 백인들의 경우와 눈을 크게 하려고 수술을 받는 일본인들의 예시가 논지를 뒷받침하고 있다. 따라서 빈칸에 들어갈 말로 가장 적절한 것은 ① '자부심의 부족'이다.

② 유행의 양식

③ 일종의 모방

④ 만족의 방법

해석 당신은 몇몇 메스티소들이 그들의 전통적인 얼굴이 가치가 없다고 믿기 때문에 성형 수술을 한다고 말했다. 그 사람들은 모두 하나의 유행으로 새롭고 흥미로운 외모를 추구할 뿐이므로 그것은 터무니없는 생각이다. 독특하게 보이려고 아프리카인의 머리 모양을 한 미국 백인에 대해 생각해 보라. 그들은 분명 자신들의 머리 모양이 수치스럽다고 여기지는 않는다. 그리고 눈을 크게 하려고 수술을 하는 일본인도 분명히 그들이 가끔 창백한 얼굴을 한 야만인으로 묘사하는 인종이 되고 싶어 하지는 않는다. 히스패닉이나 메스티소가 백인처럼 보이려는 시도는 단지 하나의 유행임을 기억하라. 당신은 결코 그것을 자부심의 부족으로 묘사해서는 안 된다.

어휘

plastic surgery 성형 수술	preposterous 터무니없는
vogue 유행	shameful 부끄러운
obviously 명백히	pale-complexioned 창백한 안색의
barbarian 야만인	Hispanic 히스패닉
attempt 시도	imitation 모방

06 ②

해설 이 글은 아날로그 방식의 영화 제작을 프레스코 화법과 템페라 화법에 비유하고, 디지털 방식의 영화 제작을 유화 화법에 비유하고 있다. 유화 화법이 수고로운 작업으로부터 화가들을 자유롭게 해 주었던 것처럼, 디지털 기술도 영화 제작자들이 영화로 할 수 있는 일을 재정립하고 있다는 내용이 빈칸 앞의 Similarly 앞뒤로 이어지고 있으므로, 빈칸에 들어갈 말로 가장 적절한 것은 ② '영화 제작자가 유화 화법처럼 영화의 영상을 다루는 것을 가능하게 함으로써'이다.

① 유화 화법을 아날로그 영화 제작 방식과 동일시함으로써

③ 영화 제작에 있어서 유화 방식에서 프레스코화 방식으로 변화하면서

④ 템페라 화법을 영화 특수 효과에 도입하여

해석 나는 아날로그에서 디지털로의 영화 제작 방식의 변화를 초기 르네상스 시대의 프레스코 화법(석회를 바른 벽에 석회가 마르기 전에 그림을 그리는 것)과 템페라 화법(안료에 달걀노른자와 물을 섞어 그린 그림)에서 유화 화법으로의 변화에 비유하고 싶다. 프레스코화를 그리는 화가는 물감이 마르기 전에 그려야 하는 제한 시간이 있으며, 일단 물감이 마르고 나면 그림에 더 이상의 변화를 주는 것이 불가능하다. 마찬가지로, 전통적인 영화 제작자는 일단 영상이 필름에 기록되고 나면 그것을 수정할 수 있는 수단이 제한적이다. 중세의 템페라 화법은 영화를 아날로그 방식으로 제작하던 시기의 특수 효과 실행에 비유될 수 있다. 템페라화를 그리는 화가는 그림을 수정하고 다시 그릴 수 있었지만, 그 과정은 고생스럽고 느렸다. 유화로의 전환은 화가들이 필요한 만큼 오랫동안 작품을 수정하는 것뿐만 아니라 훨씬 더 큰 작품을 빠르게 그려 내는 것을 가능하게 함으로써 그들을 대단히 자유롭게 해 주었다. 마찬가지로, 디지털 기술은 영화 제작자가 유화 화법처럼 영화의 영상을 다루는 것을 가능하게 함으로써, 영화로 할 수 있는 것들을 재정립한다.

어휘

shift 변화	modify 수정하다
medieval 중세의	painstaking 고생스러운
switch 전환	liberate 해방시키다
composition 작품	redefine 재정립하다
equate A with B A와 B를 동일시하다	

07 ①

해설 이 글은 소리들 사이의 공백이 음악에 구조와 조화를 만든다고 언급한다. 빈칸이 있는 문장은 'that 이하는 오해이다'라는 의미이므로, 빈칸에는 오해의 내용이 들어가야 한다. 쉼표의 완전한 박자가 맹렬한 음표의 완전한 박자보다 더 많은 음악을 담을 수 있다는 결론으로 보아 이 글은 쉼표의 중요성을 강조함을 알 수 있다. 따라서 빈칸에 들어갈 말로 가장 적절한 것은 ① '음표가 쉼표보다 더 중요하다'이다.

② 쉼표는 음악에 직접적인 기준점을 제공한다

③ 음악에서 침묵은 소리 못지않게 의미 있다

④ 멜로디는 소리의 집합에 지나지 않는다

해석 음표가 쉼표보다 더 중요하다는 것은 많은 음악가와 비음악가 모두에게 똑같이 흔한 오해이다. 이것은 놀라운 일이 아닌데, 그 이유는 음악을 음표 사이의 조용한 공백과 연관시키는 것보다 멜로디를 만들어 내는 소리와 연관시키는 것이 더 자연스럽기 때문이다. 쉼표는 조용하기 때문에, 사람들은 종종 비어 있는 시간을 중요하지 않은 것으로 잘못 해석한다. 그러나 만약 노래가 쉼표 없이 오직 음표로만 이루어져 있다면 무슨 일이 일어날지 상상해 보라. "쉼표는 더 이상 존재하지 않는다."(말장난이 의도됨)라는 사실과는 별도로, 음악에 있어서 기준점이나 식별할 수 있는 중추가 없는 소리의 벽이 있을 것이다. 그 이유는 소리들 사이의 공백이 작품에 기준치와 대조를 제공하며, 음악에 구조와 조화를 주기 때문이다. 사실, 쉼표의 완전한 박자가 맹렬한 음표의 완전한 박자보다 더 많은 음악을 담을 수 있다는 것은 경험 많은 음악가들 사이에서 흔한 격언이다.

어휘

misconception 오해, 잘못된 생각	associate A with B A와 B를 연관시키다
note 음표, 음	rest (음악) 쉼, 쉼표
misinterpret 잘못 해석하다, 오해하다	aside from ~과는 별도로
pun 말장난, 익살	reference point 기준점
discernible 식별할 수 있는	backbone 중추, 척추
baseline 기준치, 기준선	texture 질감, 조화
measure (음악) 박자, 소절	blistering 맹렬한, 격렬한

01	①	02	①	03	③	04	①	05	②

01 ①

해설 however 앞에서는 바닷물고기를 집안 수조에서 기르는 것의 장점을 이야기하지만, 그 뒤에서는 바닷물고기가 수질과 온도의 변화에 적응하지 못하기 때문에 기르기 어렵다고 언급한다. 따라서 빈칸에 들어갈 말로 가장 적절한 것은 ① '내성'이다.
② 차별
③ 효과
④ 영향

해석 바닷물고기를 가정의 수조에서 기를 만한 좋은 이유가 있다. 바닷물고기는 다양하며 아름다운 색깔인 경우가 많고, 그들의 생활상과 행동은 끝없이 흥미롭다. 그러나 바닷물고기는 수족관에서 해수의 질과 온도를 안정적으로 유지하는 것이 어렵기 때문에 숙련된 민물고기 사육사에게도 도전적인 일이다. 민물고기와 달리, 많은 바닷물고기는 물의 질과 온도의 변화에 내성이 거의 없다. 그러므로 바닷물고기를 집안 수조에서 기르는 것은 더 많은 관찰과 세세한 것에 대한 주의가 필요하다.

어휘
marine fish 바닷물고기
diverse 다양한
fascinating 흥미로운
aquarist 수족관 관리사
species 종
aquarium 수족관
biology 생활 현상
freshwater 민물의
stable 안정된
variation 변화

02 ①

해설 ①의 앞에서는 치아를 하얗게 보이기 위해 치아 미백을 많이 한다는 내용이 나오고 ① 뒤에는 그에 따른 부작용을 설명하고 있다. 주어진 문장은 however가 이끌면서 치아 미백과 관련된 위험들을 말하고 있으므로 주어진 문장이 들어갈 위치로 가장 적절한 것은 ①이다.

해석 대부분의 사람들은 그들의 얼굴에서 치아가 하얗게 빛나고 아름다운 미소를 지니기를 원한다. 새로운 미모에 대한 이러한 요구는 치아 미백에 대한 높은 인기를 이끌어 왔다. 그러나 치아 미백과 관련된 위험 요소들이 있다. 두 가지의 가장 보편적인 부작용들은 치아 민감도와 잇몸 염증이 일시적으로 증가한다는 것이다. 치아 내부의 민감성 문제는 보통 치아 미백 과정의 첫 단계에서 일어난다. 잇몸 염증은 마우스피스 트레이를 맞추는 동안 종종 일어난다. 치아 미백과 관련된 일부 다른 위험들로는 과다 복용 혹은 남용, 중독, 그리고 비위생적이거나 부적절한 기구의 사용이 있다.

어휘
associated with ~와 관련된
sparkling 빛나는
temporary 일시적인
irritation 염증
mouthpiece 마우스피스
overuse 남용
unhygienic 비위생적인
whitening 미백
side effect 부작용
sensitivity 민감성
gum 잇몸
overdose 과다 복용
addiction 중독
improper 부적절한

03 ③

해설 주어진 문장은 수면 시간의 변화, 병, 손님의 존재가 아이의 수면에 방해가 될 수 있다는 내용이므로 잠을 잘 못 자는 아이에 관한 언급이다. However 뒷부분은 잠을 못 자는 아이들도 수면 패턴이 유지되면 잠을 잘 잔다는 내용이므로 주어진 문장은 However 앞에 위치하여 잠을 잘 못 자는 아이들에 대한 특성을 부연 설명해야 한다. 따라서 주어진 문장이 들어갈 위치로 가장 적절한 것은 ③이다.

해석 몇몇 아이들은 태어날 때부터 아주 잠이 많다. 초기 몇 주에는 수유를 위해 그들을 깨워야 할지 모른다. 성장해 감에 따라 그들은 계속해서 잠을 많이 잘 뿐만 아니라 누가 깨워도 잘 일어나지 않을 정도가 된다. 그들은 밤에 밝든 어둡든, 조용하든 시끄럽든, 평온하든 혼란스럽든 다양한 상황에도 곤히 잘 잔다. 그들은 가끔 그들의 수면 일정이 틀어져도 견딜 수 있고 심지어 감정적으로 스트레스를 받고 있는 와중에도 잠을 잘 잔다. 반면, 다른 아이들은 선천적으로 더 잠에 들지 못하는 것처럼 보인다. 이런 아이들은 그들의 수면 패턴이 방해받을 때 좀 더 민감한 반응을 보인다. 수면 시간의 변화, 질병, 심지어 집을 방문한 손님들의 존재가 수면 패턴을 더 나쁘게 만들 수 있다. 하지만, 이러한 아이들이 언제나 '잠을 자지 못하는 사람'으로 여겨지더라도 그들의 (수면) 습관이 존중되면, 그들 또한 상당히 만족스러운 수면을 취할 수 있을 것이다. 어떤 경우든, 두 유형의 아이들이 정신적, 육체적 건강을 보장하는 적절한 양의 수면을 취하기 위해서는 규칙적인 (수면) 습관이 유지되어야 한다.

어휘
soundly 곤히
tolerate 견디다
disruption 방해
restless 잠들지 못하는
consistent 일관된
ensure 보장하다
chaotic 혼란스러운
occasional 가끔의
inherently 선천적으로
susceptible to ~에 민감한
adequate 적절한

04 ①

해설 주어진 문장에서는 이것들이 유일한 또는 중요한 이유가 아닐지도 모른다고 하였으므로 앞 문장에는 이유들이 언급되어 있어야 한다. 또한 주어진 문장 뒤에는 앞서 언급되지 않은 새로운 이유가 서술되어야 한다. 따라서 주어진 문장이 들어갈 위치로 가장 적절한 것은 ①이다.

해석 왜 쿠키를 먹는가? 몇몇 이유로는 당신의 배고픔을 만족시키기 위해서, 당신의 혈당을 높이기 위해서, 또는 단지 씹을 무엇인가를 갖기 위해서가 있을 것이다. 그러나 최근 포장 쿠키 시장에서의 성공은 이것들이 유일한 또는 아마도 심지어 가장 중요한 이유가 아닐지도 모른다는 것을 시사한다. 쿠키 제조회사들은 몇몇 다른 영향들을 인식하게 되었으며, 그 결과 그 인식에서 비롯된 상품들을 시장에 내놓고 있는 것처럼 보인다. 이 상대적으로 새로운 상품 제공물은 보통 더 전형적인 바삭거리는 종류로부터 구별되기 위해 '부드러운' 또는 '쫄깃한' 쿠키라고 불린다. 왜 그것들의 도입에 호들갑인가? 분명히 그 매력의 많은 부분은 계단 뒤에 앉아 오븐에서 바로 엄마가 가져다준, 입에서 살살 녹는 쿠키를 그것이 아직 부드러울 때 게걸스럽게 먹던 어린 시절의 기억과 관계가 있다.

어휘
awareness 인식
offering 제공물
distinguish A from B A와 B를 구별하다
typical 전형적인
fuss 호들갑
devour 게걸스럽게 먹다
relatively 상대적으로
refer to A as B A를 B라고 부르다
crunchy 바삭바삭한
appeal 매력

05 ②

해설 주어진 문장은 어머니가 항상 같이 있어서 자신들을 도울 수 있었던 것에 대해서 고마워하는 내용이므로 전업주부인 어머니를 두었던 조사 대상에 관한 부분에 해당한다. 따라서 On the other hand를 통해 내용이 전환되기 이전에 들어가야 하는데, ②의 뒤 문장에 also가 나오기 위해서는 그 전에 전업주부인 어머니를 둔 조사 대상에 관한 설명이 제시되어야 하므로 주어진 문장이 들어갈 위치로 가장 적절한 것은 ②이다.

해석 나의 연구는 어머니가 일을 하는 것과 그녀의 딸이 자신의 아이를 가졌을 때 일을 하고 싶어 하는 것에는 밀접한 상관관계가 있다는 것을 지적한다. 내가 만나보았던 집에 있는 어머니(전업주부)의 4분의 3이 집 밖에서 전혀 일을 해보지 않았던 어머니 아래서 자랐다. 그들은 어머니의 변함없는 존재와 항상 도움을 받을 수 있음에 대해 고맙게 생각했다. 그들은 또한 직업을 갖는 것이 필수가 아닌 선택사항이라고 생각했다. 반면, 나는 밖에서 일했던 어머니를 둔 여성들을 만나보았는데 그들은 모두 아이를 가졌을 때 그들 역시 일을 할 것이라는 사실을 알고 있었다. 이들 여성들은 대부분 이러한 결정을 내리는 데 거의 주저하지 않았다. 그들은 직업을 갖는 것이 당연하다고 생각했다.

어휘

appreciate 고맙게 생각하다	availability 도움을 받을 수 있음
overwhelming 굉장한	correlation 상관관계
hesitation 주저함	

Reading Skill 03 예시·나열 ACTUAL TEST

01	②	02	③	03	④	04	③	05	④
06	②								

01 ②

해설 빈칸에는 가난한 나라가 부유한 나라를 빠르게 따라잡을 수 있는 이유가 들어가야 한다. For instance 이후에 이러한 예시가 나열되어 있는데, 도로와 교육, 기술의 발전이 부유한 나라보다는 가난한 나라에서 더 큰 효과를 가져온다고 하였으므로 빈칸에 들어갈 말로 가장 적절한 것은 ② '새로운 투자가 훨씬 더 큰 성과를 낸다'이다.

① 대중교통 체계가 잘 되어 있다

③ 사람들은 빈곤의 고리를 끊기 위해서 열심히 일한다

④ 임금이 부유한 국가들에 비해 상대적으로 낮다

해석 전통적인 이론에 따르면, 가난한 나라일수록 새로운 투자가 훨씬 더 큰 성과를 내기 때문에 빠르게 따라잡을 수 있다. 예를 들어, 가난한 나라에서는 도로를 몇 군데 놓으면 완전히 새로운 거래 지역이 생길 수 있다. 부유한 나라에서는 도로를 몇 군데 더 놓는다 하더라도 교통 혼잡을 조금 해소해 줄 수 있을 뿐이다. 가난한 나라에서는 교육을 조금만 더 해도 대단한 변화를 가져온다. 부유한 나라에서는 학위 소지자들도 일자리를 찾지 못할 때가 많다. 그리고 물론, 부유한 나라가 기술을 개발하는 것보다 (가난한 나라가) 그 기술을 모방하는 것이 더 쉽다. 세계의 몇몇 개발도상국을 보면 따라잡기 이론이 그럴듯해 보인다.

어휘

catch up 따라잡다	relieve 해소하다
congestion 혼잡	degree 학위
reasonable 합당한	

02 ③

해설 For instance 뒤에 나온 예시들을 잘 살펴봐야 한다. 교통 체증이 탁 트인 도로보다 기억 속에 더 오래 남는 것과 무례한 점원이 친절한 점원보다 더 오래 기억되는 것은 결국 우리가 일반적으로 나쁜 일을 더 오랫동안 기억하는 경향이 있음을 나타내는 예시이다. 또한 마지막 문장에서 '좋은 일은 나쁜 일만큼이나 많이 존재하지만, 우리는 종종 그것을 놓치는 경향이 있다'고 했으므로, 빈칸에 들어갈 말로 가장 적절한 것은 ③ '나쁜 일이 종종 우리의 생각에서 더 큰 부분을 차지한다'이다.

① 탁 트인 도로가 항상 좋은 것은 아니다

② 우리는 쉬운 길을 택하려는 경향이 있다

④ 좋은 일이 우리의 삶에서 긍정적인 역할을 한다

해석 좋은 일과 나쁜 일 중 어떤 것이 더 중요한가? 당신이 어떤 것을 올바른 답이라고 생각하는지와 관계없이, 나쁜 일이 종종 우리의 생각에서 더 큰 부분을 차지한다. 예를 들어, 우리의 하루를 수렁에 빠지게 하는 교통 체증은 우리를 빠르게 가도록 해 준 탁 트인 도로보다 우리의 생각 속에 더 오래 남는다. 친절한 점원이 기억에서 사라진 후로도 무례한 점원은 오랫동안 기억에 남는다. 좋은 일을 보고 좋은 일에 대해 생각하고 좋은 일을 기억하라고 스스로에게 일깨우라. 좋은 일은 나쁜 일만큼이나 많이 존재하지만, 우리는 종종 그것을 놓치기 쉽다.

어휘

regardless of ~와 관계없이	bog down 수렁에 빠뜨리다
speed ~을 빠르게 가게 하다	memorable 잊히지 않는
be prone to ~하기 쉽다	

03 ④

해설 인간의 도식적 지식이 이해와 기억이 도움이 된다는 주어진 글 뒤에는 도식이 해가 될 수도 있음을 역접의 연결사로 연결한 내용인 (C)가 온 후, 알아차리지 못한 내용을 도식이 어떻게 채워주는지를 설명한 (B)가 온 다음, 이와 마찬가지로 기억하지 못하는 내용을 도식이 어떻게 채워주는지를 설명하는 (A)가 와야 가장 자연스러운 흐름이 된다. 따라서 글의 순서로 가장 적절한 것은 ④ '(C) - (B) - (A)'이다.

해석 분명히, 도식적인 지식은 여러분의 이해를 이끌어주고 여러분으로 하여금 기억할 수 없는 것들을 재구성할 수 있게 해주어서 여러분에게 도움을 준다. (C) 하지만 도식적인 지식은 또한 인식과 기억에서 실수를 유발시켜서 여러분에게 해를 끼칠 수 있다. 게다가 도식에 의해 만들어지는 실수의 유형은 꽤나 예측가능하다. 도식이 여러분의 경험의 광범위한 형태를 요약해주고 따라서 그것은 본질적으로 주어진 상황에서 무엇이 전형적인지 혹은 일반적인지를 여러분에게 말해준다는 점을 명심해라. (B) 고로, 도식에 대한 어떠한 의존이라 하더라도, 그것은 어떤 것이 '정상적'인지에 대한 이 정보에 의해 형성될 것이다. 따라서 한 상황이나 사건을 보면서 여러분이 알아차리지 못하는 것이 있다면, 여러분의 도식이 그 상황에서 보통 무엇이 적절한지에 대한 지식으로 이러한 '공백'을 채우도록 이끌 것이다. (A) 마찬가지로, 여러분이 기억해낼 수 없는 것들이 있다면 여러분의 도식이 그 상황에서 무엇이 전형적인지에 관한 지식으로 그 알아차리지 못하는 것을 채울 것이다. 결과적으로 도식에의 의존은 불가피하게 세상을 실제보다 더 '정상적'으로 보이게 할 것이고, 과거를 실제 그랬던 것보다 더 '규칙적'으로 보이게 할 것이다.

어휘

schematic 도식의	reconstruct 재구성하다
inevitably 불가피하게	reliance 의존
in place 적절한	promote 조장하다, 촉진하다
perception 인식, 지각	summarize 요약하다

04 ③

해설 주어진 글에서 박쥐가 밤에 날아다니는 곤충을 잡아먹으며, 자연에서 곤충의 균형을 잡는 중요한 역할을 한다고 했다. 따라서 주어진 글 다음에 박쥐가 곤충을 잡아먹는 내용이 이어져야 하는데 이를 언급한 (A)와 (C) 중 보다 일반적인 내용의 (C)가 바로 이어지는 것이 적절하다. (C)에 이어 덩치가 큰 박쥐와 작은 박쥐를 분류하여 예시를 드는 (A)가 이어지는 것이 자연스럽다. 그다음으로 연결사 In addition으로 시작하여 박쥐가 곤충을 잡아먹는 것뿐만 아니라 가루받이 역할을 한다는 내용을 추가 설명한 (B)가 이어지는 것이 흐름상 자연스럽다. 따라서 글의 순서로 가장 적절한 것은 ③ '(C) - (A) - (B)'이다.

해석 박쥐는 밤에 날아다니는 곤충을 잡아먹는 주된 포식자로 자연에서 곤충의 균형을 유지하는 데 중요한 역할을 한다. (C) 박쥐 한 마리는 자신의 몸무게의 1/3을 먹으며, 한 시간에 600마리의 모기를 잡을 수 있다. 그리고 다양한 박쥐 종들은 다양한 높이에서 사냥을 하며, 다양한 종류의 곤충들을 먹이로 잡아먹는다. (A) 덩치가 큰 박쥐는 농업과 임업에 해로운 여러 나방과 벌레들을 잡아먹는다. 크기가 작은 박쥐들은 모기와 날개가 둘 달린 다른 곤충들, 즉 말라리아 같은 질병들의 매개체들을 잡아먹는다. (B) 게다가 과일이나 꽃을 먹는 박쥐는 씨앗을 퍼뜨리고 500종 이상의 열대 나무들과 관목들의 꽃에 가루받이를 해 준다. 박쥐가 없다면, 바나나와 파인애플 같은 열대 과일들의 수확은 60%나 감소할 것이다.

어휘

primary 주된	predator 포식자
vital 중요한	moth 나방
harmful 해로운	forestry 임업
carrier 매개체	disperse 퍼뜨리다
pollinate 수분하다	shrub 관목

05 ④

해설 이 글은 만리장성 건설과 로마 제국의 몰락이라는 두 가지 역사적 사건을 사례로 들어 '두 가지 사실과 그 사실들 간의 인과관계'에 대해 설명하고 있다. 서로 무관해 보이는 만리장성의 건설과 로마 제국의 몰락은 좀 더 조사해 보면 서로 깊게 관련되어 있음을 알 수 있다. 그러므로 빈칸에 들어갈 말로 가장 적절한 것은 ④ '겉보기에는 관련이 없는 것처럼 보이는 사실들도 실제로는 보이는 것보다 더 관련이 있을 수 있다'이다.

① 로마 제국의 몰락은 세계사에 영향을 미쳤다

② 두 가지 사실 간의 관계는 쉽게 확인할 수 있다

③ 역사가들은 우연한 사실들과 필연적인 결과들을 구별해야 한다

해석 어떤 특정한 사실이 다른 특정한 사실의 원인이라고 주장할 때, 그 두 가지 사실 사이에는 실질적인 인과관계가 존재해야 한다. 그러나 그 관련성을 보기가 항상 쉬운 것은 아니다. 예를 들어, 만약 어떤 역사가가 로마 제국 몰락의 원인을 조사하고 있다면, 그는 중국의 만리장성이 건설된 날짜를 알아야 할까? 이것은 관련이 있는 사실인가? 좀 더 조사해 보면, 그렇다는 것을 알게 된다. 만리장성의 건설과 로마 제국의 몰락 사이에는 정말로 인과관계가 있어 보인다. 중국인들은 그들의 국경을 보호하기 위해 만리장성을 건설했다. 그것이 건설된 후에, 훈족은 중국에 진출할 수 없었다. 동쪽으로 이동할 수 없게 되자, 그들은 서쪽으로 방향을 틀었고 마침내 로마 지역에 도달했다. 거기서 그들은 로마 제국이 몰락하는 데 커다란 원인을 제공했다. 이것은 겉보기에는 관련이 없는 것처럼 보이는 사실들도 실제로는 보이는 것보다 더 관련이 있을 수 있다는 점을 보여준다.

어휘

relevance 관련성	decline 몰락
contribute 원인을 제공하다, 기여하다	distinguish 구별하다
casual 우연적인	inevitable 피할 수 없는, 필연적인

06 ②

해설 이 글은 코요테의 영역 확장과 그 요인을 설명하는 글이다. 주어진 글은 코요테가 지역 토종이라고 언급하는데, 이는 연결사 However로 시작하여 코요테가 영역을 확장해 왔다고 언급하는 (B)로 이어지는 것이 자연스럽다. 또 (C)에서 언급하는 코요테의 '성공'은 (B)에 언급된 코요테의 이동과 영역 확장을 의미하므로 (B) 뒤에는 (C)가 위치하는 것이 적절하다. 마지막으로 (C)에 언급된 코요테의 먹이에 이어 가축이라는 새로운 먹이를 언급하는 (A)가 위치하는 것이 자연스럽다. 따라서 글의 순서로 가장 적절한 것은 ② '(B) - (C) - (A)'이다.

해석 대부분의 사람들은 아마도 코요테를 미국 서부와 연관 지어 생각할 것이다. 실제로, 미끈하고 적응력 좋은 이 동물은 그 지역의 토종(동물)이다. (B) 하지만 과거 백 년에 걸쳐 그 종은 자기 영역을 크게 확장해 왔다. 그것은 꾸준히 동쪽으로 이동하여 사람들이 좀 더 밀집하여 사는 지역들로 옮겨 왔다. 오늘날 노래 선율 같은 코요테의 울음소리는 미국 전역과 캐나다, 중미의 일부 지역에서도 들을 수 있다. (C) 코요테는 어떻게 그렇게 성공했을까(성공적으로 퍼져 나갔을까)? 그들의 '잡식성 식습관'은 분명히 도움이 되었다. 그들은 곤충, 뱀, 개구리, 풀, 사과, 선인장 열매, 심지어 수박까지 포함하여 거의 모든 것을 먹는 것으로 알려져 있다. (A) 그러나 코요테는 가축 또한 잡아먹는다. 이런 이유로, 어떤 사람들은 그 숫자를 줄이려고 하거나 심지어 완전히 없애 버리려고까지 한다. 미국 서부의 목장주들은 오랫동안 코요테에게 적대감을 느껴 왔는데, 그 이유는 매년 그 동물들이 양을 수십만 마리씩 죽이기 때문이다.

어휘

associate 연상하다, 연관 짓다	adaptable 적응할 수 있는
livestock 가축	eliminate 없애다, 제거하다
rancher 목장 주인	hostility 적대감
enlarge 확대(확장)하다	territory 지역, 영토
densely 빽빽이, 밀집하여	melodious 듣기 좋은, 음악 같은
howl (늑대 등의) 길게 짖는 소리	omnivorous 잡식성의

Reading Skill 04

원인-결과 / 실험 구조
(Cause & Effect)

ACTUAL TEST

01	①	02	②	03	②	04	②	05	①
06	③								

01 ①

해설 이 글은 태양이 더 뜨거워지며 지구를 가열하여 그 결과 대양의 물이 증발해 대기권 밖으로 사라져 간다는 내용이다. 빈칸 앞부분에서 성층권으로 이동한 물이 산소와 수소로 분해된 후, 수소가 우주 공간으로 날아간다고 했다. 물의 구성원소의 일부분인 수소가 사라지는 것이므로 빈칸에 들어갈 말로 가장 적절한 것은 ① '새어 없어지다'이다.

② 얼어버리다

③ 흘러넘치다

④ 축적되다

해석 중심핵이 수축하고 뜨거워지면서 태양이 서서히 더 밝아지고 있다. 10억 년 후에는 그것이 오늘날보다 약 10% 더 밝아져서, 불편할 정도로까지 지구를 가열하게 될 것이다. 대양으로부터 증발하는 물은 지구를 습한 형태의 금성으로 바꾸는 통제 불능의 온실 효과를 유발하여, 영구적으로 두꺼운 흰 구름 막에 둘러싸여 있게 할 수도 있다. 혹은 그 변화가 어느 정도 시간이 걸리고 더 완만해서 한동안은 미생물을 보호해 줄 수 있는 점점 더 무덥고 구름 낀 대기를 유지할 수도 있다. 어느 쪽이 되든지 간에, 물은 성층권 속으로 달아나 자외선에 의해 산소와 수소로 분해될 것이다. 산소는 성층권에 남아서, 어쩌면 외계인들이 지구에 여전히 생명체가 살고 있다고 착각하게 만들 수도 있지만, 수소는 아주 가벼워 우주 공간으로 달아나게 된다. 그래서 우리의 물은 점차 새어 없어질 것이다.

어휘

core 핵, 중심부	contract 수축하다
evaporate 증발하다	set off 유발하다
runaway 통제 불능의	damp 습한, 축축한
transformation 변형	shelter 보호하다
microbial 미생물의	stratosphere 성층권

02 ②

해설 'One study showed' 등의 표현을 통해 이 글이 실험 구조의 글임을 알 수 있다. For instance 이후에서 결혼 여부, 성별, 나이에 따라 꿈을 꾸는 빈도가 달라진다고 하였으므로, 빈칸에 들어갈 말로 가장 적절한 것은 ② '얼마나 많은 꿈을 꾸는지'이다.

① 왜 꿈을 꾸는지

③ 꿈이 무엇을 의미하는지

④ 어떤 꿈을 꾸는지

해석 꿈은 잠의 자연적인 일부분이고 그들이 꿈을 기억하든 못하든 간에 모든 사람들이 꿈을 꾼다. 그러나 얼마나 많은 꿈을 꾸는지는 그들이 누구인지 그리고 그들이 몇 살인지에 달려 있다. 예를 들어서, 결혼은 꿈을 꾸는 데 영향을 미친다. 한 연구는 기혼의 여성보다도 미혼의 여성이 꿈을 더 많이 꾼다는 것을 보여주었다. 남성은 그들이 기혼이든지 미혼이든지 간에 여성보다 꿈을 적게 꾼다. 젊은 사람은 꿈을 꽤 많이 꾸는 경향이 있다. 반면에 은퇴할 나이에 이를 때면 사람들은 꿈을 훨씬 덜 꾼다.

어휘

marriage 결혼	retirement 은퇴

03 ②

해설 빈칸 앞뒤의 'This is why', 'which is why'로 미루어 보아 빈칸에 들어갈 내용은 앞 문장의 결과이자 뒤 문장의 원인이 된다. 빈칸 앞 문장에서 온도가 높을수록 맛이 더 강렬하다고 하였고, 뒤 문장에서 아이스크림 제조사들이 아이스크림에 많은 양의 설탕을 첨가한다고 하였으므로, 빈칸에 들어갈 말로 가장 적절한 것은 ② '냉장고에서 막 꺼낸 아이스크림이 그렇게 달콤한 맛이 나지 않는다'이다.

① 차의 향이 첨가되었을 때 아이스크림이 더 맛있다

③ 뜨거운 차를 마시는 동안은 아이스크림을 먹는 것이 권장되지 않는다

④ 아이스크림이 겨울에 특히 더 달콤하다

해석 중국 음식에서는, 그것이 끓을 정도로 뜨거워야 한다고 생각하는데, 그것이 음식의 풍미에 결정적이기 때문이며, 이는 'wok hei'라는 어구에 구체적으로 표현되어 있는데, 이것은 뜨거운 중국 요리용 냄비에 의해 더해진 결합된 맛의 '숨결' 또는 진수를 의미한다. 2005년에 Leuven 대학의 벨기에 연구진들은 온도와 맛 사이의 연결이 어떻게 작용하는지를 확인했다. 그들은 우리 혀의 미뢰에 있는 극히 작은 경로들을 확인했는데, 그것들은 다른 온도에서 다르게 반응하는 것처럼 보인다. 분명히, 온도가 더 높을수록, 풍미는 더 강렬하다. 이것이 냉장고에서 막 꺼낸 아이스크림이 그렇게 달콤한 맛이 나지 않는 이유이며, 당신이 아이스크림이 녹을 때 너무나 분명하게 알 수 있듯이 아이스크림 제조사들이 다량의 설탕을 첨가하는 이유이다. 비슷하게, 차와 같은, 어떤 쓴맛들은 그것이 뜨거울 때 맛이 더 강해지기 때문에 맛이 더 좋다.

어휘

crucial 결정적인	embody 구체화하다
essence 진수, 정수	combination 결합
confirm 확인하다	microscopic 미세한, 극히 작은
taste bud 미뢰	intense 강렬한

04 ②

해설 (B)의 his garden에서 he는 주어진 글의 a man이므로 (B)가 가장 처음에 오게 된다. 그다음 (A)의 them은 (B)의 끝부분에 나온 they(prickly pears)이며 (A)의 결과가 (C)에서 언급되므로, 글의 순서로 가장 적절한 것은 ② '(B) - (A) - (C)'이다.

해석 잡초 제거에 관한 놀랄 만큼 성공적이고 경제적인 예를 호주에서 찾아볼 수 있다. 1787년경 어떤 사람이 선인장의 일종인 prickly pear를 호주에 들여왔다. (B) prickly pear 중에서 일부가 그의 정원을 빠져나갔다. 이 새로운 지역에는 자연적인 통제 수단이 없었기 때문에 그것들이 엄청나게 퍼져나가 결국 약 6천만 에이커를 차지하게 되었다. (A) 그것들을 제거하고자, 호주의 과학자들이 prickly pear의 천적을 연구하기 위해 북미와 남미로 파견되었다. 몇 가지 종으로 실험을 한 끝에 아르헨티나 나방의 알 30억 개를 호주에 풀어 놓았다. (C) 7년 후에 prickly pear의 밀집 군락이 파괴되었으며, 전에는 거주할 수 없었던 지역이 다시 거주지와 목초지로 이용할 수 있게 되었다. 그 모든 과정은 에이커당 1페니도 채 들지 않았다.

어휘

extraordinary 놀랄 만한	economical 경제적인
weed 잡초	prickly 가시로 뒤덮인
cactus 선인장	eliminate 제거하다
territory 영역, 지역	immensely 막대하게
eventually 마침내	dense 빽빽한
uninhabitable 거주할 수 없는	grazing 방목
operation 과정	

05 ①

해설 아이들이 세부 사항을 그릴 공간을 남기기 위해 얼굴을 크게 그린다는 글의 내용을 통하여, 아이들은 그림을 그릴 때 향후 그릴 내용에 대하여 미리 생각하고 계획하고 있음을 유추할 수 있다. 따라서 빈칸에 들어갈 말로 가장 적절한 것은 ① '일종의 미리 계획하는 모습'이다.

② 형편없는 그림 실력의 증거

③ 크기에 대한 형편없는 감각의 표시

④ 성장을 바라는 그들의 희망 표현

해석 사람 형상을 그릴 때 아이들은 종종 머리를 신체의 나머지 부분과 비교해서 지나치게 크게 그린다. 최근 한 연구는 아이들의 그림에서 보이는 이러한 일반적인 불균형에 대한 어떤 통찰력을 보여준다. 그 연구의 일부로 연구자들은 네 살에서 일곱 살 사이의 아이들에게 어른들을 몇 장 그릴 것을 요구했다. 아이들이 어른들의 정면을 그릴 때는 머리의 크기가 눈에 띄게 커졌다. 하지만 아이들이 어른들의 뒷모습을 그릴 때는 머리의 크기가 그렇게 과장되지는 않았다. 연구자들은 아이들이 얼굴의 세부 사항들을 위한 공간을 남겨야만 한다는 사실을 알 때 머리를 크게 그린다고 말한다. 그들은 아이들 그림의 왜곡된 머리 크기는 일종의 미리 계획하는 모습이라고 말한다.

어휘

insight 통찰	disproportion 불균형
frontal 정면의	markedly 현저하게
enlarge 확대하다	rear 뒤쪽의
exaggerate 과장하다	distorted 왜곡된
indication 표시	scale 규모, 범위

06 ③

해설 이 글은 긍정적인 상상과 실제 현실의 결과를 비교하고 그 상관관계를 분석하고 있다. 환상적이고 긍정적인 것을 상상했던 사람들이 현실적이거나 부정적인 것을 상상했던 사람들보다 실제 현실에서 더 나쁜 경험을 한다는 실험 결과를 먼저 제시하고, 그 원인으로 빈칸 다음에 나온 단서(목표를 추구하고 달성할 열정이 생길 동기를 소진시킨다)를 제시하고 있다. 따라서 긍정적 상상을 한 사람들이 실제로는 그것을 달성하지 못한 원인에 대해 설명하는 빈칸에 들어갈 말로 가장 적절한 것은 ③ '마음을 속여서 목표가 달성되었다고 생각하게 만든다'이다.

① 여러분이 실제 삶을 있는 그대로 평가하도록 촉구한다

② 장밋빛 꿈을 실제의 성취로 변화시킨다

④ 여러분이 장애물은 극복할 수 없는 것이라고 믿게 한다

해석 연구원들은 대학생 자원자들에게 판타지 형태의 경험(하이힐을 신고 멋있어 보이거나, 에세이 대회에서 우승을 하거나, 시험에서 A학점을 받는 것)을 하는 생각을 하라고 요청하고 나서, 판타지가 실험 대상자와 현실에서 어떻게 일이 전개되는가에 끼친 영향에 대해 평가했다. 참여자들이 가장 긍정적인 결과를 상상했을 때, 혈압으로 측정한 그들의 에너지 수준은 떨어졌고, 그들은 보다 현실적이거나 심지어 부정적인 모습을 떠올렸던 사람들보다 실제 사건에서 더 나쁜 경험을 했다고 보고했다. 실험 대상자들의 실제 경험을 평가하기 위해, 연구원들은 실험 대상자들 스스로가 설정했던 목표들의 목록과 그들이 실제로 성취했던 것을 비교하였고, 또한 자기 보고서에 의존했다. "우리가 그것에 대해 환상을 가질 때, 특히 여러분이 아주 긍정적인 것에 환상을 가질 때 그것은 거의 실제로 그것(환상한 것)을 경험하는 것과 같다."라고 그 연구의 공동 저자 중 한 명이 말했다. 그것은 마음을 속여서 목표가 달성되었다고 생각하게 만들고, '그것을 추구하고 달성할 열정이 생길' 동기를 소진시킨다고 그녀는 설명한다. 실험 대상자들은 장애물을 무시하는 대신 극복할 방법을 상상하는 것이 나을지도 모른다.

어휘

unfold 전개되다, 진행되다	envision 상상하다
conjure 떠올리다, 상상하다	drain 소진시키다, 쏟아내다
incentive 동기, 유인	be better off ~ing ~하는 것이 낫다
surmount 극복하다	

Reading Skill 05 필자의 강조·지시 형용사 ACTUAL TEST

01	①	02	③	03	①	04	④	05	①
06	④								

01 ①

해설 달걀과 초콜릿의 예를 통해 몸에 나쁜 것으로 알려진 음식일지라도 체질에만 맞는다면 적당량을 섭취해도 좋다고 말하고 있다. 따라서 필자의 주장으로 가장 적절한 것은 ① '자신의 체질에 맞는 음식은 즐겨라.'이다.

해석 환자들은 종종 나에게 "왜 내가 즐기는 모든 것은 나에게 나쁘지요?"하고 묻는다. 글쎄, 비록 그것이 종종 그렇게 보이지만 반드시 사실은 아니다. 예를 들어 당신의 몸이 추가의 칼로리를 견딜 수 있는 한 당신은 좋아하는 초콜릿을 모두 먹어도 된다. 당신은 달걀을 좋아하는가? 만약 당신의 콜레스테롤 수치가 정상이라면 일주일에 세 개, 네 개, 또는 심지어 다섯 개의 달걀을 먹어도 좋다. 사람들은 식사에 있는 콜레스테롤에 다르게 반응한다. 어떤 경우에는 그것이 혈류 속 콜레스테롤 수준을 높이지만 반면에 다른 경우에는 그것은 그렇지 않다. 그래서 당신이 달걀과 초콜릿을 좋아한다면 조금은 먹어라. 단지 지나치게는 먹지 마라.

어휘

patient 환자	necessarily 반드시
stand 견디다	cholesterol 콜레스테롤
go overboard 정도가 지나치다	

02 ③

해설 주어진 문장의 such evidence가 ③ 앞 문장의 1974년 캐나다 연방 선거 결과를 가리키며 ③ 뒤에 유권자들이 자신의 편견을 깨닫지 못했다는 예시가 이어지므로 주어진 문장이 들어갈 위치로 가장 적절한 것은 ③이다.

해석 한 연구에서 우리는 재능, 다정함, 정직, 그리고 지성과 같은 좋은 특성들을 잘생긴 사람들에게 무의식적으로 부여한다는 것이 밝혀졌다. 더군다나, 우리는 신체적인 매력이 그러한 과정에 원인으로 작용했다는 인식 없이 이러한 판단을 한다. "잘생긴 것이 좋은 것이다."라는 이러한 무의식적인 가정으로 인한 어떤 결과들은 나를 두렵게 한다. 예를 들어, 1974년 캐나다 연방 선거에 대한 한 연구에서는 매력적인 후보자들이 매력적이지 않은 후보자들보다 2.5배 이상을 득표했다는 것을 밝혀냈다. 잘생긴 정치인들을 향해 치우친 애정에 대한 그와 같은 증거에도 불구하고, 후속 연구는 유권자들이 자신들의 편견을 깨닫지 못했다는 것을 보여 주었다. 사실, 조사에 참여한 캐나다 유권자들 중 73%가 자신들의 투표가 신체적인 외모에 영향을 받았다는 것을 가능한 한 가장 강력한 어조로 부인했으며, 14%만이 그러한 영향의 가능성을 인정할 정도였다. 유권자들은 (신체적인) 매력이 선출될 가능성에 미치는 영향력을 자신들이 원하는 만큼 마음껏 부인할 수는 있겠지만, 증거가 그것의 성가신 존재를 계속해서 확인시켜 왔다.

어휘

favoritism 편애	follow-up 후속의
bias 편견	assign 부여하다
favorable 좋은	trait 특성
consequence 결과	unconscious 무의식적인
assumption 가정	federal 연방의
candidate 후보자	terms 표현, 말하는 방식
appearance 외모	electability 당선 가능성

03 ①

해설 첫 문장에서 TV 메시지를 처리하는 것은 눈으로 정보를 처리하는 직선 방식보다는 귀로 듣고 즉시 처리하는 방식에 더 가깝다고 말하며, 이어지는 실험 결과를 통해 TV가 청각적 매체라는 주장을 뒷받침하고 있다. 따라서 글의 제목으로 가장 적절한 것은 ① 'TV 메시지: 보다 시각적인가, 보다 청각적인가?'이다.

② 선호하는 TV 프로그램에 대한 조사들

③ 청각 장애인을 위한 효과적인 도구로서의 TV

④ 더 곤혹스러운 상황: 볼 수 없는 상황

해석 TV 메시지를 처리하는 것은 인쇄된 면을 읽는 눈의 단선적인 처리 과정보다는 귀의 일괄 처리 과정과 훨씬 더 흡사하다. McLuhan에 따르면, 텔레비전은 기본적으로 청각적 매체이다. 이 점을 명확히 하기 위하여, 그는 사람들이 단순한 실험을 해 보도록 초대했다. 우선, 당신이 가장 좋아하는 프로그램 방영 중에 1분 동안 TV 소리를 줄여라. 이제 또 다른 1분 동안, 당신은 소리는 들을 수 있지만 화면은 전혀 볼 수 없도록 TV를 조정해라. 어떤 상태가 더 좌절감을 일으키는가? 어떤 상태가 당신에게 더 적은 정보를 주는가? McLuhan은 이 작은 실험을 해 본 사람들이 화면은 볼 수 있지만 소리는 들을 수 없는 상태에서 항상 더 많은 좌절감을 보고할 것이라고 확신했다.

어휘

all-at-once 동시에	processing 처리 과정
linear 직선의, 1차의	fundamentally 근본적으로
acoustic 청각의	medium 매체
turn down 낮추다, 줄이다	invariably 변함없이, 항상
inaudible 들을 수 없는	

04 ④

해설 주어진 문장에서 this trade라는 지시어가 쓰였으므로, 앞 문장에는 반드시 '교역(trade)'에 관한 내용이 있어야 한다. 또한 주어진 문장에서 식물의 다양성이 퍼진다는 결론이 있으므로 앞 문장에 이에 대한 원인이 제시되어야 논리적으로 알맞다. 이 조건들로 비추어 볼 때, ①~③은 모두 앞 문장에서 식물의 저장에 대해서만 이야기하고 있으므로 주어진 문장이 들어갈 수 없다. ④의 경우, 앞 문장에서 농부들이 남은 저장물을 이웃끼리, 혹은 지역 시장에서 교역한다는 내용이 있고, 또한 이 내용이 식물의 다양성을 퍼뜨린다는 원인으로도 적합하다. 따라서 주어진 문장이 들어갈 위치로 가장 적절한 것은 ④이다.

해석 수천 년 동안 수확 시기에 농부들은 다음 파종을 위해서 보관해야 하는 씨앗들, 줄기들, 덩이줄기들을 우수한 식물들로부터 선별해왔다. 농부들은 종종 진흙 항아리들에 그것들을 봉하거나 재로 뒤덮인 바구니들 안에 그것들을 묻어서 보관함으로써 저장된 씨앗을 벌레들이나 동물들로부터 보호하였다. 그들은 또한 종종 서늘한 곳들에 덩이줄기들을 보관하고 즉시 그 가지들을 옮겨 심거나 다음 파종 시기까지 그것들을 건조시켜두었다. 농부들은 따라서 그들의 유전적인 저장물들을 계절마다 보존하였다. 그들은 남은 저장물들을 이웃들과 교환하거나 지역 시장에서 그것들을 교환할 수 있었다. 이러한 교역 덕분에, 식물의 다양성은 한 지역 안에서 널리 퍼졌다. 그러나 체계적인 종자 생산은 1900년대 초에서야 비로소 시작하였다.

어휘

harvest 수확, 추수	select 선별하다, 선택하다
cutting 줄기, 가지	tuber 덩이줄기
seal 봉하다, 봉인하다	ash 재
replant 옮겨 심다	organized 체계적인, 조직화된
production 생산	

05 ①

해설 이 글은 시장이 빠르게 변화하고 있으며 과거의 전통적인 산업 모델에 도전하여 변화할 필요가 있다고 주장하고 있다. 따라서 새로운 시대에서의 번창을 위한 노력에 해당하는 빈칸에 들어갈 말로 가장 적절한 것은 ① '관습에 얽매이지 않게 생각하고 행동하는 것을 배우다'이다.

② 그들 자신을 실패하게 만들었던 낡은 습관을 없애다

③ 성공에 대해 생각하는 방식을 바꾸다

④ 새롭고 혁신적인 아이디어를 받아들이는 것을 꺼리다

해석 세계화, 압도적인 다수의 상품과 정보에 접근할 수 있는 가능성, 기술적 혁신은 이미 의미 있는 방식들로 시장을 재빨리 변화시키고 있다. 결과적으로, 소비자들은 그들이 구매하는 방식을 바꾸고 있으며 기업들은 그들이 경쟁하는 방식을 바꿀 필요가 있다. 우리는 과거에 우리를 성공하게 만든 습관들을 다시 생각해보고 우리가 사는 세계를 규정해온 전통적인 지혜와 산업 모델에 도전할 필요가 있다. 마케팅 전문가 Seth Godin의 말을 빌리면 "산업들은 매일 창조되고 있다. 혁명은 한창 진행 중이고 전 세대가 그것 때문에 모든 것을 바꾸길 열망하고 있다." 이 새로운 시대에 번창하기 위해서 조직들과 기관들, 경영 간부들과 기업가들은 관습에 얽매이지 않게 생각하고 행동하는 것을 배울 필요가 있다.

어휘

accessibility 접근하기 쉬움	overwhelming 압도적인
an array of 다수의	conventional 전통적인, 관습적인
in full swing 한창 진행 중인	be eager to ~하기를 열망하다
unconventionally 비전통적으로	reluctant 꺼리다

06 ④

해설 이 글은 에페수스가 왜 유령도시가 되었는지에 대하여 설명하고 있다. 습지가 모기의 번식장소를 제공하고 그 모기들이 말라리아를 옮겼다는 내용의 주어진 문장은, 습지가 만들어졌다는 문장과 그 병으로 많은 사람들이 죽었다는 문장 사이에 와야 하므로, 주어진 문장이 들어갈 위치로 가장 적절한 것은 ④이다.

해석 동지중해에서 한때 에페수스는 로마제국의 가장 중요한 항구였다. 그러나 로마의 점령기 600년 동안 에페수스는 유령도시가 되었다. 로마인들은 자연의 균형을 망쳐 놓았고, 이는 도시의 몰락을 야기했다. 로마인들은 도시 주변의 거대한 숲이 더 많은 곡물을 위해 자리를 내어주도록 없앴고, 결국 이것은 에페수스라는 도시를 바다로부터 영원히 단절시켰다. 숲에 의해 차단되지 못한 비로 인해 물이 비옥한 표토를 쓸어가 버렸고, 그것은 해안가 근처로 흙을 쌓았다. 이런 퇴적물이 점점 쌓여가면서, 도시는 바다로부터 단절되었고, 이것은 항구도시에 재앙이었다. 한때 바닷물이 자유롭게 들어왔던 그곳은 현재 거대한 습지가 되었다. 게다가 습지는 모기에게 완벽한 번식지를 제공했고, 모기는 치명적인 병인 말라리아를 옮겼다. 많은 에페수스 사람들이 그 병으로 죽자, 로마 제국은 그 땅을 보유할 수 없었기에 위대한 신전과 기념물들을 뒤로한 채 그 도시를 떠났다.

어휘

swamp 습지	breeding ground 번식지
mosquito 모기	deadly 치명적인
malaria 말라리아	the Mediterranean 지중해
seaport 항구 도시	occupation 점령

downfall 몰락
cut off 단절시키다
topsoil 표토
abandon 떠나다
monument 기념물
make way for ~에게 자리를 내주다
fertile 비옥한
sediment 침전물
temple 사원

PART 02 글의 중심 내용 파악하기

Reading Skill 06 주제·제목 추론 ACTUAL TEST

01	④	02	①	03	③	04	③	05	④
06	①	07	③	08	④	09	③	10	③

01 ④

해설 개인 생산성 증가를 통한 효율성 최적화에 관한 글이다. 글의 중반부부터 멀티태스킹을 할 때 시간이 더 오래 걸리므로 그것을 중단시킴으로써 생산성을 높일 수 있다고 진술하며, 마지막 문장에서도 더 생산적이려면 연속으로 한 가지 일을 하라고 인용구를 통해 강조하고 있다. 따라서 글의 제목으로 가장 적절한 것은 ④ '더 큰 효율성을 위해 한 번에 한 가지 일을 하라'이다.
① 인생에서 더 많은 선택지를 만드는 방법
② 일상적인 신체 기능을 향상시키는 방법
③ 멀티태스킹은 더 나은 효율성을 위한 답이다

해석 효율성을 최적화할 수 있는 분야 중 하나는 노동력으로, 한 직원이 주어진 시간 내에 처리하는 작업량(제품 생산량, 응대 고객 수)으로 정의되는 개인 생산성을 증가시키는 것을 통해 가능하다. 최적의 성과를 보장하기 위해 적절한 장비, 환경 및 교육에 투자했는지 확인하는 것과 더불어, 직원들이 현대의 에너지 낭비인 멀티태스킹을 중단하도록 장려함으로써 생산성을 높일 수 있다. 연구들은 동시에 다른 프로젝트들을 수행하려고 할 때 한 작업을 완료하는 데 25~40% 더 오래 걸린다는 것을 보여준다. 컨설팅 회사 The Energy Project의 사업개발 부사장인 Andrew Deutscher는 더 생산적이기 위해, "지속적인 기간에 연속으로 한 가지 일을 하세요."라고 말한다.

어휘
optimize 최적화하다
staffer 직원
simultaneously 동시에
uninterrupted 중단되지 않은, 연속된
optimal 최적의
drain 고갈, 낭비
vice 부(副)-
sustained 지속된

02 ①

해설 이 글은 레이저의 발생 원리를 빛과 전자의 상호작용 방식을 구체적으로 제시하여 설명하고 있다. 따라서 글의 제목으로 가장 적절한 것은 ① '레이저는 어떻게 만들어지는가?'이다.
② 레이저는 언제 발명되었는가?
③ 레이저는 어떤 전자를 방출하는가?
④ 전자는 왜 빛을 반사하는가?

해석 레이저는 빛이 전자와 상호작용하는 방식 때문에 (발생이) 가능하다. 전자는 그 특정 원자 또는 분자 특유의 특정 에너지 준위 혹은 상태에 존재한다. 에너지 준위는 핵 주위의 고리 또는 궤도로 상상할 수 있다. 외부 고리의 전자는 내부 고리의 전자보다 에너지 준위가 높다. 전자는 예를 들어 빛의 섬광과 같은, 에너지 주입에 의해 더 높은 에너지 준위로 상승될 수 있다. 전자가 바깥쪽에서 안쪽 준위로 떨어지면, "과잉" 에너지가 빛으로 방출된다. 방출되는 빛의 파장 또는 색상은 방출되는 에너지의 양과 정확히 관련되어 있다. 사용되는 특정 레이저 발진 물질에 따라, (전자에 에너지를 주거나 그것을 들뜨게 하도록) 특정 파장의 빛이 흡수되고 (전자가 초기 준위로 떨어질 때) 특정 파장이 방출된다.

어휘
electron 전자
molecule 분자
nucleus 핵
injection 주입
wavelength 파장
lase 레이저 광을 발하다
atom 원자
orbit 궤도
bump up ~을 올리다
give off 발하다
emit 방출하다
absorb 흡수하다

03 ③

해설 이 글은 일본과 미국 학생들에게 같은 수중 풍경 사진을 보여주었을 때 서로 다른 것에 초점을 두었다는 예시를 들어, 서로 다른 문화권의 사람들이 세상을 어떻게 다르게 보는지에 관해 설명하고 있다. 따라서 글의 제목으로 가장 적절한 것은 ③ '인지의 문화적 차이'이다.
① 일본인과 미국인 사이의 언어 장벽
② 뇌 속의 물체와 배경의 연관성
④ 꼼꼼한 사람들의 우월성

해석 다른 문화권의 사람들은 세상을 다르게 보는가? 한 심리학자는 일본과 미국 학생들에게 물고기와 다른 수중 물체들의 사실적인 영상화된 장면들을 보여주고 그들이 본 것을 보고하도록 요구했다. 미국인들과 일본인들은 그 초점에 있는 물고기를 거의 같은 수로 언급했지만, 그 일본인들은 물, 바위, 거품, 그리고 비활동적인 식물과 동물들을 포함한 배경 요소들에 대해 60% 이상 더 많이 언급했다. 게다가 일본과 미국의 참가자가 활동적인 동물들을 포함한 움직임을 거의 같은 수로 언급한 반면, 그 일본 참가자들은 비활동적인 배경 물체를 포함한 관계에 대해 거의 두 배 더 많이 언급했다. 아마 가장 현저하게도, 일본인 참가자들의 가장 첫 문장은 환경을 언급하는 것이었을 반면, 미국인들의 첫 문장은 초점에 있는 물고기를 언급하는 것이었을 가능성이 세 배 더 컸다.

어휘
animated 동영상으로 된, 만화로 된
reference 언급
inert 활발치 못한
superiority 우월성
scene 장면
focal 초점에 있는, 중심의
tellingly 강력하게, 현저하게
oriented ~을 지향하는

04 ③

해설 이 글은 해양 온난화로 인해 물고기들이 산소를 더 많이 필요로 하지만 동시에 산소 이용 가능성은 작아지면서, 다양한 어종과 수중 호흡 생물들의 크기가 줄어들 것이라는 내용이다. 이에 대한 부연 설명으로 과학자들과 William Cheung의 주장이 제시되고 있다. 따라서 글의 제목으로 가장 적절한 것은 ③ '기후 변화가 세계의 물고기를 줄어들게 할 수 있다'이다.

① 물고기는 이제 그 어느 때보다 더 빨리 자란다
② 산소가 해양 온도에 미치는 영향
④ 바다 생물들이 낮은 신진대사로 살아남는 방법

해석 바다의 온난화와 산소 손실이 참치와 농어에서 연어, 환도상어, 해덕, 대구까지 수백 어종을 이전에 생각했던 것보다 훨씬 더 많이 줄어들게 할 것이라고 새로운 연구는 결론 내렸다. 따뜻한 바다는 물고기들의 신진대사를 가속화하기 때문에, 물고기, 오징어 그리고 다른 수중 호흡 생물들은 바다에서 더 많은 산소를 끌어내야 할 것이다. 이와 동시에, 바다 온난화는 이미 바다의 많은 부분에서 산소의 이용 가능성을 줄이고 있다. British Columbia 대학의 과학자 두 명은 물고기의 몸통이 아가미보다 더 빨리 자라기 때문에, 이 동물들은 결국 정상적인 성장을 지속하기에 충분한 산소를 얻을 수 없는 지경에 이를 것이라고 주장한다. "우리가 발견한 것은 물고기의 몸통 크기가 수온이 섭씨 1도 상승할 때마다 20~30% 줄어든다는 것입니다."라고 저술가 William Cheung은 말한다.

어휘

shrink 줄어들게 하다, 감소시키다
grouper 농어
thresher shark 환도상어
cod 대구
metabolism 신진대사
availability 이용 가능성
gill 아가미
sustain 지속하다

05 ④

해설 20세기 후반 시장 자본주의의 특성과 그 반향에 관한 글이다. 20세기 후반 사회주의가 쇠퇴하고 시장 자본주의가 진화하여 '세계화'되었는데, 이는 무역을 활성화하고 생산성을 향상시켰으나 저임금 노동자와 환경을 착취하고 제3세계를 독점적 자본주의에 종속시키는 문제점도 있었기에, 그에 반대하는 자들이 비정부단체에 가입하고 연합하여 환경 운동을 일으키게 되었다는 내용이다. 따라서 글의 주제로 가장 적절한 것은 ④ '세계 자본주의의 착취적 특성과 그에 맞선 다양한 사회적 반응'이다.

① 과거 개발도상국에서의 세계화의 긍정적 현상
② 20세기 사회주의의 쇠퇴와 자본주의의 출현
③ 세계 자본시장과 좌파 정치조직 사이의 갈등

해석 20세기 후반 사회주의는 서구와 개발도상국의 넓은 지역에서 후퇴하고 있었다. 시장 자본주의 진화의 이 새로운 국면에서, 세계 무역 패턴은 점점 더 상호 연결되었고, 정보 기술의 발전은 규제가 철폐된 금융 시장이 몇 초 만에 국가 경계를 넘어 거대한 자본의 흐름을 바꿀 수 있다는 것을 의미했다. '세계화'는 무역을 활성화하고, 생산성 향상을 장려하고, 가격을 낮췄지만, 비판자들은 그것이 저임금 노동자들을 착취하고, 환경 문제에 무관심하며 제3 세계를 독점적인 형태의 자본주의에 종속시켰다고 주장했다. 이 과정에 반대하고자 했던 서구 사회 내의 많은 급진주의자들은 좌파의 뒤처진 정당들보다는 자발적 단체, 자선단체, 그리고 다른 비정부기구들에 가입했다. 환경 운동 자체는 세계가 서로 연결되어 있다는 인식에서 비롯되었으며, 비록 흩어져 있지만, 분노한 이익집단들의 국제 연합이 출현했다.

어휘

retreat 후퇴
phase 단계, 국면
deregulate 규제를 철폐하다
massive 거대한
boost 북돋우다
allege 주장하다
exploit 착취하다
indifferent 무관심한
subject 종속시키다
monopolistic 독점적인
radical 급진주의자
charity 자선단체
marginalize 소외시키다, 처지게 하다
diffuse 분산된
coalition 연합
affirmative 긍정적인
decline 쇠퇴

06 ①

해설 이 글은 변화하는 미래 상황 속에서 예술이 어떻게 변할 것인지에 대해 말하고 있다. 미래의 예술은 더 다양해질 것이고, 우리가 기대하는 예술과는 다를지도 모른다고 했고, 글의 마지막 부분에서 개인적이기보다는 집단적이고 경험적일 것이라고 말하고 있다. 따라서 글의 제목으로 가장 적절한 것은 ① '예술은 미래에 어떤 모습일까?'이다.

② 지구온난화는 우리의 삶에 어떤 영향을 미칠까?
③ 인공지능이 환경에 어떤 영향을 미칠까?
④ 정치 운동으로 인해 어떤 변화가 일어날까?

해석 미래는 불확실할지 모르지만 기후 변화, 변하는 인구 통계, 지정학 같은 어떤 것들은 명백하다. 유일한 보장은 변화가 있을 것이라는 것인데, 그 변화는 멋질 수도, 끔찍할 수도 있다. 현재와 미래에 예술이 어떤 목적에 기여하는지뿐만 아니라 예술가들이 이러한 변화에 어떻게 반응할지를 고려해 볼 가치가 있다. 보고서는 2040년까지 인간이 초래한 기후 변화의 영향이 피할 수 없게 되어 20년 후 예술과 삶의 중심에서 큰 이슈가 될 것이라고 제시하고 있다. 미래의 예술가들은 포스트휴먼과 인류세 이후의 가능성, 즉 인공지능, 우주에 있는 인간의 식민지, 그리고 잠재적 파멸과 씨름할 것이다. #미투(MeToo)와 흑인 인권 운동(Black Lives Matter)을 둘러싼 예술에서 보이는 정체성 정치는 환경 결정론, 국경 정치, 이주가 더욱 첨예하게 집중되면서 더욱 커질 것이다. 예술은 점점 더 다양해질 것이고 우리가 기대하는 것처럼 '예술처럼 보이지' 않을 것이다. 미래에, 우리가 온라인에서 모든 사람들이 볼 수 있는 우리의 삶이 보이는 것에 싫증이 나고 사생활이 거의 없어지면, 익명성이 명성보다 더 바람직할지도 모른다. 수천, 아니 수백만의 '좋아요'와 '팔로워'가 아니라, 우리는 진실성과 관계에 굶주릴 것이다. 예술은 결국 개인적이기보다는 더 집단적이고 경험적이게 될 수 있다.

어휘

demographics 인구 통계
geopolitics 지정학
Anthropocene 인류세(인류로 인한 지구온난화 및 생태계 침범을 특징으로 하는 현재의 지질학적 시기)
environmentalism 환경 결정론
anonymity 익명성
authenticity 진실성
collective 집단의
experiential 경험상의

07 ③

해설 이 글은 태블릿 컴퓨터에서 사용되는 터치스크린 기술이 작동하는 방식과 그 원리에 대해서 설명하고 있다. 이러한 구체적인 예로 두 금속 표면을 덮는 유리 패널을 가진 저항성 스크린의 작동 방식에 대한 설명과 유리 패널 아래에 하나의 전기가 통하는 금속층을 가진 용량성 스크린의 작동 방식에 대한 설명이 나오고 있다. 따라서 글의 주제로 가장 적절한 것은 ③ '터치스크린 기술이 작동하는 방식'이다.

① 사용자가 새로운 기술을 배우는 방식
② 전자책이 태블릿 컴퓨터에서 작동하는 방식
④ 터치스크린이 어떻게 진화해 왔는가

해석 태블릿 컴퓨터에서 사용할 수 있는 전자책 애플리케이션은 터치스크린 기술을 이용한다. 일부 터치스크린은 마주 보고 누운 전자 충전된 두 개의 금속 표면을 덮는 유리 패널을 특징으로 한다. 화면을 터치하면 두 금속 표면이 압력을 감지하고 전류를 연결한다. 이러한 압력은 컴퓨터로 전기 신호를 보내서 그 터치를 명령으로 변환시킨다. 터치스크린의 이 버전은 화면이 손가락의 압력에 반응하기 때문에 저항성 스크린으로 알려져 있다. 다른 태블릿 컴퓨터들은 유리 패널 아래에 하나의 전기가 통하는 금속층을 특징으로 한다. 사용자가 화면을 터치하면 일부 전류가 유리를 통과해 사용자의 손가락으로 전해진다. 전하가 전달되면 컴퓨터는 전력 상실을 명령어로 해석하고 사용자가 원하는 기능을 수행한다. 이러한 유형의 화면을 용량성(容量性) 스크린이라고 한다.

어휘

available 사용할 수 있는
command 명령
electrify 전기를 통하게 하다
capacitive 용량성의, 전기 용량의
translate 옮기다
resistive 저항성의
pass through ~을 관통하다, 거쳐 가다

08 ④

해설 지도 작성 기술이 생물학, 지구물리학, 해양학 등 다양하고 새로운 분야에서 사용되고 있다는 내용의 글이다. 더 나아가 관념적인 측면에서도 아이디어 간의 관계를 도식화 할 수 있다고 서술하기 때문에 글의 제목으로 가장 적절한 것은 ④ '새로운 분야를 도식화하기'이다.

① 전산화된 지도 vs 전통적 지도
② 지도 제작은 어디서부터 시작되는가?
③ DNA 비밀을 푸는 방법을 찾기

해석 매핑(도식화) 기술은 많은 새로운 응용 분야에 사용되고 있다. 생물학자들은 DNA의 분자구조("게놈 지도")를 분석하고, 지구물리학자들은 지구 핵의 구조를, 그리고 해양학자들은 해저를 매핑하고 있다. 컴퓨터 게임은 다양한 상상 속의 "땅"이나 규칙, 위험, 보상이 변하는 단계를 가지고 있다. 전산화는 이제 훈련과 오락에 유용할 수도 있는 특수한 상황을 자극하는 인위적인 환경인 "가상현실"로 현실에 도전한다. 지도 기술은 아이디어의 영역에서도 사용되고 있다. 예를 들어, 아이디어 간의 관계가 개념지도라 불리는 것을 사용하면서 나타날 수 있다. 일반적이거나 "중심" 생각으로부터 출발하여, 주요 개념 주위에 웹을 구축하면서, 관련된 생각들은 연결될 수 있다. 이것은 어떠한 전통적인 정의에 의한 지도는 아니지만, 그것을 생산하기 위해 지도 제작의 도구와 기법을 이용하고 있으며, 어떤 면에서 이것은 지도를 닮았다.

어휘

application 지원, 적용
computerization 전산화
stimulate 자극하다
cartography 지도 제작(법)
molecular 분자의
artificial 인위적인
realm 영역
employ 쓰다, 이용하다

09 ③

해설 이 글은 상업적 어업의 지속을 위해서는 과학적이고 체계적인 물고기 개체 수 유지가 필요하다고 서술하고 있다. 글의 첫 번째 문장에서 상업적 어업이 과학적으로 이루어져야 한다고 했으며, 이후 개체 수가 유지된 물고기와 남획된 물고기의 사례를 들어 적절한 연간 생산량을 유지하기 위해서는 과학이 필요하다고 주장한다. 따라서 글의 제목으로 가장 적절한 것은 ③ '왜 어업에 과학이 필요한가?'이다.

① 상업적 어업을 거부하라
② 수상한 사업으로 여겨지는 양식 어업
④ 남획된 동물들: 불법 어업의 사례

해석 과학자들의 도움으로, 상업적 어업은 그 어업이 지속되려면 과학적으로 이루어져야 한다는 것을 알아냈다. 물고기 개체 수에 어업으로 인한 압박이 없다면, 물고기의 수는 예상 가능한 풍부함의 수준에 도달하고 거기에 머무를 것이다. 유일한 변동은 먹이 획득 가능성, 적정한 온도 따위와 같은 자연스러운 환경적 요인 때문일 것이다. 만일 이러한 물고기들을 잡도록 어장이 개발될 경우, 어획량이 적다면 그들의 개체 수는 유지될 수 있다. 북해의 고등어가 좋은 예시다. 만약 우리가 어장을 늘리고 해마다 더 많은 물고기를 잡는다면, 우리는 우리가 매년 잡는 모든 물고기를 다시 채울 수 있는 이상적인 수준 아래로 개체 수를 감소시키지 않도록 조심해야 한다. 만일 우리가 이 '최대 유지 생산량'이라고 불리는 수준으로 물고기를 잡는다면, 매년 우리는 가능한 최대의 생산량을 유지할 수 있다. 만일 우리가 너무 많이 잡는다면, 물고기의 수는 우리가 스스로 일자리를 잃게 만들 때까지 해마다 줄어들 것이다. 심각하게 남획된 동물의 예로는 남극의 흰긴수염고래와 북대서양의 넙치가 있다. 최대 연간 생산량을 유지하기 위해 딱 정확한 양의 물고기를 잡는 것은 과학이면서 기술이기도 하다. 물고기 개체 수와 그것을 격감시키지 않으면서 최대한 활용하는 방법을 우리가 더 잘 이해하도록 돕기 위해 연구는 계속해서 이루어지고 있다.

어휘

fluctuation 변동
mackerel 고등어
overfished 남획된
halibut 큰 넙치
sea farming 양식 어업
fishery 어장, 양식장
fish A out of ~에서 A를 빼내다
blue whale 흰긴수염고래
deplete 격감시키다, 고갈시키다
fishy 수상한

10 ③

해설 이 글은 과학자, 예술가 등은 서로 다른 것을 창조하지만, 그들의 창조는 모두 '사고의 도구'를 이용한다는 공통점이 있다고 언급하고 있다. 따라서 글의 주제로 가장 적절한 것은 ③ '창조 과정의 공통성'이다.

① 창의적인 사고의 방해물들
② 예술과 과학의 차이점
④ 다양한 직종의 독특한 특징

해석 사람들이 만들어낸 다양한 것들을 보고 그것들의 차이점을 설명하는 것은 쉽다. 명백하게 시는 수학 공식이 아니며, 소설은 유전학 실험이 아니다. 작곡가는 확실히 시각 예술가들의 언어와는 다른 언어를 사용하며, 화학자들은 극작가들이 하는 것과는 매우 다른 것들을 결합한다. 그러나 사람들을 그들이 만드는 다른 것들로 특징짓는 것은 그들이 창조하는 방식에 대한 보편성을 놓치는 것이다. 창조 과정의 수준에서, 과학자, 예술가, 수학자, 작곡가, 작가, 그리고 조각가는 소위 '사고의 도구'라고 부르는 공통된 조합을 사용하는데, 거기에는 정서적 느낌, 시각적 이미지, 육체적 감각, 재현 가능한 패턴, 유추 등이 포함된다. 그리고 모든 창의적으로 생각하는 사람들은 이러한 주관적인 사고의 도구들로 생성된 아이디어들을 그들의 통찰을 표현하기 위해 대중적인 언어로 번역하는 법을 배우는데, 그것은 이어서 다른 사람의 마음속에 새로운 아이디어를 불러일으킬 수 있다.

어휘

playwright 극작가
universality 보편성
what we call 소위, 이른바
analogy 유추, 비유
subjective 주관의, 주관적인
distinctive 독특한, 특유의
characterize 특징짓다
sculptor 조각가
reproducible 재현[재생] 가능한
imaginative 창의적인, 상상력이 풍부한
give rise to ~를 불러일으키다

01	①	02	①	03	②	04	③	05	②
06	④								

01 ①

해설 사람들이 자신과 비슷한 복장의 타인에게 더 긍정적으로 반응한다는 것을 두 실험을 예로 들어 설명하는 글이다. 실험자가 학생과 비슷하게 입었을 때 동전을 더 잘 빌려주었고, 시위자와 비슷하게 입었을 때 탄원서에 더 잘 서명해주었다는 것이다. 따라서 글의 요지로 가장 적절한 것은 ① '사람들은 그들처럼 입는 사람들을 도울 가능성이 더 크다.'이다.

② 정장을 차려입는 것은 탄원서에 서명할 가능성을 높인다.

③ 전화를 거는 것은 다른 학생들과 교제하는 효율적인 방법이다.

④ 1970년대 초반의 몇몇 대학생들은 독특한 패션으로 동경 받았다.

해석 젊은이들이 "히피"나 "스트레이트" 패션으로 입는 경향이 있던 1970년대 초에 행해진 한 연구에서, 실험자들은 히피나 스트레이트 복장을 하고 교내의 대학생들에게 전화를 걸기 위한 10센트짜리 동전을 요구했다. 실험자가 학생과 같은 방식으로 입었을 때, 그 요청은 3분의 2 이상 허락되었고, 학생과 요청자가 서로 다르게 입었을 때, 10센트짜리 동전은 절반 미만으로 제공되었다. 또 다른 실험은 비슷한 타인에 대한 우리의 긍정적인 반응이 얼마나 자동적인지를 보여주었다. 반전 시위에 참여한 시위자들은 비슷한 복장을 한 요청자의 탄원서에 서명할 가능성이 더 크고, 그것을 우선 읽어보려 하지도 않고 서명할 가능성이 더 큰 것으로 밝혀졌다.

어휘

don 입다
dime 10센트짜리 은화
dissimilarly 다르게
marcher 시위 참가자
petition 탄원서
attire 의상, 복장
grant 들어주다, 허락하다
automatic 자동의
demonstration 시위
admire 감탄하다, 동경하다

02 ①

해설 제안을 받았을 때 그에 대해 원하는 수정사항들을 어떻게 제시해야 하는지 설명하는 글이다. 원하는 수정사항이 여러 개라면 그것들을 한꺼번에 제안하고, 또 그것들의 상대적 중요성을 표현해야 한다고 말한다. 따라서 글의 요지로 가장 적절한 것은 ① '여러 문제를 연속적으로가 아닌 동시에 협상해라.'이다.

② 성공적인 협상을 위해 민감한 주제를 피해라.

③ 당신의 협상을 위해 적절한 시간을 골라라.

④ 급여를 협상할 때 너무 직설적으로 굴지 마라.

해석 만약 누군가가 당신에게 제안을 하고 당신이 정당하게 그것의 일부에 대해 걱정된다면, 당신은 보통 당신의 모든 수정사항을 한꺼번에 제안하는 것이 더 낫다. "급여가 좀 적어요. 어떻게 좀 해주시겠어요?"라고 말하고 그에 대해 그녀가 작업을 마치면 "고맙습니다. 이제 제가 원하는 다른 두 가지가 있는데..."라고 다시 말하지 마라. 처음에 당신이 한 가지만 요구한다면, 그녀는 그 하나를 들어주면 당신이 제안을 받아들일 (또는 적어도 결정을 내릴) 준비가 될 것으로 생각할 수 있다. 만약 당신이 계속해서 "그리고 한 가지 더..."라고 말한다면, 그녀는 관대하거나 이해심 있는 기분을 유지하지 않을 가능성이 크다. 더욱이, 하나보다 많은 요구사항이 있다면, 당신이 원하는 그 모든 것들을 A, B, C, D로 단순히 언급하지 말고, 당신에게 있어 각각의 상대적 중요성을 표해라. 그렇지 않으면, 그녀는 당신이 가장 덜 중요하게 여기는 두 가지를 당신에게 주기 꽤 쉽다는 이유로 고르고 당신과 타협했다고 느낄지도 모른다.

어휘

legitimately 합법적으로, 정당하게
initially 처음에
understanding 이해심 있는
relative 상대적인
negotiate 협상하다
serially 연속적으로
salary 급여
generous 관대한
signal 표하다
meet sb halfway ~와 타협하다
simultaneously 동시에

03 ②

해설 이 글은 대화를 의미 있게 만드는 방법에 대해서 말하고 있다. 글의 중반부에서, 의견을 말하는 것은 중요하지만, 듣지 않고 의견을 내는 것은 냄비와 팬을 함께 쾅쾅 두드리는 것과 같다고 했으므로, 상대방의 말을 듣는 것에 대한 중요성을 강조하고 있다. 따라서 글의 요지로 가장 적절한 것은 ② '우리는 의사소통을 잘하기 위해 듣고 의견을 말해야 한다.'이다.

① 우리는 다른 사람들을 설득하기 위해 더 단호해져야 한다.

③ 우리는 우리가 보는 세상에 대한 믿음을 바꾸는 것을 꺼린다.

④ 우리는 우리가 선택한 것만 듣고 다른 의견을 무시하려고 노력한다.

해석 다른 사람의 생각을 듣는 것은 당신이 자기 자신과 세상 속 당신의 위치뿐만 아니라, 세상에 대해 믿는 이야기가 온전하게 남아 있는지를 알 수 있는 하나의 방법이다. 우리 모두는 우리의 신념을 들여다보고, 환기시켜 숨 쉬게 할 필요가 있다. 다른 사람들이, 특히 우리가 기초적인 것으로 간주하는 개념에 대해 말하는 것을 듣는 것은 우리의 마음과 정신의 창을 여는 것과 같다. 의견을 말하는 것은 중요하다. 그러나 듣지 않고 이야기하는 것은 냄비와 프라이팬을 쾅쾅 두드리는 것과 같다: 비록 그것이 당신을 주목받게 하더라도, 존중받게 하지는 않을 것이다. 대화가 의미 있게 되기 위해서는 다음과 같은 세 가지 전제조건이 있다. 1. 당신이 무슨 말을 하고 있는지 알아야 한다. 즉, 당신은 독창적인 요점을 가지고 있고 낡고 진부하거나 미리 만들어진 논거를 그대로 따라하지 않는다는 것을 의미한다. 2. 당신은 당신이 말하고 있는 사람들을 존경하고, 비록 당신이 그들의 입장에 동의하지 않더라도 그들을 진정으로 정중하게 대할 의향이 있어야 한다. 3. 당신은 끊이지 않는 좋은 유머와 분별력을 가지고 주제에 대한 당신 자신의 관점을 다루면서 상대방의 말을 들을 수 있을 만큼 똑똑하고 잘 알아야 한다.

어휘

intact 온전한
prerequisite 전제조건
hand-me-down 진부한
authentically 진정으로
discernment 분별력, 안목
bang 치다, 때리다
worn-out 낡은
pre-fab 미리 만들어진
uninterrupted 끊임없는

04 ③

해설 이 글은 피드백을 할 때 피드백 수신자의 과거나 미래의 잠재력까지 잘 고려해야 한다는 내용이다. 수용자가 high performers(훌륭한 수행자), adequate performers(평범한 수행자), 그리고 poor performers(형편없는 수행자) 중 어느 부류인지에 따라 피드백을 다르게 해야 한다는 내용이 진술되었으므로 글의 요지로 가장 적절한 것은 ③ '피드백을 사람에게 맞춰라'이다.

① 피드백을 적당한 시기에 하라

② 부정적인 피드백을 개개인에게 맞춰라

④ 목표 지향적인 피드백은 피하라

해석 성과 피드백을 제공할 때, 당신은 (피드백을) 받는 사람의 이전의 성과와 빈도, 정도, 그리고 내용을 계획하는 데 있어 그 사람의 미래 잠재성에 대한 당신의 평가를 고려해야 한다. 성장가능성이 있는 훌륭한 수행자의 경우, 피드백은 그들이 시정 조치를 취할 수 있을 정도로 자주 주어져야 하지만 너무 (피드백을) 자주해서 그것이 통제하는 것처럼 느껴지고 그들의 진취성을 무너뜨리게 해서는 안 된다. 자신의 직업에 정착하고 승진 가능성이 제한적인 적절한 수행자들에게 피드백은 거의 필요하지 않다. 왜냐하면 그들의 일을 알고 무엇을 해야 하는지 깨닫고 있으면서, 과거에 믿음직스럽고 착실한 행동을 보였기 때문이다. 형편없는 성과자들 — 성과가 개선되지 않으면 직장에서 퇴출되어야 할 사람들 — 에게 피드백은 자주 그리고 매우 구체적이어야 하며, 피드백에 대한 행동과 일시 해고 또는 해고와 같은 부정적인 제재 사이의 연관성을 명시해야 한다.

어휘

recipient 수령인
corrective 정정하는
initiative 계획, 진취성
explicit 분명한
prod 쿡 찌르다, 재촉하다
sap 차츰 무너뜨리다
sanction 제재

05 ②

해설 이 글은 훌륭한 인적 네트워크를 만들기만 하면 본인의 업적이 향상될 것이라고 믿는 사람들의 통념을 반박하는 글이다. 스스로 본인의 업적을 위해 이루어놓은 것이 없다면 훌륭한 인적 네트워크를 형성하기 쉽지 않으며, 이를 위해서 어떤 분야의 전문가가 되는 것이 필수적이라고 주장한다. 따라서 글의 요지로 가장 적절한 것은 ② '좋은 (인적) 네트워크 만들기는 당신의 성과에서 시작한다.'이다.

① 후원은 성공적인 경력을 위해 필수이다.

③ 강력한 (인적) 네트워크는 당신의 성취의 전제 조건이다.

④ 당신이 (인적) 네트워크 형성의 전문가가 될 때, 당신의 통찰력과 성과는 증가한다.

해석 나의 학생들은 종종 그들이 단순히 좀 더 중요한 사람들을 만난다면 그들의 성과가 개선될 것이라고 믿는다. 그러나 여러분이 이미 가치 있는 무언가를 세상에 내어놓았던 것이 아니라면, 그러한 사람들과 관계를 맺는 것은 매우 어려운 일이다. 그것이 바로 조언자들과 후원자들의 호기심을 자극하는 것이다. 성취한 것들은 여러분이 단지 받기만 하는게 아니라 줄 수 있는 무언가를 갖고 있다는 것을 보여준다. 삶에서 적절한 사람들을 아는 것은 분명히 도움이 된다. 그러나 그들이 여러분을 위해 얼마나 열심히 도와주는지와 그들이 여러분을 위해 얼마나 위험을 무릅쓰는지는, 여러분이 무엇을 주는지에 달려 있다. 강력한 인적 네트워크를 만드는 것은 여러분이 인맥 쌓기의 전문가가 될 것을 요구하지 않는다. 그것은 단지 여러분이 무언가에 전문가가 될 것을 요구한다. 만약 여러분이 훌륭한 관계들을 만든다면, 그것들이 당신의 경력을 발전시켜 줄지도 모른다. 만약 여러분이 훌륭한 성과를 만들어낸다면, 그러한 관계들은 만들기 더 쉬워질 것이다. 여러분의 명함이 아니라 여러분의 통찰력과 성과가 대변하게 하라.

어휘

remarkably 매우, 두드러지게
pique (호기심 등을) 자극하다
stick one's neck out 위험을 무릅쓰다
insight 통찰력
do the talking 대변하다, 말하다
engage with ~와 관계를 맺다
go to bat for ~를 도와주다
advance 성공을 돕다, 진전하다
output 성과, 산출
prerequisite 전제 조건

06 ④

해설 이 글은 뇌가 반복적이고 평범한 자극보다 새롭고 특이한 자극이 더 오래 지속되는 것처럼 느낀다고 주장하며 그 이유를 설명하고 있다. 따라서 글의 요지로 가장 적절한 것은 ④ '새로운 자극은 주관적인 시간 확장을 일으킨다.'이다.

① 자극에 대한 반응은 두뇌 훈련의 중요한 부산물이다.

② 자극의 강도는 그것이 반복됨에 따라 증가한다.

③ 자극에 대한 우리의 신체적 반응은 우리의 생각에 영향을 준다.

해석 새로움으로 유발되는 시간 확장은 실험실 조건하에 조사될 수 있는 잘 특징지어진 현상이다. 그저 사람들에게 자신들이 일련의 자극에 노출된 시간을 가늠하도록 요청하면, 새로운 자극은 반복적이거나 평범한 자극보다 정말로 더 오래 지속되는 것처럼 보인다는 사실을 보여준다. 사실, 적당히 반복적인 연속들 중에서 첫 번째 자극이기만 해도 주관적인 시간 확장을 유발하기에 충분한 것으로 보인다. 물론, 우리의 뇌가 이런 식으로 작동하도록 진화한 이유를 생각해내는 것은 쉽다. 짐작건대 새롭고 특이한 자극은 익숙한 자극보다 더 많은 생각과 숙고를 요하므로, 뇌가 그것들에 더 많은 주관적 시간을 배당하는 것은 말이 된다.

어휘

novelty 새로움, 참신함
a train of 일련의
unremarkable 평범한
exotic 이국적인, 특이한
by-product 부산물
induce 유발하다, 유도하다
repetitive 반복적인, 되풀이하는
presumably 아마, 짐작건대
allocate 할당하다, 배당하다
give rise to ~을 일으키다

PART 03 글의 논리 전개 파악하기

Reading Skill 08 빈칸 완성 ACTUAL TEST

01	②	02	④	03	①	04	②	05	④
06	①	07	②	08	③	09	①	10	④
11	②	12	①						

01 ②

해설 선전 기법의 목표는 선전자가 일반적인 사람과 같은 견해를 가지고 있으며 자신도 대중들 중 한 명일 뿐이라는 인상을 주는 것이라고 했으므로, 빈칸에 들어갈 말로 가장 적절한 것은 ② '우리 같은 평범한 사람들'이다.

① 화려한 추상어를 넘어선

③ 남들과는 다른 무언가

④ 대중보다 더 잘 교육받은

해석 가장 자주 사용되는 선전 기법 중 하나는 선전자의 견해가 일반인의 견해를 반영하고 있으며 그 또는 그녀가 최선의 이익을 위해 일하고 있다는 것을 대중에게 확신시키는 것이다. 블루칼라 청중에게 말하는 정치인은 소매를 걷어붙이고 넥타이를 풀고 대중의 특정 관용구를 사용하려고 시도할 수 있다. 그는 심지어 자신이 "그 사람들 중 한 명일 뿐"이라는 인상을 주기 위해 일부러 언어를 잘못 사용할 수도 있다. 이 기법은 또한 보통 정치가의 견해가 연설을 듣는 대중의 견해와 같다는 인상을 주기 위해 화려한 추상어를 사용한다. 노조 간부들, 사업가들, 성직자들, 교육자들, 그리고 광고주들은 우리 같은 평범한 사람들인 것처럼 보임으로써 우리의 신뢰를 얻기 위해 이 기법을 사용해왔다.

어휘

propaganda 선전
sleeve 소매
idiom 관용구, 표현 양식
folks 사람들
minister 성직자
plain 평범한
blue-collar 블루칼라[육체노동자]의
undo 풀다, 벗기다
on purpose 일부러
glittering generality 화려한 추상어
confidence 신뢰

02 ④

해설 빙하 아래에 흐르는 따뜻한 바닷물이 빙하를 훨씬 더 빨리 녹게 한다는 연구 결과에 관한 글이므로, 빈칸에 들어갈 말로 가장 적절한 것은 ④ '가속하는'이다.

① 분리하는

② 지연시키는

③ 방지하는

해석 과학자들은 더 높은 기온으로 인해 그린란드 빙상의 표면이 녹고 있다는 것을 오랫동안 알고 있었다. 하지만 한 새로운 연구가 아래로부터 얼음을 공격하기 시작한 또 다른 위협을 발견했는데, 광대한 빙하 아래에서 움직이는 따뜻한 바닷물이 빙하를 훨씬 더 빨리 녹게 하고 있다는 것이다. 그 연구 결과는 그린란드 북동부에 있는 빙하 79N(Nioghalvfjerdsfjorden Glacier)의 많은 "빙설" 중 하나를 연구한 연구자들에 의해 'Nature Geoscience'지에 실렸다. 빙설은 육지의 얼음에서 떨어지지 않고 물에 떠 있는 길쭉한 얼음 조각이다. 이 과학자들이 연구한 그 거대한 빙설은 길이가 50마일 가까이 된다. 그 조사는 대서양에서 온 따뜻한 물이 빙하를 향해 곧장 흐를 수 있는, 폭이 1마일 이상인 해류가 많은 양의 열을 얼음과 접촉시켜 빙하가 녹는 것을 가속하는 것을 밝혔다.

어휘

ice sheet 빙상
glacier 빙하
break off 떨어지다, 분리되다
underwater current 해류
vast 광대한
strip 길쭉한 조각
massive 거대한

03 ①

해설 이 글은 영국 사회에 만연한 의류 과소비와 낭비에 대한 우려를 표하고 있다. 영국인들은 일 년에 많은 돈을 새 옷에 소비하고 그만큼 많은 의류가 쓰레기 매립지로 들어간다고 했으므로, 그들에게 꼭 필요하지 않은 물건도 생각 없이 구매한다는 것을 알 수 있다. 따라서 빈칸에 들어갈 말로 가장 적절한 것은 ① '그들에게 필요하지 않은'이다.

② 생활필수품인

③ 곧 재활용 될

④ 그들이 다른 사람들에게 물려줄 수 있는

해석 소셜 미디어, 잡지, 상품진열창은 매일 사람들에게 구매할 물건들을 쏟아붓고, 영국 소비자들은 그 어느 때보다도 더 많은 옷과 신발을 사고 있다. 온라인 쇼핑은 고객들이 생각 없이 구매하기 쉽다는 것을 의미하는 한편, 주요 브랜드들은 두세 번 입고 나면 버리는 일회용품처럼 취급될 수 있을 만큼 매우 값싼 옷을 제공한다. 영국에서, 보통 사람은 일 년에 1,000파운드 이상을 새 옷에 소비하는데, 이는 그들 수입의 약 4%에 해당한다. 별로 크게 들리진 않겠지만, 그 수치는 사회와 환경에 대한 훨씬 더 걱정스러운 두 가지 추세를 감추고 있다. 첫째는, 그 소비자 지출의 많은 부분이 신용카드를 통해 이루어진다는 것이다. 영국인들은 현재 신용카드 회사에 성인 1인당 약 670파운드의 빚을 지고 있다. 이는 평균 의류 예산의 66%에 해당한다. 또한, 사람들은 가지고 있지 않은 돈을 쓸 뿐만 아니라, 그들에게 필요하지 않은 물건들을 사는 데 돈을 쓰고 있다. 영국은 1년에 30만 톤의 의류를 버리고, 그 대부분은 쓰레기 매립지로 들어간다.

어휘

bombard 쏟아 붓다
figure 수치
wardrobe 의상, 옷
hand down ~을 물려주다
disposable 일회용의
via ~을 통하여
landfill 쓰레기 매립지

04 ②

해설 이 글은 고급 식당의 경영자는 식당을 효율적으로 만들기 위해 가능한 모든 것을 하려 하지만, 가격이 비싸기 때문에 손님들은 더 뛰어난 음식과 서비스를 요구한다고 말한다. 식당은 결국 사람이 운영하는 것이라 조금 더 빨리 움직이는 등의 미미한 개선만이 가능하며 이를 통해서는 적당한 절약만이 가능하기에 가격이 오를 수밖에 없다는 내용이므로, 빈칸에 들어갈 말로 가장 적절한 것은 ② '불가피한'이다. 참고로 ①, ③, ④의 보기 단어가 전부 '터무니없는, 상상도 할 수 없는'이라는 뜻의 유의어이므로 정답이 되기 어렵다는 것을 알 수 있다.

① 터무니없는

③ 터무니없는

④ 상상도 할 수 없는

해석 고급 식당에서는 청구되는 가격이 반드시 높기 때문에 뛰어남이 절대적 전제 조건이다. 경영자는 식당을 효율적으로 만들기 위해 가능한 모든 것을 할지도 모르지만, 손님들은 여전히 정성 들인 개개인을 위한 서비스, 즉 매우 숙련된 요리사가 주문에 따라 준비하고 전문 서버가 전달하는 음식을 기대한다. 이 서비스는 말 그대로 수작업이기 때문에 생산성에 있어서 미미한 개선만이 가능하다. 예를 들어, 요리사, 서버, 또는 바텐더가 인간 수행능력의 한계에 도달하기까지 겨우 조금 더 빨리 움직일 수 있을 뿐이다. 따라서 향상된 효율성을 통해서는 겨우 적당한 절약만이 가능하고, 이는 가격 상승을 불가피하게 만든다. (가격이 오를수록 소비자들이 더 분별력 있어진다는 것은 경제학의 자명한 이치다.) 따라서, 고급 식당의 손님들은 뛰어남을 기대하고, 요구하며, 그를 위해 기꺼이 비용을 지불한다.

어휘

prerequisite 전제 조건
marginal 미미한, 근소한
escalation 상승
discriminating 식별력 있는, 안목 있는
fine dining 고급 식당
moderate 중간의, 적당한
axiom 자명한 이치
clientele 고객들

05 ④

해설 이 글은 같이 업무를 하는 사람들에게 신뢰와 책임감을 주어야 한다고 말하고 있다. 어떠한 간섭 없이 일을 완전히 수행할 수 있는 권한을 부여받은 정도와 직무 만족도가 깊이 연관되어 있으며, 신뢰하는 사람에게 책임을 맡기는 것이 조직을 더 원활하게 만들고 본인에게 더 많은 시간을 주어 더 큰 문제에 집중할 수 있게 만든다고 했다. 따라서 빈칸에 들어갈 말로 가장 적절한 것은 ④ '자율성'이다.

① 일

② 보상

③ 제한

해석 점점 더 많은 리더들이 원격으로 일하거나, 컨설턴트와 프리랜서뿐만 아니라 전국이나 전 세계에 흩어져 있는 팀들과 함께 일하면서, 당신은 그들에게 더 많은 자율성을 주어야 할 것이다. 당신이 더 많은 신뢰를 줄수록, 다른 사람들은 당신을 더 신뢰한다. 나는 직무 만족도와 모든 단계마다 따라다니는 누군가 없이 일을 완전히 수행할 수 있도록 사람들이 권한을 얼마나 부여받는지 사이에 직접적인 상관관계가 있다고 확신한다. 당신이 신뢰하는 사람들에게 책임을 맡기는 것은 조직을 보다 원활하게 운영할 수 있을 뿐만 아니라 당신에게 더 많은 시간을 만들어 내어 더 큰 문제에 집중할 수 있도록 한다.

어휘

remotely 원격으로
bestow 주다
execute 수행하다
free up (특정 목적을 위해 시간·돈을) 만들어 내다
scattered 흩어져 있는
empower 권한을 주다
shadow 그림자처럼 따라다니다

06 ①

해설 이 글은 인간의 언어는 단일 소음일 때보다 다양한 음성이 결합될 때 더 일관된 메시지를 전달할 수 있다는 내용을 담고 있다. 따라서 빈칸에 들어갈 말로 가장 적절한 것은 ① '개별 음이 거의 가치가 없는 경우가 종종 있다'이다.

② 리듬감 있는 소리가 중요하다
③ 방언이 중요한 역할을 한다
④ 음성 체계가 존재하지 않는다

해석 엄밀한 언어는 그 자체로 이중층이다. 단일 소음은 오직 가끔 의미가 있다. 대부분 다양한 음성 사운드는 서로 다른 색깔의 아이스크림이 서로 녹는 것처럼 겹치는 사슬에 결합될 때만 일관된 메시지를 전달한다. 또한 새소리에서도 개별 음이 거의 가치가 없는 경우가 종종 있다. 그 순서가 중요한 것이다. 인간과 새 모두에서 이 전문화된 음계의 제어는 뇌의 절반, 대개 왼쪽 절반에 의해 행해지고, 그 체계는 비교적 일찍 학습된다. 그리고 많은 인간 언어들이 방언을 가지고 있는 것처럼, 몇몇 새 종들도 그러하다. 캘리포니아에선 흰정수리북미멧새가 지역마다 너무나 다른 노래를 가지고 있어서 캘리포니아 사람들은 이 참새들의 소리를 들어보면 그들이 주의 어디에 있는지 알 수 있을 것이다.

어휘

occasionally 가끔
coherent 일관성 있는
specialized 전문적인
convey 전달하다
sequence 순서
relatively 비교적

07 ②

해설 이 글은 Kahneman이 개별적인 요인에 의해 선택이 알려질 때까지 의사결정을 연기하는 MAP 방식을 고안했다는 내용을 담고 있다. 따라서 빈칸에 들어갈 말로 가장 적절한 것은 ② '지연시키다'이다.

① 개선하다
③ 소유하다
④ 용이하게 하다

해석 노벨상 수상자인 심리학자 Daniel Kahneman은 인간이 이성적인 의사 결정자라는 개념을 뒤집으면서, 세계가 경제에 대해 생각하는 방식을 바꾸었다. 그 과정에서, 그의 학문 분야를 초월하는 영향은 의사들이 의학적 결정을 내리고 투자자들이 월가의 위험을 평가하는 방식을 변화시켰다. 한 논문에서, Kahneman과 그의 동료들은 큰 전략적 결정을 내리는 과정을 개략적으로 설명한다. Mediating Assessment Protocol, 즉 MAP이라고 라벨을 붙인 그들의 제안된 접근 방법은 다음과 같은 간단한 목표를 가지고 있다. 여러 가지 개별적인 요인에 의해 선택이 알려질 수 있을 때까지 직감 기반 의사결정을 연기하는 것이다. Kahneman은 최근 '포스트'와의 인터뷰에서 "MAP의 본질적인 목적 중 하나는 기본적으로 직관을 지연시키는 것"이라고 말했다. 구조화된 프로세스는 이전에 선택된 6~7개의 속성을 바탕으로 결정을 분석하고, 각각에 대해 별도로 논의하고, 상대적 백분위수 점수를 할당하며, 마지막으로 그러한 점수를 사용하여 전체론적 판단을 내리는 것을 요구한다.

어휘

upend 뒤집다
rational 이성적인
evaluate 평가하다
intuition 직관
percentile 백분위수
notion 개념
alter 바꾸다, 고치다
outline 개요를 서술하다
attribute 자질, 속성
holistic 전체론의

08 ③

해설 이 글은 고슴도치 유형과 여우 유형의 사상가의 특징을 비교하고 있다. 여우 유형의 사상가에 대해 설명하는 빈칸이 prevent A from RVing 구문의 일부임에 유의하면, 빈칸에 들어갈 내용은 빈칸 앞에 언급된 'have a variegated take(더 다양한 의견을 가진다)'에 반대되는 내용임을 유추할 수 있다. 따라서 빈칸에 들어갈 말로 가장 적절한 것은 ③ '하나의 큰 구호를 분명하게 표현하는'이다.

① 합리적으로 행동하는
② 여러 가지 해결책을 찾는
④ 세계의 복잡한 문제들을 파악하는

해석 Tolstoy에 관한 유명한 에세이에서, 자유주의 철학자인 Isaiah Berlin 경은 그리스 서정시인인 Archilochus(BC 7세기)의 말이라고 여겨지는, "여우는 많은 것을 알지만, 고슴도치는 큰 하나를 안다."라는 고대의 격언을 상기시킴으로써 두 종류의 사상가들을 구분하였다. 고슴도치들은 하나의 중심 생각을 가졌으며 오로지 그 생각의 프리즘을 통해서만 세계를 본다. 그들은 복잡한 문제들과 예외들을 간과하거나, 그것들을 그들의 세계관에 맞추기 위해 틀에 끼워 넣는다. 모든 시간과 모든 환경에 맞는 하나의 진정한 답만 있다. Berlin은 여우에게 더 크게 공감했는데, 여우는 그들로 하여금 하나의 큰 구호를 분명하게 표현하지 않도록 막아주는, 세계에 관한 다양한 의견을 가졌다. 세계의 복잡성이 일반화를 막는다고 느끼기 때문에 그들은 웅장한 이론들에 대하여 회의적이다. Berlin은 Dante는 고슴도치였던 반면 Shakespeare는 여우였다고 생각했다.

어휘

liberal 자유주의의, 진보적인
attribute (말 등을) ~의 것이라고 여기다
exclusively 오로지, 배타적으로
variegated 다양한 종류로 이루어진
grand 웅장한, 원대한
hark back to ~을 상기시키다
lyric 서정시; 서정적인
mold 틀에 넣다; 틀
take 의견
articulate 분명히 표현하다

09 ①

해설 빈칸이 지문 중간에 있으므로 빈칸 주변의 연결사를 확인한다. 역접의 접속사 But이 있는 것으로 보아 빈칸에는 앞 내용과 상반되는 내용이 올 것임을 알 수 있다. 빈칸 뒤의 문장에서도, 동정심을 느껴 선행을 하는 것은 옳고 그름의 문제와는 관계가 없다고 하고 있으므로, 빈칸에 들어갈 말로 가장 적절한 것은 ① '그것은 전혀 도덕적인 행동이 아닐 것이다'이다.

② 당신의 행동은 이성에 기초한다
③ 그렇다면 당신은 윤리적 행위를 드러내고 있다
④ 당신은 그가 정직한 사람이 되도록 격려하고 있다

해석 당신의 문에 누군가 노크를 한다. 당신 앞에는 도움이 필요한 한 젊은이가 서 있다. 그는 다쳤고 피를 흘리고 있다. 당신은 그를 데리고 들어와 도와주며, 그가 편안하고 안전하게 느끼도록 한 뒤, 전화를 걸어 응급차를 부른다. 이것은 분명 올바른 일이다. 하지만 Immanuel Kant에 따르면, 당신이 그저 그에게 동정심을 느껴서 그를 돕는 것이라면, 그것은 전혀 도덕적인 행동이 아닐 것이다. 당신의 동정심은 당신의 행위의 도덕성과는 무관하다. 그것은 당신의 성품의 일부일 뿐, 옳고 그름과는 무관하다. Kant에게 도덕성이란, 그저 무엇을 하는가가 아닌, 왜 그것을 하는가에 관한 것이다. 올바른 일을 하는 사람들은 단순히 자신이 느끼는 감정 때문에 올바른 일을 하는 것이 아니다. 그 결정은 이성에, 당신이 어떤 감정을 느끼게 되었든 관계없이 당신의 의무가 무엇인지를 알려주는 바로 그 이성에 근거해야 한다.

어휘

bleed 피를 흘리다
irrelevant 무관한
character 성품
sympathy 동정심
morality 도덕성
regardless of ~와 관계없이

10 ④

해설 빈칸이 포함된 문장에서, 세계에 대한 서로 다른 주장들이 결코 '진실 혹은 거짓'으로 나뉠 수 있는 것이 아니라고 설명하고 있고, 역접의 접속사 but 이후에 빈칸이 나오므로, 빈칸에 들어갈 말로 가장 적절한 것은 ④ '서로 다른 방식으로 한 상황을 나타내는 대안적인 은유'이다.

① 모든 상황에서 항상 옳은 것으로 입증되는
② 논쟁 불가능한 되돌릴 수 없는 확정된 진실들
③ 그 진정성과 명확성에 대한 과학적 검증들의 대상인

해석 언어는 "사건은 물체이고 시간은 공간이다."와 같은 함축적인 은유들로 가득 차 있다. 과연 공간은, 단지 시간에 대해서뿐 아니라 다양한 유형의 상태나 상황에 대한 개념상의 매개체임이 드러난다. 회의가 3시에서 4시로 이동될 수 있듯이, 신호등은 녹색에서 빨간색으로 바뀔 수 있고, 한 사람이 햄버거를 뒤집는 일에서 한 기업을 운영하는 일로 옮겨 갈 수 있고, 경제는 갈수록 더 악화되어 갈 수 있다. 은유는 언어에 너무 만연해서 추상적인 개념들에 대한 은유적이지 않은 표현을 찾기란 어렵다. 이는, 우리의 가장 희미한 개념들까지도 우리가 정신적 단계에서 이리저리 움직이는 물질 덩이로 마음속에 표상된다는 것을 의미하는 것일까? 이는, 세상에 대한 서로 다른 주장들이 결코 '진실 혹은 거짓'이 아니라 그저 서로 다른 방식으로 한 상황을 나타내는 대안적인 은유만이 될 수 있음을 말하는 것일까? 삶에서 변수와 그 안의 변화의 인과관계 면에서 특징지을 수 없는 것들은 거의 없다.

어휘

be saturated with ~로 가득 차다	implicit 함축적인
metaphor 은유	conceptual 개념상의
vehicle 매개체	

flipping burgers 햄버거 뒤집기, 발전 기회가 없는 일

wispy 희미한	hunk 큰 덩어리
in terms of ~면에서	variable 변수
irreversible 되돌릴 수 없는	established 확정된
authenticity 진정성	frame 표현하다

11 ②

해설 이 글은 단순히 문자를 소리 내서 읽게 하는 교육 방식은 학생들로 하여금 행간의 숨은 의미를 이해하고, 의미를 추론하며, 작가의 편향성을 탐지하는 방법을 가르치지 못한다고 설명하고 있다. 빈칸은 마지막 문장으로, 필자의 이러한 독서관을 압축적으로 표현하는 문장이 될 것이라 예측할 수 있다. 따라서, 빈칸에 들어갈 말로 가장 적절한 것은 ② '단순히 음소의 인지와 알파벳 인식을 터득하는 것보다 훨씬 더 복잡하다'이다.

① 음소와 알파벳에 대한 지식이 일반적인 독해 과정에 더해지기 때문에 기본적으로 해독이다
③ 혼자서 또는 교사와 함께할 때보다 동료와 함께할 때 더 능률적으로 학습될 수 있다
④ 학습자가 유창하게 단어를 소리 내서 말할 줄 알 때 숙달될 수 있다

해석 주로 음소 인지와 알파벳 원칙에 대한 지식으로 해석되는 해독에 관한 강조가, 학교로 하여금 학생이 해독의 기술을 터득하도록 도와주는, 일괄적으로 구성되거나 상업적으로 생산된 읽기 프로그램을 추구하도록 이끌어 왔다. 우리와 함께 일하는 교사들에 따르면, 주로 원고를 읽는 방식의 독서 교육 접근법은 단어를 소리 내어 읽을 줄 아는 많은 학생들을 만들어 냈으나, 이들에게 있어 읽기 과정은 거기가 끝이다. 그런 학생들은 해독하고 심지어 유창하게 말하는 독서가가 될 수는 있지만, 그들은 자료를 진실로 이해하지는 못한다. 무엇보다도 그들은 행간의 숨은 의미를 이해하지 못하고, 의미를 추론하지 못하고, 작가의 편향성을 알아채지 못한다. 독서는 단순히 음소의 인지와 알파벳 인식을 터득하는 것보다 훨씬 더 복잡하다.

어휘

decode 해독하다	phonemic 음소의
awareness 인지	scripted 원고를 읽는
comprehend 이해하다	material 자료

read between the lines 행간의 숨은 의미를 이해하다
bias 편향성

12 ①

해설 과학 기술의 발달로 개인적인 생활이 가능해졌지만, 우리의 개인 정보가 타인에게 노출될 수 있는 부작용 또한 있다는 내용이므로 빈칸에 들어갈 말로 가장 적절한 것은 ① '자유롭다는 것은 또한 벌거벗는 것을 흔히 의미한다'이다.

② 사람들과 협력하는 것은 잘못된 결론을 초래한다
③ 더 많은 사람들이 부유함의 확산에 무관심해진다
④ 기술은 우리를 자연 환경으로부터 독립하게 한다

해석 부유함의 확산, 1인 가구, 텔레비전과 컴퓨터의 발명은 우리가 이전 세대들에게는 상상할 수도 없던 개인적인 생활을 누리는 것을 가능하게 했다. 우리는 더 이상 이웃들과 가까운 지역에 살지 않는다. 우리는 버스나 기차에 몰려 타지 않고서도 여기저기 돌아다닐 수 있다. 그리고 우리는 극장에 가거나 이웃들과 취미를 함께 나눌 필요도 없다. 하지만, 우리를 많은 사람들로부터 떼어놓는 것에 일조하는 바로 그 과학 기술이 또한 우리의 행동을 감시하고 기록하는 것을 가능하게 한다. 비록 우리 삶을 잘 알고 있는 사람들이 점점 더 적어지지만, 대부분 우리에게 알려지지 않은 많은 사람들이 우리에 관한 무언가를 알고 있다. 우리를 대중 사회로부터 자유롭게 해줄 것이라고 생각되던 바로 그 과학 기술이 정보의 고속도로인 것만큼이나 유리 어항과 같다는 것이 입증되어 왔다. 현대 사회에서 자유롭다는 것은 또한 벌거벗는 것을 흔히 의미한다는 것을 우리는 알게 되었다.

어휘

prosperity 부유함	single-family home 1인 가정
unimaginable 상상할 수 없는	quarter 지역
move about 돌아다니다	separate 분리시키다

have intimate knowledge of ~을 잘 알고 있다

be supposed to ~하기로 되어 있다	turn out ~로 밝혀지다

fishbowl (유리)어항

Reading Skill 09 **연결사 추론** ACTUAL TEST

01	①	02	②	03	③	04	②	05	④
06	②								

01 ①

해설 친구를 자주 보면 만나는 시간이 줄어들고 자주 보지 않으면 만나는 시간이 늘어난다는 서술 이후 (A) 뒤에서 그에 대한 구체적인 예시가 제시되므로, (A)에 들어갈 연결사로 가장 적절한 것은 For example이다. 또한 연인 관계에서는 지속 시간과 빈도가 둘 다 매우 높다는 (B) 뒤의 내용은 지속 시간과 빈도가 역관계라는 앞의 내용과 반대되므로, (B)에 들어갈 연결사로 가장 적절한 것은 Conversely이다.

해석 지속 시간은 빈도와 역관계를 공유한다. 당신이 친구를 자주 만난다면, 만남의 지속 시간은 더 짧아질 것이다. 반대로 친구를 자주 보지 않으면, 만남의 지속 시간은 보통 상당히 늘어날 것이다. 예를 들어, 만약 당신이 친구를 매일 본다면, 당신은 사건이 전개되면서 일어나는 일을 알 수 있으므로 만남의 지속 시간이 짧을 수 있다. 하지만 만약 당신이 친구를 일 년에 두 번만 본다면, 만남의 지속 시간은 더 길어질 것이다. 오랫동안 보지 못한 친구와 식당에서 저녁을 먹었던 때를 돌이켜 봐라. 당신은 아마 서로의 삶을 알아내는 데 몇 시간을 보냈을 것이다. 만약 당신이 정기적으로 그 사람을 본다면 같은 저녁 식사 시간은 상당히 더 짧을 것이다. 반대로, 연인 관계에서는 커플들, 특히 새로 생긴 커플들이 서로 가능한 한 많은 시간을 보내고 싶어 하므로 빈도와 (만남의) 지속 시간이 매우 높다. 관계의 강도 또한 매우 높을 것이다.

어휘

duration 지속 (시간)	inverse 역의, 반비례의
frequency 빈도	significantly 상당히
keep up with ~을 알다	catch up on ~을 알아내다
minted 최근에 생겨난	intensity 강도

02 ②

해설 다양한 애도 문화에 관한 글이다. (A) 앞엔 Hopi족이 고인을 최대한 빨리 잊고 삶을 이어간다는 내용이 나오고, 뒤에서 Hopi족의 장례 의식은 인간과 영혼 간의 단절이라고 자세한 내용을 덧붙이고 있으므로, (A)에 들어갈 연결사로 적절한 것은 In fact 또는 Therefore이다. 또한 (B)의 앞뒤로 슬픔을 극대화하는 이집트와 최소화하는 발리가 대조되어 서술되므로, (B)에 들어갈 연결사로 가장 적절한 것은 By contrast이다. 따라서 (A), (B)에 들어갈 연결사로 가장 적절한 것은 ②이다.

해석 죽은 사람들과의 유대를 유지하는 것에 대한 믿음은 문화마다 다르다. 예를 들면, 일본의 종교의식에서는 고인과 유대를 유지하는 것이 수용되고 지속된다. 하지만 Arizona의 Hopi 인디언들 사이에서는 고인이 가능한 한 빨리 잊히고 삶은 평소와 같이 계속된다. 실제로, Hopi의 장례 의식은 인간과 영혼 사이의 단절로 끝난다. 애도의 다양성이 이집트와 발리, 두 이슬람교 사회에서보다 더 명확한 곳은 없다. 이집트의 이슬람교도 사이에서 유족들은 비슷하게 비극적인 이야기와 관련 있고 자신의 슬픔을 표현하는 다른 사람들에게 둘러싸여 그들의 슬픔을 길고 찬찬히 생각하도록 권해진다. 반대로, 발리에서는 이슬람교 유족들이 슬퍼하기보다는 웃고 기뻐하도록 권해진다.

어휘

ties 유대	deceased 사망한
ritual 의식	funeral 장례식(의)
break-off 단절	mortal 인간
grieve 슬퍼하다, 애도하다	bereaved 사별한, 유족이 된
dwell on ~을 곱씹다, 찬찬히 생각하다	account 이야기
sorrow 슬픔	

03 ③

해설 이 글은 부정적 사고를 권고하는 스토아학파의 견해를 말하고 있다. (A) 앞에서 최악의 상황을 가정할 때 미래에 대한 불안감이 줄어들고, (A) 뒤에서 현재 누리는 것들을 잃을 수도 있다고 가정할 때 감사함이 커진다는 부정적 사고의 긍정 효과들이 나열되고 있으므로, (A)에 들어갈 연결사로 적절한 것은 Furthermore 또는 Besides이다. 또한 (B) 뒤에서는 현재의 기쁨을 무시하고 미래에만 기대는 긍정적 사고의 단점이 언급되므로, (B) 앞의 내용들과는 대조됨을 알 수 있다. 따라서 (B)에 들어갈 연결사로 가장 적절한 것은 by contrast이다.

해석 고대 철학자들과 영적 스승들은 긍정과 부정, 낙관주의와 비관주의, 성공과 보장을 위한 노력과 실패와 불확실성에 대한 개방의 균형을 유지할 필요성을 이해했다. 스토아학파는 "악을 미리 생각하기" 즉 최악의 상황을 의도적으로 시각화하는 것을 권고했다. 이것은 미래에 대한 불안감을 줄이는 경향이 있다. 상황이 실제로 얼마나 나쁘게 돌아갈지 냉정하게 상상할 때, 당신은 대개 대처해낼 수 있을 것이라고 결론짓는다. 게다가, 그들은 당신이 현재 누리고 있는 관계와 소유물을 잃게 될 수도 있다고 상상하는 것이 지금 그것들을 가지고 있는 것에 대한 감사함을 증가시킨다고 언급했다. 이에 반하여, 긍정적인 생각은 항상 현재의 기쁨을 무시한 채 미래에 기댄다.

어휘

spiritual 영적인	optimism 낙관주의
pessimism 비관주의	strive 노력하다
Stoics 스토아학파	premeditation 미리 생각하기
deliberately 의도적으로	visualize 시각화하다
soberly 냉정하게	cope 대처하다
gratitude 감사	

04 ②

해설 이 글은 홈스쿨링을 찬성하는 입장과 반대하는 입장에 대해서 각각 설명하고 있다. (A) 앞에서는 홈스쿨링을 찬성하는 입장에 대한 이야기가 나오고 있고, (A) 뒤에서는 홈스쿨링을 반대하는 입장에 대한 이야기가 나오고 있으므로, (A)에 들어갈 연결사로 가장 적절한 것은 In contrast이다. (B) 앞에서는 홈스쿨링을 하는 학생들도 다른 학생들만큼 사회 정서 발달이 이루어진다는 연구 결과를 보여주면서 홈스쿨링을 찬성하는 입장에 대해서 말하고 있는데, (B) 뒤에서는 부모가 효과적으로 아이들을 가르칠 수 없다는 우려를 말하면서 홈스쿨링을 반대하는 입장에 대해서 말하고 있다. 따라서 (B)에 들어갈 연결사로 가장 적절한 것은 In spite of this이다.

해석 홈스쿨링을 지지하는 사람들은 아이들이 안전하고 사랑이 넘치는 환경에 있을 때 더 잘 배운다고 믿는다. 많은 심리학자들이 집을 가장 자연적인 학습 환경으로 보고 있으며, 원래 집은 학교가 설립되기 훨씬 전부터 교실이었다. 홈스쿨링을 하는 학부모들은 자녀의 교육을 감시할 수 있고 전통적인 학교 환경에서는 부족한 관심을 줄 수 있다고 주장한다. 학생들은 또한 무엇을 공부할지, 언제 공부할지 고르고 선택할 수 있기 때문에, 자신의 속도에 따라 배울 수 있다. 그에 반해서, 홈스쿨링을 비판하는 사람들은 교실에 없는 아이들은 또래와의 상호작용이 거의 없기 때문에 중요한 사회적 기술을 배우는 것을 놓친다고 말한다. 그러나 몇몇 연구들은 가정에서 교육 받는 아이들이, 그들의 복지에 신경을 쓰는 부모들의 지도와 함께 가정의 편안함과 안정감 속에서 더 많은 시간을 보내면서, 다른 학생들만큼 사회 정서적 발달에 있어서 잘하는 것처럼 보인다는 것을 보여주었다. 그럼에도 불구하고, 많은 홈스쿨링 비판자들은 그들의 아이들을 효과적으로 가르칠 수 있는 부모들의 능력에 대한 우려를 제기해왔다.

어휘

advocate 옹호자, 지지자	psychologist 심리학자
setting 환경	miss out on ~을 놓치다
peer 또래	welfare 복지

05 ④

해설 이 글은 가상현실 체험의 청각적 구성요소의 한계를 서술한다. (A) 뒤에는 시각적인 것과 청각적인 것이 확실하게 일치하지 않는 이상 가상 경험은 산산조각 난다는 내용이 담겨 있으므로 (A)에 들어갈 연결사로 가장 적절한 것은 Unless이다. (B) 뒤에는 오늘날의 오디오 장비의 음향 효과가 설득력 있는 소리 재현을 하지 못한다는 내용이 이어지므로, (B)에 들어갈 연결사로 가장 적절한 것은 Unfortunately이다.

해석 오늘날 VR(가상현실) 경험의 시각적 구성요소를 만드는 기술은 널리 접근 가능하고 저렴하게 전환되고 있다. 그러나 강력하게 작동하기 위해서는 가상현실은 시각적인 것 이상의 것이 필요하다. 당신이 듣고 있는 것이 확실하게 시각적인 것과 일치하지 않는다면, 가상 경험은 산산조각이 난다. 농구 경기를 예로 들어 보자. 만약 선수들, 코치들, 아나운서들, 그리고 관중들이 모두 코트에 앉아 있는 것처럼 들린다면, 여러분은 텔레비전으로 경기를 보는 것이 좋을 것이다. 여러분은 그것으로 충분히 여러분이 "거기"에 있다는 느낌을 받을 것이다. 불행하게도, 오늘날의 오디오 장비와 널리 사용되는 녹음 및 재생 형식은 단순히 먼 행성의 전쟁터 소리, 코트의 농구 경기, 또는 위대한 공연장의 첫 번째 줄에서 들려오는 교향곡 소리를 설득력 있게 재현하는 임무에 적합하지 않다.

어휘

component 요소	accessible 접근이 쉬운
affordable 저렴한, 입수 가능한	convincingly 납득이 가도록
equipment 장비	inadequate 불충분한
symphony 교향곡	

06 ②

해설 (A)가 있는 문장의 앞에서는 역사의 특정 시기에는 감정을 통제하는 능력을 갖추는 것을 당연시한다고 하였고, (A)가 있는 문장에서 이에 해당하는 구체적인 시대를 예시로 들고 있으므로, (A)에 들어갈 연결사로 가장 적절한 것은 for example이다. 한편 (B)를 포함하는 문장의 앞 문장에서는 감정 통제를 못하는 사람은 사회 구성원으로서의 권리가 박탈됐다고 한 반면, (B)가 있는 문장에서는 다른 시대의 경우 감정 통제 능력이 항상 존중받는 것은 아니라고 하였다. 따라서 (B)에 들어갈 연결사로 가장 적절한 것은 however이다.

해석 역사상 특정 시기에 사람이 생각과 느낌을 완벽히 제어하는 법을 배우지 못한다면 완전한 인간이 아니라는 것을 당연시하던 문화가 있었다. 예를 들어, 고대 스파르타 시대에서, 로마 공화정 시대에서, 빅토리아 시대의 영국 상류계층들 사이에서는 사람들이 자신의 감정을 통제할 책임이 있었다. 평정심을 너무나 쉽게 잃어버리는 사람은 누구든지 사회 구성원으로서 수용될 권한을 박탈당했다. 그러나, 지금 우리가 살고 있는 것과 같은 역사의 다른 시기에는, 자신을 통제할 수 있는 능력이 항상 높게 존중받는 것만은 아니다. 그러한 것을 시도하는 사람들은 종종 이상하게 생각된다.

어휘

take ~ for granted ~을 당연하게 생각하다

fully 충분히	upper 상류의
responsible 책임이 있는	temper 기분, 성질
deprive A of B A에게서 B를 빼앗다	community 공동체
historical 역사의	attempt 시도하다

Reading Skill 10 순서 배열 ACTUAL TEST

01	③	02	③	03	③	04	①	05	③
06	③	07	③	08	②	09	③	10	②

01 ③

해설 시각 장애인을 위한 Aira 서비스에 관한 글이다. 시각 장애인들에겐 일상적인 일들이 어렵다는 내용의 주어진 글 다음엔, 역접 접속사 But으로 시작하여 어려움이 있지만 누군가의 눈을 빌릴 수 있다는 대안을 언급하는 (B)가 오는 것이 자연스럽다. 그다음에는 그 대안을 That으로 받아 Aira의 기반이 되는 생각이라고 하며 그 서비스의 내용을 설명하는 (A)가 오고, 마지막으로 (A)에서 an on-demand agent로 언급된 Aira 에이전트의 업무 내용을 then을 사용해 추가로 설명하는 (C)가 와야 한다. 따라서 글의 순서로 가장 적절한 것은 ③ '(B) - (A) - (C)'이다.

해석 시각 장애인들에게 우편물을 분류하거나 한 무더기의 빨래를 하는 것과 같은 일상적인 일은 어려운 일이다. (B) 하지만 만약 그들이 볼 수 있는 누군가의 눈을 "빌릴" 수 있다면 어떨까? (A) 그것은 수천 명의 사용자들이 스마트폰이나 Aira의 전매특허 안경을 사용하여 그들 주변 환경의 실시간 영상을 맞춤형 에이전트(직원)에게 스트리밍할 수 있게 해주는 새로운 서비스인 Aira의 배경이 되는 생각이다. (C) 연중무휴로 이용할 수 있는 Aira 에이전트들은 그리고 질문에 답하거나, 사물을 설명하거나, 사용자에게 위치를 안내할 수 있다.

어휘

sort through ~을 분류하다	laundry 세탁물
on-demand 맞춤형의	agent 대리인, 직원
proprietary 전매특허의	

02 ③

해설 Lamarck의 획득 형질 유전설에 관한 내용이다. Lamarck가 유기체는 특정 신체 부위의 사용 및 미사용으로 특정 형질을 발달시킨다고 제안했다는 내용의 주어진 글 뒤엔, certain characteristics를 these characteristics로 받아 이것이 자손에게 전해진다는 Lamarck의 주장을 덧붙이는 (B)가 와야 한다. 그다음엔 For example로 시작하여 그 유전에 관한 자세한 예를 제시하는 (C)가 오고, 이후 캥거루의 강력한 뒷다리가 유전된 것이라는 (C)의 내용을 this로 받아 증거는 없지만 Lamarck의 가설에 중요한 의의가 있다고 마무리 짓는 (A)가 와야 한다. 따라서 글의 순서로 가장 적절한 것은 ③ '(B) - (C) - (A)'이다.

해석 오늘날, Lamarck는 적응이 어떻게 진화하는지에 대한 잘못된 설명으로 많은 부분에 있어 부당하게 기억된다. 그는 유기체가 특정 신체 부위를 사용하거나 사용하지 않음으로써 특정 형질을 발달시킨다고 제안했다. (B) Lamarck는 이러한 형질이 자손에게 전해질 것이라고 생각했다. Lamarck는 이 생각을 '획득 형질 유전'이라고 불렀다. (C) 예를 들어, Lamarck는 캥거루의 강력한 뒷다리가 조상들이 뛰면서 그들의 다리를 강화하고 그 획득한 다리 힘을 자손에게 전한 결과라고 설명할 수 있다. 그러나 획득 형질은 유전되기 위해선 특정 유전자의 DNA를 어떻게든 수정해야 할 것이다. (A) 이것이 일어난다는 증거는 없다. 그럼에도 불구하고, Lamarck가 유기체가 자신의 환경에 적응할 때 진화가 일어남을 제안한 것에 주목하는 것은 중요하다. 이 생각은 Darwin을 위한 장을 마련하는 데 도움이 되었다.

어휘

adaptation 적응	organism 유기체
characteristic 특질, 형질	note ~에 주목하다
pass on 물려주다	offspring 자식, 자손
inheritance 유전	acquired 획득한
hind 뒤의	ancestor 조상
modify 수정하다	

03 ③

해설 주어진 글은 인간의 언어가 원숭이와 유인원을 포함한 다른 동물들의 의사소통보다 훨씬 더 정교하다는 내용으로, 그다음에 인간과 가장 가까운 영장류조차 인간 언어를 제대로 습득할 수 없으며 그 복잡한 언어가 종 특이성이라는 내용의 (C)가 오는 것이 자연스럽다. 그 이후에는 역접 접속사 That said로 시작하여 그래도 자연에서 많은 종이 각자의 복잡한 의사소통 체계를 가진다고 설명하는 (A)가 오고, 마지막으로 (A)의 many species를 they로 받아 많은 종이 인위적인 상황에서는 훨씬 더 복잡한 체계를 배울 수 있다고 마무리하는 (B)가 와야 한다. 따라서 글의 순서로 가장 적절한 것은 ③ '(C) - (A) - (B)'이다.

해석 확실히, 인간의 언어는 원숭이와 유인원의 확연히 제한된 발성으로부터 두드러진다. 게다가, 그것은 어느 다른 형태의 동물 의사소통을 훨씬 능가하는 정도의 정교함을 보여준다. (C) 심지어 우리의 가장 가까운 영장류 사촌들조차 몇 년 동안 집중적인 훈련을 받은 후에도 기초 의사소통 체계 그 이상은 습득할 수 없는 것처럼 보인다. 언어라는 복잡성은 확실히 종의 고유 특성이다. (A) 그렇긴 해도, 많은 종들은 인간의 언어에는 크게 못 미치지만, 그럼에도 불구하고 자연환경에서 인상적으로 복잡한 의사소통 체계를 참으로 보여준다. (B) 그리고 그들은 인간과 함께 길러지는 경우와 같이, 인위적인 상황에서 훨씬 더 복잡한 체계들을 배울 수 있다.

어휘

stand out from ~에서 두드러지다	decidedly 확실히
restricted 제한된	vocalization 발성(법)
ape 유인원	sophistication 정교함
fall short of ~에 못 미치다	impressively 인상적으로
artificial 인위적인	alongside ~와 함께
primate 영장류	incapable of ~할 수 없는
rudimentary 기초의	intensive 집중적인
species-specific 종 특이(성)의	trait 특성

04 ①

해설 환경운동의 일환인 재생 에너지 지원 조직들에 관한 글이다. 기후 변화에 대한 우려가 커지면서 환경운동가들이 재생 에너지 지원 캠페인까지 조직하게 되었다는 주어진 글 이후엔, 그에 대한 구체적인 예시로 영국의 환경운동가들이 풍력발전소 소유자들로 구성된 the Westmill Wind Farm Co-operative를 결성했다는 내용의 (C)가 오는 것이 자연스럽다. 그다음에는 (C)의 마지막 문장에서 언급된 the Westmill Solar Co-operative를 This solar cooperative로 받아 이 태양광 협동조합이 의미하는 바를 설명하는 (A)가 오고, 마지막으로 Similarly로 이어서 미국에서도 재생 에너지를 지지하는 Clean Energy Collective가 설립되었다는 내용의 (B)가 와야 한다. 따라서 글의 순서로 가장 적절한 것은 ① '(C) - (A) - (B)'이다.

해석 지구 기후 변화에 대한 우려가 커지면서 운동가들은 화석 연료 추출 소비 반대 캠페인뿐만 아니라 재생 에너지 지원 캠페인까지 조직하게 되었다. (C) 영국 정부가 재생 에너지 산업의 성장을 빠르게 가속화하지 못한 것에 실망한 환경운동가들은 Westmill Wind Farm Co-operative를 결성했는데, 이는 2,500가구가 사용하는 정도의 전기를 1년간 생산하는 것으로 추산되는 육상 풍력발전소를 소유한 2,000명 이상의 회원을 거느린 지역사회 소유 단체이다. Westmill Wind Farm Co-operative는 지역 시민들에게 Westmill Solar Co-operative를 결성하도록 격려했다. (A) 이 태양광 협동조합은 1,400가구에 전력을 공급하기 충분한 에너지를 생산하여 국내 최초의 대규모 태양광 발전소 협동조합이 되었으며, 회원들의 말에 따르면 태양광 발전이 "일반인들이 자신의 옥상에서뿐만 아니라 유틸리티 규모로도 청정 전력을 생산할 수 있는 지속 가능하고 '민주적인' 에너지 공급의 새로운 시대"를 나타낸다는 것을 눈에 띄게 상기시켜준다. (B) 마찬가지로, 미국의 재생 에너지 지지자들은 Clean Energy Collective를 설립했는데, 이는 "참여형 유틸리티 고객들이 공동으로 소유하는 중규모 시설을 통해 청정 전력 발전을 제공하는 모델"을 개척한 회사이다.

어휘

fossil fuel 화석 연료	extraction 추출
era 시대	democratic 민주적인
enthusiast 열렬한 지지자	pioneer 개척하다
onshore 육지의	inspire 고무하다

05 ③

해설 주어진 글은 과거 연구에 따르면 빈번한 심리적 스트레스를 경험하는 것이 심혈관 질환의 중요한 위험 요소가 될 수 있다는 사실을 보여주고 있다. 그러한 심리적 스트레스에 대한 구체적인 예가 (C)에서 운전(driving)으로 나오고 있다. 그 후 (A)에서 운전하는 사람들에 대한 이야기로 이어지고, 운전의 스트레스를 줄일 방법에 있는가에 대한 질문의 답으로 (B)에서 있다고(there is) 연결되는 것이 자연스럽다. 따라서 글의 순서로 가장 적절한 것은 ③ '(C) - (A) - (B)'이다.

해석 과거의 연구는 빈번한 심리적 스트레스를 경험하는 것이 심혈관 질환의 중요한 위험 요인이 될 수 있다는 것을 보여주었는데, 이것은 미국의 20세 이상 사람들 중 거의 절반에 영향을 미치는 질환이다. (C) 잦은 스트레스의 한 가지 요인은 운전인데, 이는 교통체증과 관련된 스트레스 요인이나 미숙한 운전자들에게 흔히 동반되는 불안감 때문이다. (A) 하지만 이것은 매일 운전하는 사람들이 심장 질환에 걸릴 것을 의미하는 것인가, 아니면 운전의 스트레스를 완화시킬 수 있는 간단한 방법이 있는가? (B) 새로운 연구에 따르면, 있다. 연구원들은 운전하면서 음악을 듣는 것이 심장 건강에 영향을 미치는 스트레스를 해소하는 데 도움이 된다고 언급했다.

어휘

cardiovascular 심혈관의	stressor 스트레스 요인
accompany 동반하다	ease 완화시키다

06 ③

해설 주어진 글에서 산업화 이전에는 시간을 알기 위해 태양이나 달을 사용했다고 나오는데, 이러한 자연적 방법과 반대되는 개념으로 (B)에서 기계식 시계의 등장과 연결되는 것이 자연스럽다. 그 후 (C)에서 나오는 These clocks가 (B)에 나오는 기계식 시계를 받아 연결시키는 것이 자연스럽다. (C)의 마지막에 시계를 반복적으로 재설정해야 한다는 말과, 약 70개의 다른 시간대가 있었다는 내용이 (A)에서 시간 기준이 없다는 내용과 이어지는 것이 자연스럽다. 따라서 글의 순서로 가장 적절한 것은 ③ '(B) - (C) - (A)'이다.

해석 요즘에는 시계가 우리의 삶을 너무나 지배하고 있어서 시계가 없는 삶은 상상하기 어렵다. 산업화 이전에 대부분의 사회는 시간을 알기 위해 태양이나 달을 사용했다. (B) 기계식 시계가 처음 등장했을 때, 그것들은 즉시 인기가 있었다. 벽에 거는 시계나 손목에 차는 시계를 가지는 것이 유행이었다. 사람들은 시간을 알려주는 이 새로운 방법을 언급하기 위해 "of the clock" 또는 "o'clock"이라는 표현을 발명했다. (C) 이 시계들은 매력적이었지만 항상 유용한 것은 아니었다. 마을과 지방, 심지어 이웃 마을까지도 시간을 알 수 있는 방법이 달랐기 때문이었다. 여행자들은 한 장소에서 다른 장소로 이동할 때 시계를 반복적으로 재설정해야 했다. 미국에서는 1860년대에 약 70개의 다른 시간대가 있었다. (A) 커져가는 철도망에 있어, 시간 기준이 없다는 사실이 재앙이었다. 종종, 몇 마일 떨어져 있는 역들은 다른 시간에 시계를 맞추었다. 여행자들에게는 많은 혼란이 있었다.

어휘

industrialization 산업화
tell the time 시간을 보다, 알다
repeatedly 반복적으로
disaster 재앙
confusion 혼란

07 ③

해설 주어진 문장은 biofeedback(생체 자기 제어)이라는 개념을 소개하고 있다. (A), (B), (C)는 각각 이 biofeedback이 어떻게 작동하는지에 대해 설명한다. (B)의 마지막 부분에 나온 'such variables as ~'를 (A)에서 'such a variable'로 받고 있으므로 (A)는 (B) 다음에 등장해야 한다. 또한 (C)에 나오는 'the displays'는 (A)에서 언급한 'visual or audible displays'를 가리키므로, 글의 순서로 가장 적절한 것은 ③ '(B) - (A) - (C)'이다.

해석 자율적이거나 불수의적인 신체 기능들의 전자적 측정을 관찰함으로써 그 기능들에 대하여 개인이 어느 정도 수의적인 통제를 얻을 수 있도록 해주는 기술은 생체 자기 제어라고 알려져 있다. (B) 전자 센서가 심박수, 혈압, 그리고 피부 온도와 같은 변수들을 측정하기 위하여 몸 곳곳에 부착된다. (A) 그러한 변수가 원하는 방향대로 움직일 때 (예를 들어, 혈압 저하) 그것은 시각적 혹은 청각적 표현을, 즉 텔레비전 세트, 측정기, 조명과 같은 장치에 반응을 발생시킨다. (C) 생체 자기 제어 훈련은 그 표현을 발생시킨 생각의 패턴이나 행동을 재형성해서 원하는 반응을 만들어내도록 가르친다.

어휘

voluntary 수의적인(몸을 마음대로 움직일 수 있는), 자발적인
autonomic 자율적인
involuntary 불수의적인
trigger 유발하다
display 표현, 표시

08 ②

해설 Moreno의 사이코드라마(심리극)에 관한 글이다. 주어진 글의 마지막 문장에서 사이코드라마가 프로이트의 세계관에 상반되는 전제로 출발했다고 하였으므로, 주어진 글 다음에는 이러한 내용을 'his theoretical difference from the mainstream viewpoint'로 받은 (B)가 와야 한다. 창조적 생활이 인간의 건강과 직결된다는 (B)의 마지막 문장 다음에는 이러한 창의성은 사회적 상호작용을 통해 발생한다는 (A)가 와야 하고, (A)의 마지막 부분에 언급된 연극적 기법을 부연하는 (C)가 마지막에 위치해야 한다. 따라서 글의 순서로 가장 적절한 것은 ② '(B) - (A) - (C)'이다.

해석 가장 획기적인 집단치료 접근법은 Jacob L. Moreno의 독자적 아이디어인 심리극(사이코드라마)이었다. 집단치료요법으로서의 사이코드라마는 정신적 질병은 본질적으로 정신 또는 마음 내에서 발생한다는 프로이트의 세계관에 꽤 상반되는 전제조건으로 시작되었다. (B) 주류 관점과는 다른 그의 이론적 차이에도 불구하고, 20세기에 심리학적 의식을 형성하는 데 있어 Moreno의 영향력은 상당했다. 그는 인간의 본질은 창조하는 것이며, 창조적인 생활이 곧 인간의 건강과 복지의 핵심이라고 믿었다. (A) 그러나 그는 또한 창조성이란 좀처럼 혼자 행하는 과정이 아니며 사회적인 상호작용을 통해 발생하는 것이라고 믿었다. 그는 창조성과 일반적인 사회적 신뢰를 증대시키는 수단으로 역할극과 즉흥극을 포함한 연극적 기법에 상당히 의존했다. (C) 그의 가장 중요한 연극적 도구는 그가 역할 바꾸기라고 불렀던 것인데, 참가자들에게 다른 사람의 모습을 하도록 요구하는 것이었다. '마치' 한 사람이 다른 사람의 입장이 된 것처럼 하는 행동은 공감적인 자극을 이끌어내는 데 도움을 주고 그것을 더 높은 수준의 표현으로 발전시키기 위해 고안되었다.

어휘

group therapy 집단치료
psychodrama 사이코드라마(심리극)
brainchild 아이디어
premise 전제
alien 이질적인
psyche 정신
solitary 혼자 하는
theatrical 연극의
improvisation 즉흥극
theoretical 이론의
mainstream 주류의
psychological 심리학적인, 정신의
consciousness 의식
persona 모습
empathic 감정 이입의
impulse 자극

09 ③

해설 제시문은 동물들이 의식을 갖고 있는지에 대한 질문을 제기한다. (B)의 경우, 동물들이 제한적인 형태의 의식을 가지고 있을 것이라는 과학자들의 견해를 제시하며, 주어진 글의 마지막 부분에 언급된 질문, "Do animals have consciousness?"에 대한 답을 제시하고 있다. (B)의 마지막 문장에서는, 동물들에게 언어가 없다는 사실을 지적하고 있는데, 이는 동물들이 자신의 꿈을 (말로) 전하지 못한다는 내용인 (C)의 첫 문장과 연결된다. 그리고 (C)의 마지막 문장에는 지각, 기억, 감정의 세 가지 요소가 언급되고 있는데, 이는 (A)의 'These are three of the key aspects'이라는 Signal로 연결된다. 따라서 글의 순서로 가장 적절한 것은 ③ '(B) - (C) - (A)'이다.

해석 모든 동물들은 인간과 동일한 방식으로 수면 중에 뇌가 활성화된다. 그들이 꿈을 꾸는지의 여부는 다른 문제인데, 이는 다른 질문, 즉 '동물은 의식을 가지고 있는가?'라는 질문을 제기해야만 해결될 수 있다. (B) 오늘날 많은 과학자들이, 동물에게는 아마도, 언어와 명제적, 혹은 상징적인 사고가 없다는 측면에서 우리의 의식과는 꽤나 다른, 제한된 형태의 의식이 있을 것이라고 생각한다. (C) 동물은 분명, 꿈을 꾸더라도 그 꿈을 전하지는 못한다. 하지만 그 어느 애완동물 주인이, 자신이 가장 좋아하는 동물 친구에게 지각력과 기억력, 감정이 있다는 것을 의심하겠는가? (A) 이는 의식의 3가지 주요 측면이고, 그것은 동물이 우리처럼 음성 언어를 가지고 있든 없든 간에 경험될 수 있다. 자는 동안 동물의 뇌가 활성화될 때, 그 동물도 모종의 지각적, 감정적, 그리고 기억과 관련된 경험을 하고 있다고 가정하면 어떨까?

어휘

activation 활성화
consciousness 의식
verbal 언어의
capacity 능력
symbolic 상징의
pose (문제를) 제기하다
aspect 측면
perceptual 지각의
propositional 명제의

10 ②

해설 주어진 글에서 글의 소재가 뇌우의 발생임을 알 수 있다. This라는 Signal이 있는 (A)를 먼저 살펴보면, This more buoyant air가 가리키는 내용을 주어진 글에서는 찾을 수 없으므로 맨 처음에 올 수 없다. 한편 (B)는 주어진 글에서 언급된 '상승기류'에 대한 설명을 이어가고 있으므로 가장 먼저 와야 한다. 앞에서 살펴보았던 (A)의 This more buoyant air는 (B)의 마지막 문장의 내용과 이어지므로 (B) 다음에 와야 한다. (A)의 마지막 문장에 언급된 the draft에 대한 내용이 (C)의 첫 문장에서 이어지고 있으므로 (C)가 마지막에 위치해야 한다. 따라서 글의 순서로 가장 적절한 것은 ② '(B) - (A) - (C)'이다.

해석 뇌우는 세계의 많은 지역들, 예를 들어, 북미 대부분에 걸쳐 대단히 흔하다. 따뜻한 공기의 상승기류가 이런 폭풍을 발생시킨다. (B) 상승기류는 그 지역을 둘러싸고 있는 육지보다 태양에 의해 더욱 집중적으로 데워진 지면 위에서 시작할 수 있다. 예를 들어 황량하고, 바위가 많고, 또는 포장된 (도로의) 지역들은 보통 그 위에 상승기류가 있다. 지면과 접촉한 공기는 뜨거워지고 따라서 그것을 둘러싸고 있는 공기보다 더 가볍고, 더 부유하기 쉬워진다. (A) 이러한 더 부유하기 쉬운 공기는 그 후 상승해 수증기를 더 높은 고도로 실어 나른다. 공기는 그것이 상승함에 따라 식고, 수증기는 응결되어 비로 떨어지기 시작한다. 비가 내림에 따라, 그것은 그 주변의 공기를 끌어당기고 그 바람의 일부를 아래쪽으로 돌려놓는다. (C) 그 바람은 다시 위로 방향을 틀어 이리저리 휘돌고 있는 비를 구름 안으로 보낼 수 있다. 그것의 일부는 얼어서 우박이 될 수 있다. 이내, 작은 물방울들은 그 상승기류에 저항할 정도로 충분히 무겁게 성장하고 그것들과 함께 하강기류의 형태로 공기를 끌어당기면서 지면으로 떨어진다.

어휘

updraft 상승기류
buoyant 부유하는
condense 응결되다
in contact with ~와 접촉하는
hail 우박(이 쏟아지다)
downdraft 하강기류
set off 발생시키다
water vapor 수증기
paved (도로가) 포장된
churn 마구 휘돌다
droplet 작은 방울

Reading Skill 11 **문장 삽입** ACTUAL TEST

01	③	02	④	03	④	04	②	05	④
06	④	07	③	08	②				

01 ③

해설 주어진 문장은 심장을 펌프에 빗대는 것이 '진정한' 비유라는 내용으로, 그 이전에는 진정하지 않은 비유가 제시되었을 것을 유추할 수 있다. ③ 앞에는 장미와 카네이션이 같은 속이기에 비유할 만하지 않다는 내용이 나오고, 뒤부터 These는 본질적으로 서로 다른 존재지만 중요한 특성을 공유한다는 내용이 나오므로, These가 주어진 문장의 심장과 펌프임을 알 수 있다. 또한 ③ 뒤 문장에서 언급되는 특성들은 전부 심장과 펌프에 해당하는 내용이므로, 주어진 문장이 들어갈 위치로 가장 적절한 곳은 ③이다.

해석 비유는 두 가지가 매우 근본적인 많은 면에서 비슷하다고 주장되는 수사적 표현이다. 그것들의 구조, 그것들의 부분의 관계, 또는 그것들이 기여하는 본질적인 목적은 유사하지만, 그 두 가지는 또한 크게 다르기도 하다. 장미와 카네이션은 비유할 만하지 않다. 그것들은 둘 다 줄기와 잎을 가지고 있으며 둘 다 빨간색일 수 있다. 그러나 그것들은 같은 속이기 때문에, 같은 방식으로 이러한 특성들을 드러낸다. 하지만 심장을 펌프에 빗대는 것은 진정한 비유이다. 이것들은 본질적으로 서로 다른 것들이지만, 그것들은 기계적인 장치(기관), 밸브(판막)의 보유, 압력을 증가시키고 감소시키는 능력, 유체를 이동시킬 수 있는 능력 등 중요한 특성들을 공유한다. 그리고 심장과 펌프는 다른 방식으로 다른 맥락에서 이러한 특성들을 드러낸다.

어휘

genuine 진짜의
figure of speech 수사적 표현
fundamental 근본적인
genus 속(屬)
apparatus 장치, 기관
fluid 유체
analogy 비유
assert 주장하다
stem 줄기
disparate 본질적으로 다른
valve 밸브, 판막

02 ④

해설 중력의 세 가지 유형에 관한 글로, Thus로 시작하는 주어진 문장은 심장이 피와 산소를 뇌로 순환시키기 더 쉽다는 내용이다. 지속적인 중력은 피가 다리로 몰려 신체에 치명적이지만, 신체를 수평으로 하면 피가 등에 고여서 괜찮다는 내용 뒤에 혈액 순환이 더 쉽다는 내용이 오는 것이 자연스러우므로, 주어진 문장이 들어갈 위치로 가장 적절한 곳은 ④이다.

해석 사람들은 다양한 방식으로 중력(g-force)에 노출될 수 있다. 그것은 등이 두드려지는 것처럼 신체의 한 부위에만 영향을 미치면서 국부적일 수 있다. 그것은 또한 자동차 충돌 사고 시 겪는 강한 힘처럼 순간적일 수 있다. 중력의 세 번째 유형은 계속되거나 최소 몇 초 동안 지속된다. 지속적이고 전신에 걸친 중력이 사람들에게 가장 위험하다. 신체는 보통 국부적이거나 순간적인 중력을 지속적인 중력보다 더 잘 견뎌내는데, 지속적인 중력은 피가 다리로 몰려 신체 나머지에서 산소를 빼앗기 때문에 치명적일 수 있다. 앉거나 서 있는 대신 신체를 수평으로 하거나 누워있는 동안 가해지는 지속적인 중력은 피가 다리가 아닌 등에 모이기 때문에 사람들에게 더 괜찮은 경향이 있다. 그리하여 피, 그리고 생명을 주는 산소는 심장이 뇌로 순환시키기에 더 쉽다. 우주 비행사와 전투기 조종사와 같은 몇몇 사람들은 중력에 대한 신체 저항을 증가시키기 위해 특수 훈련 연습을 받는다.

어휘

circulate 순환시키다 gravitational 중력의
localized 국부[국지]적인 portion 부분
slap 철썩 때리다 momentary 순간적인
crash 충돌 사고 withstand 견디다
deprive 빼앗다 horizontal 수평의
tolerable 견딜 만한, 괜찮은 편인 pool 고이다
astronaut 우주 비행사 undergo 겪다, 받다

03 ④

해설 이 글은 기록 보관소의 경이로움과 방대함을 도서관과의 대조를 통해 설명하고 있다. 주어진 문장은 뉴저지의 주 기록 보관소를 예로 들어 그곳에 엄청난 양의 문서와 마이크로필름이 보관되어 있다는 내용으로, ④ 앞 문장의 많은 주 및 지역 기록 보관소들에 경이롭고 다양한 공공 기록물들이 있다는 내용의 사례로 연결되는 것이 자연스럽다. 따라서 주어진 문장이 들어갈 위치로 가장 적절한 것은 ④이다.

해석 기록 보관소는 오디오에서 비디오, 신문, 잡지 및 인쇄물에 이르기까지 자료의 보고이며, 이로 인해 어느 역사 탐정 조사에든 필수적이다. 도서관과 기록 보관소가 똑같아 보일 수도 있지만, 차이점은 중요하다. 기록 보관소의 소장품들이 거의 항상 1차 자료로 구성되는 반면, 도서관은 2차 자료로 구성된다. 한국 전쟁에 대해 더 알기 위해, 당신은 역사책을 찾아 도서관에 갈 것이다. 만약 당신이 정부 문서나 한국 전쟁 병사들이 쓴 편지를 읽고자 한다면, 당신은 기록 보관소에 갈 것이다. 만약 당신이 정보를 찾고 있다면, 아마 당신을 위한 기록 보관소가 있을 것이다. 많은 주 및 지역 기록 보관소들이 경이롭고 다양한 자료인 공공 기록물들을 보관한다. 예를 들어, 뉴저지의 주 기록 보관소는 30,000입방피트 이상의 문서와 25,000릴 이상의 마이크로필름을 보유하고 있다. 당신의 주 기록 보관소에 대한 온라인 검색은 그곳에 입법부 회의록보다 훨씬 더 많은 것이 있다는 것을 빠르게 보여줄 텐데, 찾아볼 수 있는 상세한 정부 공여 토지의 정보, 구시가지 지도, 범죄 기록 및 행상 면허 신청서와 같은 특이 사항들이 있다.

어휘

archive 기록 보관소 reel 릴(영화용 필름 길이의 단위)
indispensable 필수적인 be made up of ~로 구성되다
the minutes 회의록 legislature 입법부
oddity 특이한[이상한] 것[사람] peddler 행상인

04 ②

해설 주어진 문장은 일이 재정적 보장 이상을 제공한다는 내용이다. ② 앞에서 재정적 보장을 의미하는 급여에 관한 내용이 나오고, ② 뒤에서 자신감을 준다는 내용이 나오는데, 바로 이 자신감이 주어진 문장의 재정적 보장 이상을 의미한다. 따라서 주어진 문장이 들어갈 위치로 가장 적절한 것은 ②이다.

해석 왜 일 중독자들은 그들의 일을 그렇게나 즐기는가? 주로 일하는 것이 몇 가지 중요한 이점들을 제공하기 때문이다. 그것은 사람들에게 생계를 유지하는 방법인 급여를 준다. 그리고 일하는 것은 재정적 보장 이상을 제공한다. 그것은 사람들에게 자신감을 준다. 그들이 힘든 작업물을 만들어내고 "내가 만든 거야"라고 말할 수 있을 때, 그들은 만족감을 느낀다. 심리학자들은 일이 또한 사람들에게 정체성을 준다고 주장한다. 그들은 자의식과 개성을 느낄 수 있도록 일한다. 게다가, 대부분의 직업은 사람들에게 사회적으로 용인되는 다른 사람들을 만나는 방법을 제공한다. 일하는 것은 긍정적인 중독이라고 말할 수 있다. 아마도 일 중독자들은 그들의 일에 대해 강박적일 수 있지만, 그들의 중독은 안전한, 심지어는 이로운 것으로 보인다.

어휘

paycheck 급여 challenging 힘든
individualism 개성 addiction 중독
compulsive 강박적인

05 ④

해설 이 글은 프랑스의 한 화학자가 안전유리를 만든 과정에 대해서 설명하고 있다. 주어진 글에 나온 then은 ④ 앞에 나온 several weeks later를 말하고, 특별한 코팅이 씌워질지도 모른다는 상상 이후에, ④ 뒤에 나온 얼마 지나지 않아 세계 최초의 안전유리를 제작하는 데 성공했다는 내용이 이어지는 것이 자연스럽다. 따라서 주어진 문장이 들어갈 위치로 가장 적절한 것은 ④이다.

해석 1903년 프랑스의 화학자 Edouard Benedictus는 어느 날 단단한 바닥에 유리 플라스크를 떨어뜨려 깨뜨렸다. 그러나, 그 화학자에게 놀라움을 안기며, 플라스크는 산산조각이 나지 않고, 여전히 원래의 모양 대부분을 유지하고 있었다. 그가 플라스크를 검사했을 때 플라스크 안에 필름 코팅이 들어 있는 것을 발견했는데, 플라스크가 함유하고 있던 콜로디온 용액에서 잔여물이 남아 있었다. 그는 이런 특이한 현상을 메모했지만, 몇 주 후에 자동차 사고에서 앞 유리창이 날아와 심하게 다친 사람들에 대한 이야기를 신문에서 읽고 나서야 그것에 대해 더 생각을 했다. 그가 유리 플라스크에 대한 자신의 경험을 떠올린 것이 그때였고, 재빨리, 앞 유리창이 깨지지 않도록 특별한 코팅이 씌워질지도 모른다는 상상을 했다. 그 후 얼마 지나지 않아 그는 세계 최초의 안전유리를 제작하는 데 성공했다.

어휘

astonishment 깜짝 놀람 shatter 산산조각 나다
retain 유지하다, 보유하다 residue 잔여물
windshield 전면유리 apply 바르다, 도포하다

06 ④

해설 주어진 문장에 나온 But을 통해, 바로 앞에 나온 내용과 반대되는 내용이 와야 함을 알 수 있다. ④ 앞에 나온 1965년에서 1980년에 태어난 X세대의 순자산이 높다는 내용과, 주어진 문장의 1981년과 1996년 사이에 태어난 밀레니엄 세대가 저축을 더 하고 있다는 내용이 오는 것이 자연스럽다. 게다가, ④ 뒤에 나온 that은 주어진 문장의 내용을 받아 추측하는 것보다 그들의 재정 상태가 더 낫다는 내용으로 자연스럽게 이어진다. 따라서 주어진 문장이 들어갈 위치로 가장 적절한 것은 ④이다.

해석 밀레니엄 세대는 현대에 가장 가난하고 경제적으로 부담이 가장 큰 세대라는 꼬리표가 붙는 경우가 많다. 그들 중 많은 수가 대학을 졸업하고, 미국이 봐왔던 최악의 노동 시장 중 하나로 들어가는데, 그것도 엄청난 양의 학자금 대출을 가지고 말이다. 놀랄 것도 없이, 밀레니엄 세대는 X세대가 비슷한 삶의 단계에서 누렸던 것보다 적은 부를 축적해 왔는데, 그 이유는 주로 그들 중 소수만이 집을 소유하기 때문이다. 그러나 다른 세대의 미국인들이 저축하는 것에 대한 현재까지 가장 상세한 상황을 제공하는 새로이 사용 가능한 데이터는 그러한 평가를 복잡하게 만든다. 그렇다, 1965년에서 1980년 사이에 태어난 X세대는 순자산이 더 높다. 그러나 1981년과 1996년 사이에 태어난 밀레니엄 세대는 같은 나이대인 22~37세의 X세대에 비해 은퇴를 위해 더 적극적으로 저축하고 있다는 명백한 증거도 있다. 그리고 그것은 많은 사람들이 추측하는 것보다 그들을 더 나은 재정적 상태에 놓을 수도 있다.

어휘

burden 부담을 지우다, 부담
staggering (대단히) 충격적인, 믿기 어려운
to boot 게다가, 더구나 accumulate 축적하다
primarily 주로 to date 지금까지
assessment 평가 net worth 순자산

07 ③

해설 주어진 문장은 야구선수에게 물리학 필기시험을 보게 한다면 점수를 잘 받지 못할 것이라는 내용이다. 따라서 물리학적 지식을 실제로는 잘 알고 있다는 내용 다음에 들어가야 문맥상 적절하다. ③ 뒤부터 필기시험은 이론을 이해했는지 평가하기에 적절하지만 선수들에게는 현장 시험이 공정하고 정확할 것이라는 내용이 나오므로, ③을 기점으로 내용이 전환됨을 알 수 있다. 따라서 주어진 문장이 들어갈 위치로 가장 적절한 것은 ③이다.

해석 매체의 차이에 대한 우리의 이해는 측정되고 있는 기술이나 지식의 유형과 그것들이 평가되고 있는 매체 사이의 상호 관계를 분명하게 한다. 예를 들어, 야구장에서 Chicago Cubs 선수들에게 실기 시험이 주어질 때 그들이 물리학 지식에 대해 보여주는 것을 생각해보자. 공이 땅으로 떨어지는 정확한 장소에서 야구공을 잡을 수 있는 그들의 능력은 그들이 속도와 궤도 등에 대해 이해하고 있음을 분명히 보여준다. 그러나 야구선수에게 물리학 원리에 대해 필기시험을 보게 한다면 아마도 점수를 그만큼 잘 받지 못할 것이다. 물리학 이론을 얼마나 제대로 이해하고 있는지를 평가하기에 필기시험은 아주 적합하다. 하지만 Chicago Cubs의 현장 지식에 대해서는 실전 시험이 그들의 이해도를 평가하는데 훨씬 더 공정하고 정확한 척도일 것이다.

어휘

medium (*pl.* media) 매체, 수단	shed light on 분명하게 하다
interrelation 상호관계	assess 평가하다
demonstrate 증명하다	physics 물리학
precise 정확한	velocity 속도
trajectory 궤도	comprehend 이해하다
hands-on 직접 해보는	accurate 정확한

08 ②

해설 주어진 문장은 번역가나 통역가가 돈이나 지속적인 고용보다 직업적 자부심과 같은 가치를 더 중요하게 여긴다는 내용이다. 따라서 주어진 문장 앞에는 돈이나 지속적인 고용을 강조하는 내용이 전개되어야 하고, 주어진 문장의 뒷부분에는 그 외의 다른 가치들을 더욱 중요하게 고려한다는 내용이 전개되어야 한다. 그러므로 주어진 문장이 들어갈 위치로 가장 적절한 것은 ②이다.

해석 사용자가 번역을, 번역가 그리고 전반적인 번역 과정뿐만 아니라 번역된 문장까지 신뢰할 수 있게 하는 것은 중요하다. 이것은 돈을 지불하는 사람에게 중요한 것이기 때문에, 번역가에게도 중요할 수밖에 없다. (기업에 고용된 경우) 직업을 유지하거나 (프리랜서의 경우) 계속 일거리를 받아야 한다는 실용적인 생각이, 고용주나 고객의 요구를 기꺼이 충족시키도록 할 것이다. 그러나 번역가나 통역가의 경우, 돈이나 지속적인 고용가능성보다 더욱 고려하는 것은 직업에 대한 자부심, 직업적 진실성, 직업적 자기만족이다. 그들 모두 자기가 하는 일이 중요하고, 그들이 잘 하고 있다고 여기고 싶어하고, 사람들이 그들이 하는 일의 가치를 알아주기를 바란다. 사실, 대부분의 사람들은 옳지 않다고 생각하는 일을 하며 부자가 되기보다는 급료가 적더라도 직업적 자부심이 높은 일을 하고 싶어 한다. 번역가들이 일반적으로 직업적 자부심을 가지는 부분은 신뢰도, 직업에의 몰두, 그리고 윤리이다.

어휘

interpreter 통역가	employability 고용가능성
integrity 진실성	significant 중요한
rely on ~에 의존하다	pragmatic 실용적인
consideration 고려사항	mandate 지시하다; 명령
willingness 기꺼이 하는 마음	typically 전형적으로
reliability 신뢰성	ethics 윤리

Reading Skill 12 문단의 일관성 ACTUAL TEST

01	③	02	③	03	④	04	②	05	④
06	③								

01 ③

해설 이 글은 좋은 논쟁의 기술이 인생에서 매우 중요하다는 것을 설명한다. 아이들의 창의력을 키우기 위해선 그들을 갈등에 노출해야 한다는 내용이므로, 그와 반대인 평화로운 환경의 노출이 중요하다는 내용의 ③이 글의 흐름상 가장 어색한 문장이다.

해석 좋은 논쟁을 하는 기술은 인생에서 매우 중요하다. 하지만 이것은 몇 안 되는 부모들만이 아이들에게 가르치는 것이다. 우리는 아이들에게 안정적인 가정을 주고 싶어서 형제자매들이 싸우는 것을 막고 우리 자신의 논쟁을 비밀리에 한다. 하지만 만약 아이들이 의견 충돌에 노출되지 않는다면, 우리는 결국 그들의 창의력을 제한할 수도 있다. (아이들은 평화로운 환경에서 많은 칭찬과 격려와 함께 자유롭게 브레인스토밍을 할 때 가장 창의적이다.) 창의력이 뛰어난 사람들은 긴장감이 넘치는 가정에서 자라는 경우가 많은 것으로 드러났다. 그들은 주먹다짐이나 인신공격에 둘러싸여 있는 것이 아니라, 진정한 의견 충돌에 둘러싸여 있는 것이다. 30대 초반의 어른들에게 상상력이 풍부한 이야기를 쓰라고 했을 때, 가장 창의적인 이야기는 25년 전에 부모가 가장 많은 갈등을 겪었던 사람들에게서 나왔다.

어휘

critical 매우 중요한	stable 안정적인
sibling 형제자매	quarrel 다투다
behind closed doors 비밀리에	praise 칭찬
fistfight 주먹다짐	insult 모욕
conflict 갈등	

02 ③

해설 수리권 시장의 현황과 발전 가능성에 관한 글로, 인구 증가와 기후 변화로 인해 물이 현재 새로운 금이나 다름없고 앞으로 더욱더 그러할 것이라고 기술된다. 따라서 증류수 음용이 모두에게 최선인 것은 아니라는 내용의 ③이 글의 흐름상 가장 어색한 문장이다.

해석 수리권 시장은 증가하는 인구가 (물) 부족을 초래하고 기후 변화가 가뭄과 기근을 야기함에 따라 발전할 가능성이 있다. 그러나 그것은 지역적이고 윤리적인 무역 관행에 기반할 것이며 대부분의 상품 거래와는 다를 것이다. 비판자들은 물을 거래하는 것이 비윤리적이거나 심지어 인권 침해라고 주장하지만, 이미 수리권은 오만에서 호주까지 세계의 건조한 지역에서 사고 팔리고 있다. (증류수를 마시는 것은 유익할 수 있지만, 특히 미네랄이 다른 공급원으로 보충되지 않는다면, 모두에게 최선의 선택은 아닐지도 모른다.) Ziad Abdelnour는 "우리는 물이 사실상 이 10년간 그리고 이후 새로운 금으로 바뀔 것이라고 굳게 믿는다."라고 말했다. "스마트 머니가 이 방향으로 공격적으로 움직이고 있는 것은 놀랍지 않다."

어휘

shortage 부족	drought 가뭄
famine 기근	ethical 윤리적인
bulk 대부분	commodity 상품
detractor 비판자, 비방자	breach 위반, 침해
arid 건조한	distill 증류[정제]하다
supplement 보충하다	aggressively 공격적으로

03 ④

해설 이 글은 번아웃의 개념과 이를 구성하는 세 가지 차원을 설명하고 있다. ④ 앞부분에서 번아웃의 두 번째 차원인 개인적인 성취의 부족, 즉 스스로를 업무 달성의 실패자로 여기는 근로자들에 대해 설명하고 있고, ④ 뒷부분에서는 세 번째 차원인 비인격화를 설명하고 있다. 따라서 감정 노동 근로자들이 왕성한 의욕을 가지고 업무를 한다는 내용의 ④가 글의 흐름상 가장 어색한 문장이다.

해석 번아웃이라는 용어는 업무의 압박으로 인한 "마모"를 의미한다. 번아웃은 일상적인 업무 스트레스 요인들이 직원들에게 타격을 주면서 발생하는 만성 질환이다. 가장 널리 채택된 번아웃의 개념화는 Maslach와 그녀의 동료들의 인적 서비스 근로자들에 대한 연구에서 전개되었다. Maslach는 번아웃이 서로 밀접하게 연관된 세 가지 차원으로 구성되어 있다고 간주한다. 첫 번째 차원인 정서적 고갈은 사실상 번아웃 현상의 핵심이다. 근로자들은 피로감, 좌절감, 기진맥진함을 느끼거나 직장에서 또 다른 하루를 맞이할 수 없을 때 정서적 고갈을 겪는다. 번아웃의 두 번째 차원은 개인적 성취감의 결여다. 번아웃 현상의 이러한 측면은 스스로를 업무 요구 사항들을 효과적으로 달성할 수 없는 실패자로 여기는 근로자들을 나타낸다. (감정 노동 근로자들은 신체적으로 지쳤을지라도 왕성한 의욕을 가지고 그들의 업무를 시작한다.) 번아웃의 세 번째 차원은 비인격화다. 이 차원은 업무의 일환으로 다른 사람들(예를 들면 고객, 환자, 학생)과 대인 관계 소통해야 하는 근로자들에게만 관련된다.

어휘

chronic condition 만성 질환	stressor 스트레스 요인
take its toll on ~에 피해를 주다	conceptualization 개념화
exhaustion 고갈, 기진맥진	fatigued 피로한, 지친
used up 기진맥진한	depersonalization 비인격화
interpersonally 대인 관계에서	

04 ②

해설 이 글은 15세기 자연 철학 발전의 중심이 되었던 아리스토텔레스에 관해 이야기하고 있다. 따라서 인쇄기의 힘을 빠르게 깨달은 인문주의자들에 대한 내용인 ②가 글의 흐름상 가장 어색한 문장이다.

해석 15세기에는 과학, 철학, 마술 사이에 구분이 없었다. 셋 모두 '자연 철학'이라는 일반 주제에 포함되었다. 고전 작가들의 회복이 자연 철학 발전의 중심이었는데, 다른 무엇보다도 가장 중요한 것은 아리스토텔레스의 작품이었다. (인문주의자들은 그들의 지식을 전파하는 인쇄기의 힘을 빠르게 깨달았다.) 15세기 초에 아리스토텔레스는 철학과 과학에서 모든 학문적 고찰의 기반으로 남아 있었다. Averroes와 Avicenna의 아랍어 번역과 주해에서 살아남은 아리스토텔레스는 인류와 자연계의 관계에 대한 체계적인 시각을 제공했다. 그의 '자연학', '형이상학', '기상학' 같이 살아남은 원문들은 학자들에게 자연계를 창조한 힘을 이해할 수 있는 논리적 도구들을 제공했다.

어휘

humanist 인문주의자	printing press 인쇄기
scholastic 학자의, 학문의	speculation 고찰, 추측
metaphysics 형이상학	meteorology 기상학

05 ④

해설 이 글은 뇌가 위협을 감지했을 때 신체에서 일어나는 일련의 과정에 대해서 설명하고 있다. 마지막 문장에서, 그 반응(투쟁 도피 반응)이 시작되면 호르몬을 통제할 수 없다고 했으므로, 그 바로 앞에서 호르몬 방출을 조절한다는 내용의 ④가 글의 흐름상 가장 어색한 문장이다.

해석 뇌가 바로 옆에 있는 주변 환경에서 위협을 감지할 때, 그것은 신체에서 복잡한 일련의 사건을 일으키기 시작한다. 그것은 화학 호르몬을 혈류로 방출하는 기관인 다양한 분비샘에 전기 메시지를 보낸다. 혈액은 이러한 호르몬을 그 후 다양한 일을 하도록 자극받는 다른 기관들로 빠르게 운반한다. 예를 들어, 신장 위의 부신은 몸의 스트레스 호르몬인 아드레날린을 뿜어낸다. 아드레날린은 위험 징후를 찾기 위해 눈을 확대하고, 혈액과 여분의 호르몬이 계속 흐르도록 심장을 더 빠르게 펌프질하고, 골격근을 긴장시켜 위협을 몰아세우거나 그로부터 달아나도록 준비하는 것과 같은 일들을 하면서 몸 전체를 돌아다닌다. 그 전 과정은 투쟁 도피 반응이라고 불리는데, 왜냐하면 그것은 그것이 신체로 하여금 삶을 위해 투쟁 또는 도주를 준비시키기 때문이다. (인간은 의식적으로 분비샘을 조절하여 다양한 호르몬의 방출을 조절한다.) 일단 그 반응이 시작되고 나면, 호르몬을 설득(통제)할 수 없기 때문에, 그것을 무시하는 것은 불가능하다.

어휘

a string of 일련의	gland (분비) 선, 샘
prompt 촉발하다	adrenal 신장 부근의, 부신의
kidney 신장	on the lookout (for) ~을 유의하여
lash out at ~을 몰아세우다	

06 ③

해설 이 글은 철학자들이나 철학을 공부하는 학생들은 인류학 공부에 큰 관심을 가지지 않는다고 말하고 있다. 따라서 위대한 철학자들이 인류학이나 심리학 같은 다른 분야로부터 영감을 이끌어낸다는 ③이 글의 흐름상 가장 어색한 문장이다.

해석 철학자들은 인류학자들이 철학에 가지고 있는 것만큼 인류학에 관심을 가지지 않았다. 영향력 있는 현대 철학자들 중 그들의 연구에서 인류학 연구를 고려하는 사람이 거의 없다. 사회과학의 철학을 전공으로 하는 사람들은 인류학 연구의 예를 고려하거나 분석할 수 있지만, 이것은 대부분 개념적 요점이나 인식론적 차이를 설명하거나 인식론적 또는 윤리적 함의에 대해 비판하기 위해 한다. (사실 우리 시대의 위대한 철학자들은 종종 인류학이나 심리학 같은 다른 분야로부터 영감을 이끌어냈다.) 철학을 공부하는 학생들은 좀처럼 인류학에 대해 공부하거나 진지한 관심을 보이지 않는다. 그들은 과학에서 실험적인 방법에 대해 배울 수 있지만, 인류학 현장 연구에 대해서는 거의 배우지 않는다.

어휘

anthropology 인류학	anthropologist 인류학자
specialize in ~을 전문으로 하다	epistemological 인식론의
implication 함의	inspiration 영감
fieldwork 현장 연구	

Reading Skill 13 내용 일치·불일치 ACTUAL TEST

01	③	02	③	03	④	04	④	05	④
06	②	07	④	08	②				

01 ③

해설 5번째 문장에서 청력이 정상적이었다고 했으므로, 글의 내용과 일치하지 않는 것은 ③ 'Christopher Nolan은 청각 장애로 인해 들을 수 없었다.'이다.

해석 Christopher Nolan은 영어로 다소 유명한 아일랜드의 작가이다. 태어날 때부터 뇌가 손상된 Nolan은 음식을 삼키기 어려울 정도로 몸의 근육을 거의 통제하지 못했다. 그는 혼자 똑바로 앉을 수 없어서 휠체어에 묶여 있어야 한다. Nolan은 알아들을 수 있는 말소리를 낼 수 없다. 그러나 다행히도, 그의 뇌 손상은 지능이 손상되지 않은 그런 것이었고 청력이 정상적이었기에, 그 결과로 그는 어렸을 때 말하기를 이해하는 것을 배웠다. 그러나 그가 10살이 되고, 읽기를 배운, 수년 후에서야 비로소 그의 첫 단어를 표현할 수 있는 수단을 갖게 되었다. 그는 글자를 가리키기 위해 머리에 부착된 막대기를 사용하여 이를 해냈다. 그가 아직 10대일 때 'Dam-Burst of Dreams'라는 시와 단편 소설로 이루어진 책 한 권 전체를 만들어 낸 것은 이런 글자 하나하나를 가리키는 '유니콘' 방식으로였다.

어휘

of renown 유명한
swallow 삼키다
strap 끈으로 묶다
utter 말하다
recognizable 인식할 수 있는
intelligence 지능
attach 붙이다
letter-by-letter 글자 하나하나씩

02 ③

해설 마지막 2번째 문장에서 일부 호주 원주민들은 자신의 이름을 사는 동안 계속해서 바꿀 수 있다고 했으므로, 글의 내용과 일치하지 않는 것은 ③ '호주 원주민 문화에서 이름을 바꾸는 것은 완전히 용납될 수 없다.'이다.

① 많은 가톨릭 국가에서 아이들은 자주 성인의 이름을 따서 이름 지어진다.
② 어떤 아프리카 어린이들은 5살이 될 때까지 이름이 지어지지 않는다.
④ 다양한 문화권에서 아이들의 이름을 각기 다른 방식으로 짓는다.

해석 많은 가톨릭 국가에서, 아이들은 종종 성인의 이름을 따서 이름 지어지는데, 실제로 일부 신부들은 부모들이 아이들의 이름을 드라마 스타나 축구 선수의 이름을 따서 짓도록 허락하지 않을 것이다. 개신교 국가들은 이에 대해 더 자유로운 경향이 있는데, 하지만 노르웨이에서는 Adolf 같은 특정 이름들은 완전히 금지된다. 아프리카처럼 유아 사망률이 매우 높은 국가에서는 부족들이 생존 가능성이 커지기 시작하는 나이인 5살이 되어야만 아이들의 이름을 짓는다. 그 때까지, 아이들은 그들의 나이로 불린다. 극동의 많은 국가들은 아이들에게 어떤 식으로든 아이의 출생 상황이나 아이를 향한 부모의 기대와 희망을 묘사하는 독특한 이름을 지어준다. 어떤 호주 원주민들은 어떤 식으로든 그들의 지혜, 창의성 또는 결단력을 증명한 몇몇 중요한 경험의 결과로 그들의 이름을 사는 동안 계속해서 바꿀 수 있다. 예를 들어, 어느 날 그들 중 한 명이 춤을 아주 잘 춘다면, 그 혹은 그녀는 자신의 이름을 '최고 춤꾼' 또는 '가벼운 발'로 다시 짓기로 할 수도 있다.

어휘

name after ~의 이름을 따서 이름 짓다
saint 성인(聖人)
priest 신부, 성직자
soap opera 연속극[드라마]
Protestant 개신교의
ban 금지하다
infant 유아
mortality 사망률
tribe 부족
aborigine 원주민
wisdom 지혜
determination 결의, 결단력
unacceptable 용납할 수 없는

03 ④

해설 마지막 문장에서 Eco는 췌장암으로 밀라노 자택에서 죽었다고 했으므로, 글의 내용과 일치하지 않는 것은 ④ 'Eco는 암으로 병원에서 죽었다.'이다.

① 'The Name of the Rose'는 역사 소설이다.
② Eco는 책을 이탈리아어로 번역했다.
③ Eco는 대학 학과를 설립했다.

해석 Umberto Eco는 이탈리아의 소설가, 문화 비평가, 철학자였다. 그는 소설 속 기호학을 성서 분석, 중세 연구, 문학 이론과 결합한 1980년 역사 미스터리 소설 'The Name of the Rose'로 널리 알려져 있다. 그는 후에 'Foucault's Pendulum'과 'The Island of the Day Before'를 포함한 다른 소설들을 썼다. Eco는 또한 번역가였으며, Raymond Queneau의 책 'Exercices de style'을 이탈리아어로 번역했다. 그는 San Marino 공화국 대학교의 미디어학과 설립자였다. 그는 2016년 2월 19일 밤에 2년간 앓아왔던 췌장암으로 밀라노 자택에서 사망했다.

어휘

philosopher 철학자
semiotics 기호학
biblical 성서의
medieval 중세의
translator 번역가
department 학과
pancreatic cancer 췌장암

04 ④

해설 마지막 문장의 slavery was also an institution in many African nations에서 노예제도가 많은 아프리카 국가들의 관습이기도 했다고 하였으므로, 글의 내용과 일치하는 것은 ④ '노예제도는 심지어 아프리카 국가들에서도 존재했다.'이다.

① 아프리카인 노동자들은 자발적으로 신대륙으로 이주했다.
② 유럽인들은 노예노동을 이용한 최초의 사람들이었다.
③ 아랍 노예제도는 더는 어떤 형태로도 존재하지 않는다.

해석 수입 노동의 가장 악명 높은 사례는 당연히 대서양 노예무역으로, 이는 대농장을 경작하도록 천만 명에 이르는 노예가 된 아프리카인들을 신대륙에 데려왔다. 그러나 유럽인들이 노예제도를 가장 대규모로 시행했을지라도, 그들은 결코 그들의 지역사회에 노예를 데려온 유일한 사람들이 아니었다. 더 일찍이, 고대 이집트인들은 노예노동을 그들의 피라미드를 건설하는 데 이용했고, 초기 아랍 탐험가들은 종종 노예무역상이기도 했고, 아랍 노예제도는 20세기까지 계속되었으며 실제로 몇 군데에서는 아직도 유지되고 있다. 아메리카 대륙에서는 몇몇 토착 부족들이 다른 부족의 구성원들을 노예로 삼았고, 노예제도는 또한 특히 식민시대 이전 많은 아프리카 국가들의 관습이기도 했다.

어휘

notorious 악명 높은
imported 수입된, 들여온
enslave 노예로 만들다
plantation 대농장
by no means 결코 ~이 아닌
tribe 부족
institution 제도, 관습
colonial 식민지의

05 ④

해설 마지막 3번째 문장에 따르면, 칠레의 아타카마 사막은 연간 강수량이 2mm 미만인 곳이 있는 가장 건조한 사막 중 하나이므로, 글의 내용과 일치하지 않는 것은 ④ '아타카마 사막은 비가 가장 많이 오는 사막들 중 하나이다.'이다.
① 각 대륙에는 적어도 하나의 사막이 존재한다.
② 사하라 사막은 세계에서 가장 큰 뜨거운 사막이다.
③ 고비 사막은 차가운 사막으로 분류된다.

해석 사막은 지구 육지 면적의 5분의 1 이상을 차지하고, 모든 대륙에서 발견된다. 연간 25cm(10인치) 미만의 비가 오는 곳은 사막으로 여겨진다. 사막은 건조 지대라고 불리는 더 광범위한 종류의 지역 중 일부이다. 이 지역들은 "수분 부족" 환경하에 있는데, 이는 그곳들이 흔히 수분을 연간 강수로 얻는 것보다 증발로 잃는 것이 더 많을 수 있다는 것을 의미한다. 사막이 뜨겁다는 일반적인 개념에도 불구하고, 차가운 사막들 또한 존재한다. 세계에서 가장 큰 뜨거운 사막인 북아프리카의 사하라 사막은 낮 동안 최고 섭씨 50도(화씨 122도)에 이른다. 하지만 아시아의 고비 사막이나 세계에서 가장 큰 남극과 북극의 극지 사막과 같이, 어떤 사막들은 항상 차갑다. 다른 사막들에는 산이 많다. 겨우 약 20%의 사막들만이 모래로 덮여있다. 칠레의 아타카마 사막과 같은 가장 건조한 사막에는 연간 강수량이 2mm(0.08인치) 미만인 곳들이 있다. 그러한 환경들은 너무 혹독하고 초자연적이어서 과학자들이 화성의 생명체에 대한 단서를 찾기 위해 그것들을 연구해오기도 했다. 반면, 몇 년에 한 번씩 유난히 비가 많이 오는 시기가 "슈퍼 블룸 현상"을 만들어낼 수 있는데, 이때는 아타카마조차도 야생화로 뒤덮이게 된다.

어휘
continent 대륙
evaporation 증발
mountainous 산이 많은
otherworldly 초자연적인, 내세의
categorize 분류하다
deficit 부족, 결핍
precipitation 강수(량)
harsh 혹독한
blanketed with ~로 뒤덮인

06 ②

해설 대화에 있어 여성과 남성의 차이에 관한 글이다. 3번째 문장에서 여성들의 대화 주제 범위가 다양하지만 그중 스포츠는 눈에 띄게 없다고 언급되므로, 글의 내용과 일치하지 않는 것은 ② '여성들의 대화 주제는 건강에서 스포츠에 이르기까지 매우 다양하다.'이다.

해석 여성들은 가십에 전문가이고, 그들은 항상 사소한 것들에 대해 이야기하거나, 아니면 적어도 남성들은 항상 그렇게 생각해왔다. 하지만 몇몇 새로운 연구는 여성들끼리 대화할 때, 그들의 대화는 시시함과는 거리가 멀고, 남성들끼리 대화할 때보다 더 많은 주제(최대 40개의 주제)를 다룬다고 제시한다. 여성들의 대화는 건강에서 그들의 집, 정치에서 패션, 영화에서 가족, 교육에서 인간관계 문제까지 다양하지만, 스포츠는 눈에 띄게 없다. 남성들은 더 제한된 범위의 주제를 가지는 경향이 있는데, 가장 인기 있는 것은 일, 스포츠, 농담, 자동차, 여성이다. 1,000명이 넘는 여성들을 인터뷰한 심리학자인 Petra Boynton 교수에 따르면, 여성들은 또한 대화 중 한 주제에서 다른 주제로 빠르게 이동하는 경향이 있는 반면, 남성들은 보통 한 주제에서 더 오랫동안 벗어나지 않는다. 직장에서, 이러한 차이는 남성들에게 이점이 될 수 있는데, 그들이 다른 문제들을 제쳐두고 논의되는 주제에 완전히 집중할 수 있기 때문이다. 반면, 이는 또한 그들이 가끔 회의에서 여러 가지를 동시에 논의해야 할 때 집중하기 힘들다는 것을 의미하기도 한다.

어휘
trivial 사소한
notably 현저히
psychologist 심리학자
frivolous 시시한, 하찮은
absent 없는, 부재한
stick to ~을 고수하다

07 ④

해설 글의 마지막 문장의 the rates of gun homicide and other gun crimes in the United States have dropped since highs in the early 1990's를 보면, 1990년대 초 최고치를 기록한 이후 미국의 총기 범죄가 감소해 왔다고 했다. 따라서 글의 내용과 일치하지 않는 것은 ④ '미국에서의 총기 범죄는 지난 30년 동안 꾸준히 증가해 왔다.'이다.
① 2008년에 미국 대법원은 워싱턴 D.C.의 권총 금지법을 뒤집었다.
② 많은 총기 옹호자들은 총을 소유하는 것은 타고난 권리라고 주장한다.
③ 가장 발전된 국가들 중에서 미국이 총기 살인 사건 발생률이 가장 높다.

해석 미국 수정 헌법 제2조는 "잘 규제된 민병대는 자유 주(州)의 안보에 필요하므로, 무기를 소지할 수 있는 국민의 권리는 침해되어서는 안 된다."고 명시하고 있다. 대법원의 판결은 이 개정안을 인용하며 총기 규제권을 유지했다. 그러나 2008년 개인의 무기 보유 및 소지 권리를 확정한 판결에서 법원은 권총을 금지하고 집에 있는 권총은 잠그거나 분해하도록 한 워싱턴 DC의 법을 폐지했다. 많은 총기 옹호자들은 소유권을 생득권이며 국가 유산의 필수적인 부분이라고 생각한다. 스위스에 기반을 두고 있는 Small Arms Survey의 2007년 보고서에 따르면, 세계 인구의 5% 미만인 미국은 세계 민간 소유 총기의 약 35~50%를 보유하고 있다. 미국은 1인당 총기 소유 1위다. 미국은 또한 세계에서 가장 발전된 국가들 중에서 총기로 의한 살인율이 가장 높다. 그러나 많은 총기 권리 옹호론자들은 이러한 통계들이 인과관계를 나타내지는 않으며 미국의 총기 살인이나 기타 총기 범죄율이 1990년대 초 최고치를 기록한 이후로 감소해 왔다고 언급한다.

어휘
infringe 침해하다
uphold 유지시키다
strike down 폐지하다
per capita 1인당
proponent 지지자
amendment 미국 헌법 수정 조항
firearms 총기
birthright 생득권
homicide 살인
overturn 뒤집다

08 ②

해설 이 글은 정부 음식 서비스 프로그램이 어떻게 시작되고 발전되었는지에 대해 설명하는 글이다. 2번째 문장의 the need to use surplus agricultural commodities에서 알 수 있듯이 미국의 음식 서비스 프로그램은 대공황 시기에 과잉된 농산물을 사용하려고 시작된 것이므로, 글의 내용과 일치하지 않는 것은 ② '미국 정부는 식량 부족에도 불구하고 대공황 동안에 빈곤 아동들에게 식량을 공급하기 시작했다.'이다.
① 근로 여성들의 수적 증가가 음식 서비스 프로그램의 확대를 신장시켰다.
③ 미국의 학교 급식 시스템은 현재 빈곤 가정의 아동들에게 음식을 제공하는 것을 돕고 있다.
④ 점심을 제공하는 기능이 가정에서 학교로 이동되었다.

해석 최초의 정부 음식 서비스 프로그램은 1900년경에 유럽에서 시작되었다. 미국의 프로그램은 가난한 가정의 아이들에게 식량을 공급하기 위한 우려와 잉여 농산물을 사용할 필요가 있었던 대공황 때부터 시작되었다. 제 2차 세계 대전 중과 그 후, 일하는 여성의 수가 폭발적으로 증가하면서 더 넓은 프로그램의 필요성이 대두되었다. 한 때 가족의 기능이었던 점심 제공은 학교 급식 시스템으로 옮겨갔다. 국립학교 급식 프로그램은 이러한 노력의 결과이다. 그 프로그램은 연방정부의 지원을 받는 급식을 취학 연령의 아이들에게 제공하도록 고안되었다. 제2차 세계대전 종전부터 1980년대 초까지 학교 급식에 대한 자금 지원은 꾸준히 확대되었다. 오늘날 그것은 미국 전역의 거의 100,000개의 학교에 있는 어린이들을 먹이는 것을 돕는다. 첫 번째 기능은 모든 학생들에게 영양가 있는 점심을 제공하는 것이다. 두 번째 기능은 소외된 어린이들에게 아침과 점심 모두에서 영양가 있는 음식을 제공하는 것이다. 오히려, 한때 가족의 기능을 대신했던 학교 급식의 역할이 확대되었다.

어휘

surplus 잉여의
explosion 폭발
nutritious 영양가가 높은
commodity 물자
federally 연합으로
underprivileged 혜택을 못 받는